T0346550

Hiking Waterfalls Colorado

A Guide to the State's Best Waterfall Hikes

Second Edition

Susan Joy Paul and Stewart M. Green

GUILFORD, CONNECTICUT

FALCONGUIDES®

An imprint of Globe Pequot, the trade division of
The Rowman & Littlefield Publishing Group, Inc.
4501 Forbes Blvd., Ste. 200
Lanham, MD 20706
www.rowman.com

Falcon and FalconGuides are registered trademarks and Make Adventure Your Story is a trademark of The Rowman & Littlefield Publishing Group, Inc.

Distributed by NATIONAL BOOK NETWORK

Copyright © 2013, 2022 The Rowman & Littlefield Publishing Group, Inc.

Photos by Susan Joy Paul and Stewart M. Green unless otherwise noted
Maps updated by Melissa Baker, The Rowman & Littlefield Publishing Group, Inc.
All rights reserved. No part of this book may be reproduced in any form or by any electronic or mechanical means, including information storage and retrieval systems, without written permission from the publisher, except by a reviewer who may quote passages in a review.

British Library Cataloguing in Publication Information available

Library of Congress Cataloging-in-Publication Data
Names: Paul, Susan Joy, author. | Green, Stewart M., author.
Title: Hiking Waterfalls Colorado : a guide to the state's best waterfall hikes / Susan Joy Paul and Stewart M. Green.
Other titles: Hiking Waterfalls in Colorado
Description: Second edition. | Guilford, Connecticut : FalconGuides, [2022] | Includes index. | Summary: "From the Front Range to the Western Slope, Colorado boasts beautiful waterfalls. This book features detailed hike descriptions, maps, and color photos for the most scenic waterfall hikes in the state. Hike descriptions also include distance, elevation gain, and GPS coordinates" — Provided by publisher.
Identifiers: LCCN 2021058380 (print) | LCCN 2021058381 (ebook) | ISBN 9781493043743 (paperback) | ISBN 9781493043750 (epub)
Subjects: LCSH: Hiking—Colorado—Guidebooks. | Waterfalls—Colorado—Guidebooks. | Colorado—Guidebooks.
Classification: LCC GV199.42.C6 P38 2022 (print) | LCC GV199.42.C6 (ebook) | DDC 796.5109788—dc23
LC record available at https://lccn.loc.gov/2021058380
LC ebook record available at https://lccn.loc.gov/2021058381

♾™ The paper used in this publication meets the minimum requirements of American National Standard for Information Sciences—Permanence of Paper for Printed Library Materials, ANSI / NISO Z39.48-1992.

The authors and The Rowman & Littlefield Publishing Group, Inc., assume no liability for accidents happening to, or injuries sustained by, readers who engage in the activities described in this book.

To the fish and the fowl who make waterfalls their home, and to the waterfall hunters and hikers who, as visitors, revel in the splendor of these magical places. Many days as we, the authors, work away at our desks, we are still there with you at the falls in mind, spirit, and soul.

Spectacular Rough Creek Falls thunders over a cliff on the edge of the South San Juan Wilderness Area.

Ouzel Falls, one of Wild Basin's best waterfalls, sprays off a rock bench onto boulders.

Contents

Overview

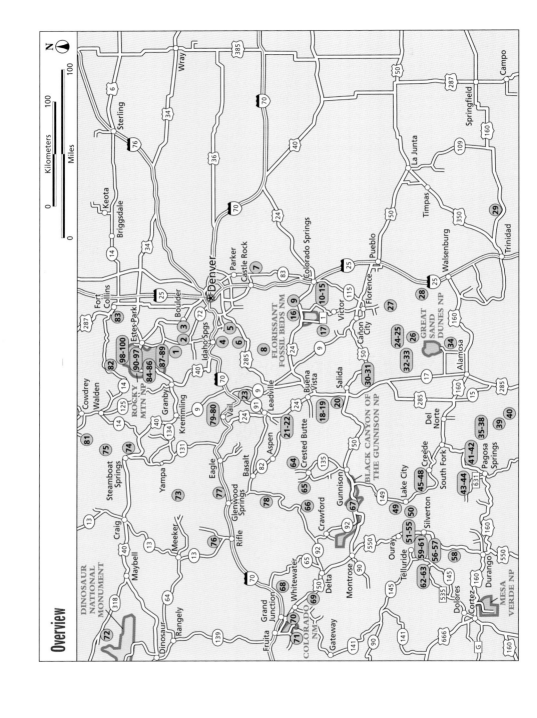

Acknowledgments

Many thanks to all the people at Rowman & Littlefield Publishing, FalconGuides, the National Book Network, and all the bookstores and outdoor recreation retailers that carry our books.

Special thanks to our acquiring editors David Legere and Mason Gadd, production editor Meredith Dias, cartographer Melissa Baker, copyeditor Ann Seifert, layout artist Melissa Evarts, and proofreader Beth Richards. We couldn't have done it without you.

—Susan Joy Paul and Stewart M. Green

High peaks tower above Lower Twin Falls in Yankee Boy Basin.

Introduction

Welcome! A Message from Your Waterfall Guides

Welcome to the wet and wild world of Colorado waterfalls! Ours is a watery state, crisscrossed by thousands of creeks, streams, and rivers. These mountain-born waterways tumble down hillsides, rest in small pools and mighty lakes, and funnel through chasms, canyons, and gorges. Along the way—to the delight of the Colorado hiker—they spill and splatter over crags and cliffs, splash off boulders, and slip over slabs in a glorious show of waterfall wonder.

Hiking Waterfalls Colorado introduces you to one hundred hikes and even more of our favorite Colorado waterfalls. The trips include drive-ups to roadside falls, short walks on easy paths, moderate hikes on bumpy trails, and strenuous treks across difficult terrain. The book guides you to dozens of national forests; national parks and monuments; state parks; and wilderness, wildlife, conservation, and recreation areas.

You'll travel through a variety of ecosystems, hike the grasslands and prairies, climb gentle foothills, meander through montane forests, reach lofty heights in subalpine zones, and top out on mountain vistas. Along the way, you'll take in views of high summits and crystal lakes, wander across desert canyons and through dense, dark forests, and cross rushing rivers and babbling creeks. You'll enjoy the sights and smells of the Rocky Mountain maple, Colorado blue spruce, and ponderosa pine. Douglas fir, Engelmann spruce, lodgepole pine, cottonwood, and aspen trees rise above you on the trails, while sagebrush, juniper, willow, prickly pear cactus, and Mormon tea lie below at your feet. You'll hear the sounds of the Colorado wilderness: the whir of the hummingbird, rat-a-tat of the woodpecker, gobble of the wild turkey, chirp of the lark bunting, clicks and clucks of the ptarmigan, and descending warble of the canyon wren. There are fish, and bugs too, and wildflowers of every shape, size, and hue. You'll catch more than a glimpse of Colorado wildlife on your outings, as mule deer, elk, bighorn sheep, mountain goats, porcupines, badgers, beavers, squirrels, chipmunks, pika, marmots, rabbits, lynx, bobcats, mountain lions, black bears, foxes, coyotes, lizards, snakes, and even moose all live in the places you will visit on your waterfall hikes.

You can do all the hikes solo, or with friends. Depending on your level of fitness, each one can be done as a day hike, but some lend themselves to overnight backpacks and camping trips.

The waterfalls vary as much as the hikes that take you to them. There are wilderness plunge pools and punchbowls, roadside cascades, and towering cataracts that will take your breath away. But with all the variety, they have one thing in common: how

◀ *"Lost Lake Falls" drops over rocky ledges before draining into Lost Lake near Kebler Pass.*

they make you feel. As you approach a waterfall, you listen, and you hear it before you see it. You might slow down to figure out where it is or hasten your step to get to it sooner. You feel your heart begin to pound, and then a big smile spreads across your face and then—there it is! It's your waterfall. I hope you enjoy them all as much as we did.

Colorado Waterfall Sources and Types

Colorado is famously known as the Rocky Mountain State. With more mountaintops above 14,000 feet than any other state in the country and a majority of the 14ers in all of North America, Colorado's topography attracts weather in the form of rain, sleet, hail, graupel, and snow showers. All that water has to go somewhere, and while some of it evaporates back into the atmosphere or is absorbed by the soil, gravity has its way with the rest. The resulting water flow is why Colorado is the source of more major rivers than any other state! The Arkansas, Platte, and Colorado Rivers, and even the mighty Rio Grande, all trace their headwaters to the state of Colorado, and their beginnings to the high peaks. This explains the state's other, lesser-known nickname: the "Mother of Rivers."

As they flow downhill, the rivers fork into streams and creeks, and the many waterways—coupled with Colorado's rugged geography—provide a perfect landscape for falling water in the form of waterfalls.

The physical forms of waterfalls depend on topography and water flow, and they are as varied as the land and waters that create them. The most common type of waterfall is a **cascade,** which tumbles over rocks and boulders, and down mountainsides, maintaining contact with the terrain. **Horsetail** waterfalls maintain some contact with the rock or earth but are more vertical and so partially airborne. **Sheet** or **block** falls are wider than they are long, while **ribbon** falls are long and thin. **Plunge** waterfalls freefall from cliffs, and the highest, most powerful plunges are known as **cataracts. Chute** falls shoot through narrow crevices, and **fan** falls spread their waters in fan-shaped falls. **Bridal veil** waterfalls are frothy and translucent, appearing as sparkling white veils over the underlying rock face. Falls can be tiered or stepped and can stream down cliffs and crags in separate segments, or serially. As their vertical progress is halted by low-angle or horizontal terrain, waterfalls can form punchbowls in the rock, or plunge pools in the earth.

Waterfall types reflect the natural traits of the earth and the water, and as nature changes, so does the type of each waterfall it forms. For this reason, the appearance of a waterfall can change from year to year and season to season, and even from one day to the next. This is especially true during times of drought, heavy rainfall, and the annual springtime melt-off of ice and snow. When you visit a waterfall, take a moment to appreciate its ever-changing beauty. You may never see that waterfall, as it appears that day, ever again.

Towering rock ridges scrape the sky above "Silver Ribbon Falls" in a cliff-lined cirque above Telluride.

Hiking Waterfalls Safety and Protocol

For your own safety, the safety of others, and protection of the environment, a general protocol should be followed when hiking Colorado's waterfalls:

- Be prepared with the appropriate clothing, gear, food, water, and supplies you'll need for a safe and enjoyable hike.
- Know where you're going, and have adequate directions to get there and the ability to find your way back to the trailhead. Share your plans with someone you trust, along with a "latest time to call" so that—in the event of an accident—someone will know your general whereabouts and can then contact the authorities with that information.
- When driving to your waterfall trailhead, be aware of changing conditions, especially during inclement weather or natural disasters. Rainfall, snowfall, rockfall, and wildfires can affect your route, so be prepared to turn around if conditions become unsafe.
- Travel in small groups to lessen impact in the backcountry. In wilderness areas, there is often a limit on the number of people allowed to hike together on a trail. When in doubt, contact the local ranger district for direction.
- Read posted warnings and restrictions at each trailhead, as these vary between public lands and can change based on conditions. It is especially important to be

mindful of campfire restrictions and required minimum camping distances from water sources.

- Do not cut switchbacks or hike off-trail where trails exist, which causes erosion and destroys vegetation. Stick to the trail, especially on delicate alpine tundra and desert cryptobiotic soil. If you do have to leave the trail, seek out hard surfaces, such as rocks and stones, to lessen your impact.
- Keep dogs on leash or on voice command, and do not allow them to chase wildlife, which can stress the native animals and cause premature death.
- Do not approach wildlife. Although attacks are rare, they can happen, and are more likely when an animal is provoked or feels threatened. Even small animals carry diseases, so don't try to pet or feed them.
- Beware of mountain beetle–killed trees, and never camp near them. They can fall without warning.
- Take extreme care when crossing streams, and never wade or stand above a moving waterfall. The current can quickly carry you downstream and over a cliff.
- Stay clear of soft or down-sloping edges over creek beds, as well as wet, icy, or slick rocks around the waterfalls. Stick to dry, solid surfaces and avoid tragedy.
- Pack out all trash and personal items, including toilet paper.
- Keep to established trails and avoid traveling off-trail or on social trails. Where the use of side trails is required to view a waterfall, be sure to adhere to the Leave No Trace principles to lessen your impact and prevent future resource damage. The Leave No Trace (www.LNT.org) principles are easy to follow and ensure a clean and pristine environment for inhabitants and future visitors to the hiking trails.
- Likewise, leave everything on the trail as you found it. Do not remove rocks, plants, wildflowers, live trees, or historical artifacts from the wilderness, but leave them for others to enjoy.

Wildfires and Colorado's Changing Climate

Scientific studies indicate that global warming, caused by greenhouse gas emissions from the burning of fossil fuels, is changing Colorado's climate. These changes include rising temperatures, decreased precipitation, lower snowpack levels, drought, an increase in insects that kill trees, increased aridification, and altered vegetation patterns. Colorado's average temperature has increased 2 degrees, faster than the global rise, since 1990. Stream flows are predicted to decrease as much as 15 percent by 2050.

The increasing dry and hot conditions and an extended fire season have led to catastrophic wildfires, with the twenty largest wildfires in Colorado history occurring after 2000, including the three largest in the devastating 2020 season—the Cameron Peak, East Troublesome, and Pine Creek Fires. Those fires damaged waterfall hikes in Rocky Mountain National Park.

Hikers need to be aware of wildfire dangers when trekking in Colorado's backcountry. Plan ahead of time to avoid areas impacted by wildfire and smoke. Follow these basic rules to avoid wildfires:

- Before hiking, check with land management agencies like the US Forest Service and the Bureau of Land Management for fire restrictions in the area. Campfires may be prohibited due to red-flag fire conditions and high fire danger. Note changing fire restrictions posted on trailhead kiosks.
- Outside of established fire rings in public campgrounds, do not build campfires except in an emergency. Never leave a fire unattended, and ensure your campfire is out completely before abandoning your campsite. Extinguish any smoldering campfires you encounter.
- Avoid hiking when the air is smoke-filled and unhealthy.
- Be aware of any active fires adjacent to your hiking location, even if they are many miles away, and monitor their progress in case you need to change plans and return to the trailhead.
- Use extreme caution when hiking in burned forests. Dead and damaged trees create unstable terrain, and a lack of vegetation can make land prone to avalanches, rockslides, landslides, and flooding.

Reservations (May Be) Required

Since the first edition of *Hiking Waterfalls Colorado* was released in 2013, the state has grown, with over a half-million people moving to Front Range cities. The population growth, coupled with increasing tourism and COVID-19 restrictions, has led to overcrowding and overuse of Colorado's iconic natural wonders. Increased recreational visits means jammed roads, parking lots, and trailheads; trail erosion caused by careless feet cutting switchbacks; and illegal camping and campfires.

In response, some popular Colorado places put limitations on visitation to protect natural resources from damage caused by overuse. Rocky Mountain National Park and Brainard Lake Recreation Area instituted timed-entry reservation systems, and while these systems may be an inconvenience, the benefit to visitors is a better hiking experience. Some other areas require parking and hiking reservations, such as Glenwood Canyon's Hanging Lake and Bridal Veil Falls. San Juan National Forest is considering a permit system to access Ice Lake Basin, home to a slew of waterfalls, to alleviate limited trailhead parking and damage to the area's fragile alpine tundra.

Before hiking to a waterfall, especially the more popular ones, call the respective land management agency listed in the "Land status/contact" section of the chapter, or go to the Appendix for more contact information including web addresses. More popular trailheads may require making camping and hiking reservations weeks or even months in advance. Plan ahead to avoid disappointment.

Each hike includes a short overview followed by details to help you choose the best adventure for you.

Start: The starting point, usually the trailhead, for the hike.

Trail or trails: The names and numbers of trails that the hike follows.

Difficulty: Refers to the level of difficulty as a guide only, as your own level of fitness will ultimately determine your experience.

Hiking time: The average time it takes to hike the route. The time is based on the total distance, elevation gain, and trail condition and difficulty. Your fitness level also affects your time.

Distance: The total distance of the recommended route from trailhead to trailhead.

Elevation trailhead to falls viewpoint: The starting elevation at the trailhead and the ending elevation at the waterfall, along with the difference in elevation between them. This does not include the cumulative elevation gain for a round-trip hike.

Trail surface: Information about what to expect underfoot, including dirt, gravel, boulders, or bedrock.

Restrictions: General info about fees, parking restrictions, hours, pets, camping, and other restrictions. Note that restrictions change often—contact the land management agency for details.

Amenities: Features at the trailhead and on the trail, including toilets, drinking water, visitor centers, benches, and interpretive signs.

Maps: A list of maps for the trail and trailhead, including the *DeLorme: Colorado Atlas & Gazetteer (2019)*, Trails Illustrated maps, and USGS topo maps.

County: The name of the county where the trail and waterfall are located.

Land status/contact: The name and phone number of the trail's land management agency. Detailed contact info for each agency, including national parklands, national forests, and state parks, is located in the Appendix.

Finding the trailhead: Driving directions and GPS coordinates to the trailhead.

The Hike: A short description of the hike.

Miles and Directions: A step-by-step guide from trailhead to waterfall, including mileage and GPS waypoints at each critical point.

Overview map: This map shows the location of each waterfall hike by hike number.

Trail maps: These maps illustrate the trailheads, roads and trails, points of interest, waterways, landmarks, geographical features, and the waterfalls.

Packing for Your Waterfall Hike

You'll want to dress appropriately for your waterfall hike, but there are other items you should carry for a safe and successful outing.

Start with a comfortable backpack to fit everything in. You don't have to spend a lot of money to get a pack that will satisfy your needs, and you can upgrade later if you need to. Try it on in the store and make sure it fits your body well, then fill it up and see if it still feels right. If waterfall hiking becomes a habit, you may be wearing it a lot!

Water is the most important item that goes into your pack, and how much or little you need depends on you and how long your hike is. You can carry it in refillable bottles or use a fancy hydration kit that allows you to sip from a tube while you're on the move. For extra-long hikes, carry a water filter, so you can filter water from nearby streams and stay hydrated if your own supply runs out.

Extra clothing is also important, and that starts with a rain jacket. If you get wet on your hike, you will get cold, and that will ruin your day. Also think about carrying extra socks; a warm knit or fleece cap; a ball cap or sun hat with a brim; gloves; a warm top layer, such as a fleece shirt; a neck gaiter, headband, scarf, or "buff"; and water shoes that you can use for stream crossings, to keep your hiking shoes and boots dry. Staying warm, dry, and thoroughly hydrated is important on any hike, but it's especially critical at higher altitudes and above timberline, when you are even more susceptible to hypothermia, dehydration, and altitude sickness. These conditions can be debilitating and deadly but can usually be avoided with proper planning, packing, and knowing when to turn around.

A first-aid kit is always a good idea. You can buy one or make your own by putting bandages, antibacterial cream, pain reliever, and any other medications you use in a resealable plastic bag. The bag is also a good place to store a pen and paper with your contact information on it, and that of your emergency contact person. If you have a CORSAR (Colorado Outdoor Recreation Search and Rescue) card, tuck it into the first-aid kit. The card may be purchased online or at local businesses, and supports the Search and Rescue Fund, to help reimburse rescue teams that assist hikers who are lost or injured. The CORSAR card is not "rescue insurance," but it is an easy and inexpensive way for responsible Colorado hikers to support backcountry rescue personnel who may one day be called upon to come to their aid.

Invest in a headlamp and extra batteries, or a flashlight. Even the easiest trails are practically impassable in the dark, and there are no streetlights to guide you once the sun goes down. If you are hiking alone, carry two headlamps so you do not have to change batteries in the dark.

Buy a compass and learn how to use it. Should you get off-trail and disoriented, a map and compass—along with route-finding skills—will get you back on the trail and headed in the right direction pronto. You may eventually want to get a GPS too, and extra batteries to go with it. Gear shops, guiding companies, and nonprofit organizations like the Colorado Mountain Club offer courses in land navigation and can provide you with the instruction you need to use these tools correctly and confidently.

The lower waterfall at "Little Dolores Falls" pours through a crevice into a crystalline pool.

Food is perhaps the most fun thing to carry on a hike, especially when you get to eat it! A combination of sweet and salty snacks—such as fresh or dried fruit and nuts, or premade, packaged energy bars—will keep you alive and alert. For longer hikes, bring a lunch. Sandwiches travel well and taste great, and you can pack them in foil and plastic bags, along with a cold pack to keep them fresh and cool. Add a bottle of your favorite beverage like juice or an electrolyte drink in summer, or a thermos full of hot chocolate in colder months.

Sun protection is important, even on cloudy days. Along with your hat, pack sunglasses, sunscreen, and lip balm, and reapply during your hike.

Be sure to use the toilet before your hike, but if you should require a bathroom break along the trail, be prepared with a kit that includes toilet paper or wet wipes, plus—for women—feminine products, and—for men—anti-chafing powder, cream, or stick. Double bag it all in resealable plastic bags to keep the items fresh and dry, step off the trail to use them, bury all solid waste, and pack out all used items in an extra plastic bag. Certain locations require that you pack out your solid waste as well, so if that is the case be prepared with a suitable, disposable container.

Winter conditions demand even more gear, including additional clothing layers, like a face mask, windproof pants and gloves, and ski goggles for extreme cold and wind; a puffy jacket to keep you warm during breaks; plus microspikes or other portable traction devices to slip over your boots for safe passage on icy trails and frozen stream crossings, and even gaiters and snowshoes to keep you high and dry in deep powder.

Extra items might include trekking poles—especially if your hike includes a lot of elevation gain or stream crossings—bug spray, a camera, and, of course, a copy of this book. Pack your guidebook in a resealable plastic bag to keep it safe and dry for your next hike.

Final Preparations

Now that you've selected your waterfall hike, and you're getting packed up and ready to go, there are just a few more things you should know.

Check the CDOT (Colorado Department of Transportation) site at www.cotrip .org for road conditions and closures along your route to the trailhead.

Check the NOAA (National Oceanic and Atmospheric Administration) site at www.noaa.gov for weather conditions. Be sure that you won't be hiking through open areas or above treeline in inclement weather, especially if there's a danger of lightning. If stormy conditions arise, be prepared to descend to the trailhead immediately.

If you plan on camping at a campground, check www.recreation.gov for availability and reservations.

If you're traveling on snow, check the Colorado Avalanche Information Center site at https://avalanche.state.co.us/index.php and avoid areas subject to avalanche danger. A thorough discussion of avalanche safety is beyond the scope of this book, but if avalanche danger exists on your planned hike, seek out the advice of an expert to determine an alternate route, choose another hike, or go another day.

Check the website of the land management agency (see Appendix) listed in the "Land status/contact" section of each hike for notifications or changes in restrictions. In the winter or springtime, ask about the effects of snow on the road to the trailhead, as some may be closed and gated, adding miles to your hike. Also find out about avalanche danger on the trail, and if there's a "winter route" that avoids that danger. Call the ranger station to get all your questions answered before you go.

If you're visiting a fee area, call ahead to find out how much it costs. Many of the parks offer annual passes, and if you plan on visiting them often it may make sense to invest in an annual National Parks pass and a Colorado State Park pass. These may be purchased at the parks, online, and at local businesses around the state. Also, bring cash or checks to pay fees if the entrance gate is unattended and you have to pay at a self-serve kiosk. Contact information for purchasing parks passes can be found in the Appendix.

For extra-long drives, bring a cooler with drinks and snacks, and two bags for your trash: one for recycling and one for composting. Carry extra change or small bills, so you can stop at local grocers or gas stations and buy items like drinks or post-cards, and then use the restrooms.

Plan on the drive and the hike taking longer than you expect, especially if you're traveling with others. Stops for gas, snacks, and restroom breaks take time, and you should work these into your schedule. Expect them, and you won't be stressed out when they happen.

Waterfall hikes may become a habit, and your favorite part of the whole week. Keep them fun, safe, and healthy, and you'll keep yourself happy doing them.

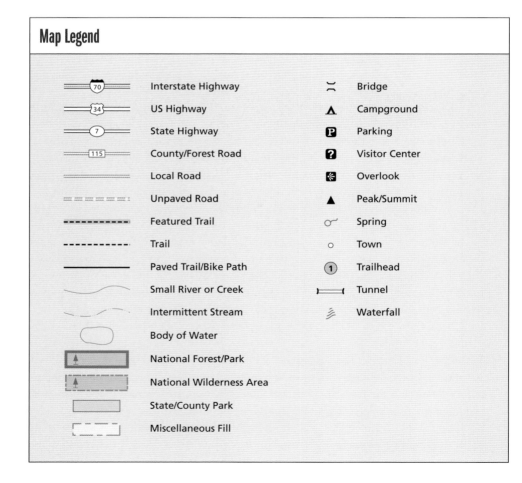

Map Legend

Interstate Highway		Bridge	
US Highway		Campground	
State Highway		Parking	
County/Forest Road		Visitor Center	
Local Road		Overlook	
Unpaved Road		Peak/Summit	
Featured Trail		Spring	
Trail		Town	
Paved Trail/Bike Path		Trailhead	
Small River or Creek		Tunnel	
Intermittent Stream		Waterfall	
Body of Water			
National Forest/Park			
National Wilderness Area			
State/County Park			
Miscellaneous Fill			

Denver and Boulder Area

Boulder, Eldorado Canyon, Idaho Springs, Conifer, Evergreen, Franktown, and Jefferson

Boulder Falls, one of Colorado's most accessible waterfalls, pours over a rock ledge in a Boulder city parkland.

1 Timberline Falls (Camp Dick)

Middle St. Vrain Creek, rising from the St. Vrain Glaciers on the Continental Divide, gushes through a gorge and drops its waters in stepped sheets and cascades at Timberline Falls.

Start: Middle Saint Vrain Trailhead
Trail: Buchanan Pass Trail #910
Difficulty: Easy/moderate
Hiking time: About 3 hours
Distance: 4.4 miles out and back
Elevation trailhead to falls viewpoint: 8,700 to 9,200 feet (+500 feet)
Trail surface: Dirt, rocks
Restrictions: No motorized vehicles; dogs prohibited Dec 1 to Apr 30

Amenities: Backcountry camping permitted beyond 0.5 mile of trailhead; vault toilets at Camp Dick and Peaceful Valley Campgrounds; services in Boulder and Allenspark
Maps: *DeLorme:* Page 29 D6; Trails Illustrated 102: Indian Peaks, Gold Hill; USGS Allens Park
County: Boulder
Land status/contact: Roosevelt National Forest, (970) 295-6600; Boulder Ranger District, (303) 541-2500

Finding the trailhead: From Boulder, take CO 93 North and turn left on Lee Hill Drive, which turns into Olde Stage Road. At 4.7 miles turn left on Lefthand Canyon Drive (which turns into James Canyon Drive, Main Street, and unpaved Overland Road) and drive 12.3 miles, then turn right on paved CO 72 West (Peak to Peak Highway). From Lyons, take CO 7 West for about 7 miles to CO 72; from Estes Park, take CO 7 South for about 18 miles to CO 72.

Drive 1.5 miles on CO 72, turn left on CR 92, and go 0.1 mile to Middle St. Vrain Road. Continue for another 1.2 miles through Peaceful Valley Campground and Camp Dick Campground, to the west end of the campground, and park at the trailhead (GPS: 40 7.793, -105 31.447).

The Hike

The waterfall hike follows the Buchanan Pass Trail across mostly easy terrain in Middle St. Vrain Creek's wooded valley. Beginning west of Peaceful Valley and Camp Dick Campgrounds, the hike initially follows a 4WD road and then cuts right on the trail along the creek's north side to the falls. After stepping across an unnamed tributary on rocks and logs, listen for the sound of falling water. A path heads left to the creek. Proceed carefully to the waterfall's base. Afterward, return to the main trail and continue to a rocky overlook above the falls. Use caution above the falls and on the steep trail down to the creek. The water runs fast, especially early in the summer, and a fall would be deadly.

Miles and Directions

0.0 Begin at the Middle St. Vrain Trailhead. Hike up 4WD Middle St. Vrain Road (FR 1141) for about 250 feet and turn right on Buchanan Pass Trail (GPS: 40 7.8182, -105 31.5372).

0.1 Cross a bridge over the creek and head west on a narrow, rocky trail on its north bank.

Timberline Falls (Camp Dick)

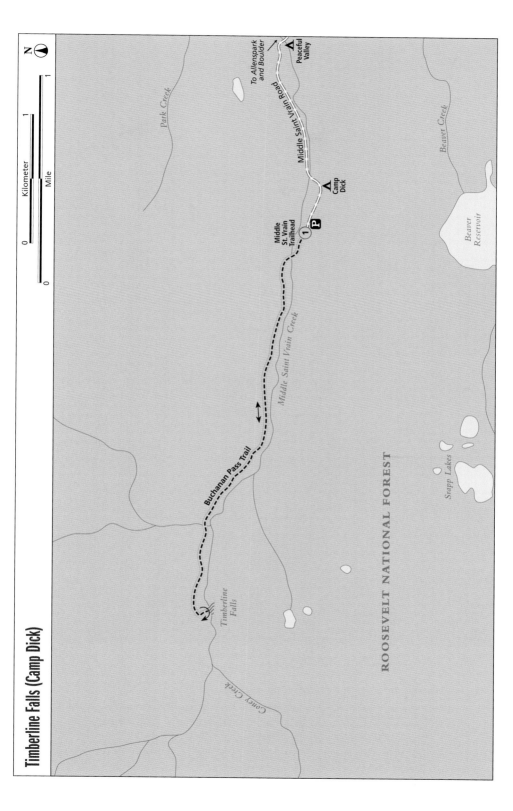

Middle St. Vrain Creek gushes through a deep gorge at Timberline Falls.

2.1 Leave main trail to left and carefully descend to falls.

2.2 Arrive at Timberline Falls (GPS: 40 8.166, -105 33.498). Return to main trail and go left to viewpoints on outcrops above falls. Alternatively, view waterfall from additional trails beyond rock outcrop. Return the way you came.

4.4 Arrive back at trailhead (GPS: 40 7.793, -105 31.447).

2 Boulder Falls

North of Boulder Canyon, North Boulder Creek twists south through a granite-walled gorge to Boulder Creek. Just north of CO 119, the creek spills over a dramatic, segmented plunge and splashes to the rocky creek bed in a grandiose horsetail spray.

Start: Boulder Falls Trailhead
Trail: Boulder Falls Trail
Difficulty: Easy
Hiking time: About 30 minutes
Distance: 0.2 mile out and back
Elevation trailhead to falls viewpoint: 6,910 to 6,930 feet (+20 feet)
Trail surface: Stone steps, rocks, dirt
Restrictions: Trail may be closed seasonally with limited hours (contact Boulder Open

Space for closure info); stay on trail; no climbing off-trail or on rocks; no wading; no glass bottles; no bicycles or motor vehicles; dogs must be leashed
Amenities: Services in Boulder
Maps: *DeLorme:* Page 39 A8; Trails Illustrated 100: Boulder, Golden; USGS Gold Hill
County: Boulder
Land status/contact: Boulder Open Space & Mountain Parks, (303) 441-3440

Finding the trailhead: From 28th Street (US 36) in Boulder, drive west on Canyon Boulevard (CO 119) for 10.4 miles to a strip parking lot on the left (south) side of the highway. Use extreme caution turning across eastbound traffic into parking spaces. Parking is limited, so visitors often park on the right shoulder past the falls trail. If parking in the lot, note that there is no crosswalk on US 36, so use caution crossing the highway to the trailhead (GPS: 40 0.2785, -105 24.3807).

The Hike

One of the Front Range's best waterfalls, 70-foot Boulder Falls lies in a 5-acre city park that was donated to Boulder in 1914 to save "this beautiful spot from the encroachment of the great tungsten boom." This short hike is dangerous, with accidents and fatalities occurring every year. Avoid scrambling on loose rocks above the overlook and waterfall, and on slick rocks along the creek. Boulder Falls isn't more dangerous than other waterfalls in this book, but because the falls are so accessible, it invites visitors with little backcountry experience. Observe posted park rules and warnings and stay on the trail.

The crux of the hike is crossing the highway from the parking strip opposite the trailhead. There is no crosswalk, so watch for speeding cars. Trailhead signs warn about waterfall dangers including wet, icy, and falling rocks. "Picture Rock" is also here, a boulder moved from the creek bed, providing a backdrop for hiker photos.

Boulder Falls

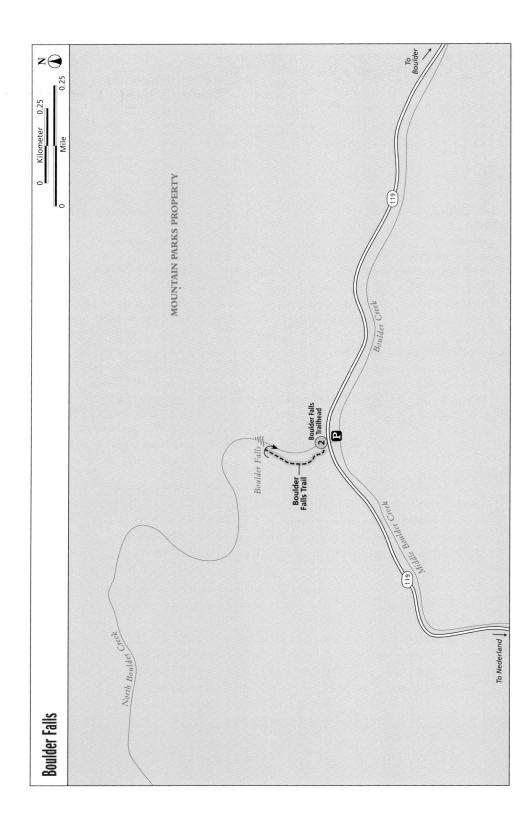

MOUNTAIN PARKS PROPERTY

North Boulder Creek

Boulder Falls

Boulder
Falls Trail

Boulder Falls
Trailhead

2

P

119

Boulder Creek

Middle Boulder Creek

119

To Nederland

To Boulder

N

0   Kilometer   0.25

0   Mile   0.25

North Boulder Creek wends through a granite-walled gorge and spills its waters at Boulder Falls.

Miles and Directions

0.0 Begin at trailhead on north side of highway. On the left, descend a stone staircase and hike north above west bank of creek.

0.1 Arrive at Boulder Falls overlook (GPS: 40 00.335, -105 24.399). Return on trail.

0.2 Arrive back at trailhead (GPS: 40 0.2785, -105 24.3807).

3 "Eldorado Falls"

South Boulder Creek flows from Gross Reservoir through Walker Ranch Park and Eldorado Canyon State Park. The reservoir's steady outflux provides a cascade that rushes over boulders in a flourish at "Eldorado Falls."

Start: Ethel Harrold Trailhead; Eldorado Canyon Trailhead
Trails: Walker Ranch Loop Trail, Eldorado Canyon Trail
Difficulty: Moderate for both hikes
Hiking time: About 2 hours for Walker Ranch hike; 4 hours for Eldorado Canyon hike
Distance: 3.3 miles out and back for Walker Ranch hike; 6.6 miles out and back for Eldorado Canyon hike
Elevation trailheads to falls viewpoints: 6,910 to 6,460 feet (-450 feet) for Walker Ranch hike; 6,100 to 6,460 feet (+360 feet) for Eldorado Canyon hike
Trail surface: Gravel road, dirt, rocks

Restrictions: Fee at Eldorado Canyon State Park; no bicycles on Eldorado Canyon Trail; both trails day use only, with no camping, ground fires, firearms, or motorized vehicles; no glass containers; dogs must be leashed
Amenities: Visitor center and restrooms at Eldorado Canyon Trailhead; vault toilets and picnic tables at Ethel Harrold Trailhead; services in Boulder
Maps: *DeLorme:* Page 39 A8; Trails Illustrated 100: Boulder, Golden; USGS Eldorado Springs
County: Boulder
Land status/contact: Eldorado Canyon State Park, (303) 494-3943; City of Boulder Open Space & Mountain Parks, (303) 441-3440

Finding the trailhead: Walker Ranch Loop Trail: From US 36 in Boulder, drive west on Baseline Road to its junction with Broadway. Continue west for 8.7 miles on Baseline and Flagstaff Mountain Road to a left turn on Pika Road. Drive east on Pika for 1.1 miles and turn right on Bison Drive. Continue 0.2 mile to Ethel Harrold Trailhead at 226 Bison Dr. (GPS: 39 57.335, -105 19.337).

Eldorado Canyon Trail: From the junction of Broadway and Baseline Road in Boulder, take Broadway (CO 93) south and go right (west) on CO 170 to the entrance to Eldorado Canyon State Park. Continue up the canyon for 0.7 mile to the road's end at the visitor center. Park in the visitor center lot or 0.1 mile to the east. Eldorado Canyon Trail starts from the road northeast of the center (GPS: 39 55.859, -105 17.641).

The Hike

South Boulder Creek crashes through a boulder-filled gap, forming "Eldorado Falls" in a deep canyon. The waterfall is impressive in late spring and early summer when snowmelt swells the creek. Two scenic hikes reach the falls, one from Ethel Harrold Trailhead in Walker Ranch Park and the other from Eldorado Canyon State Park. The hike from Harrold Trailhead descends to the falls and gains almost 800 feet of round-trip elevation, while the hike from the state park visitor center is more strenuous with over 1,000 feet of elevation gain.

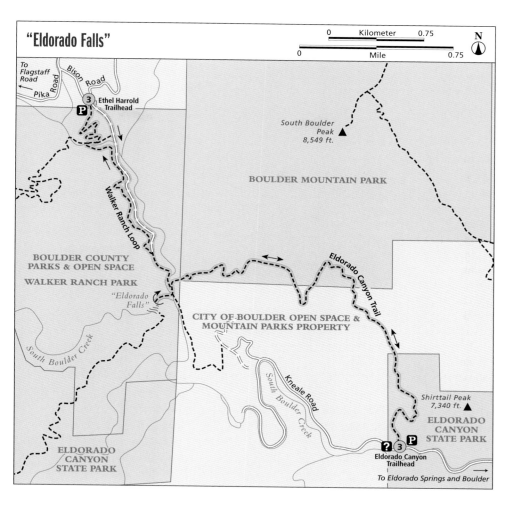

Walker Ranch Hike

From Ethel Harrold Trailhead, descend a closed road down Martin Gulch, losing 450 feet to a junction with Eldorado Canyon Trail. At the junction, bear right toward the creek, cross a bridge, and hike to a vantage point to enjoy the cascade. Return to the trailhead by reversing your footsteps to a junction with Walker Ranch Loop, which offers easy grades back to your car.

Eldorado Canyon Hike

From Eldorado Canyon Trailhead, ascend switchbacks along the western flank of Shirttail Peak. The trail winds through forest before dropping west toward the creek. Meet Walker Ranch Loop near the canyon floor and go left to the bridge and the waterfall.

Miles and Directions

From Ethel Harrold Trailhead

0.0 Begin at trailhead at gate on left side of parking lot. Hike south down old road.

0.8 Reach junction with Walker Ranch Loop Trail (return trail) on right—continue straight down road.

1.1 Reach junction with Eldorado Canyon Trail on left (GPS: 39 56.5349, -105 18.9151). Continue to South Boulder Creek and cross bridge to south bank.

1.3 Arrive at "Eldorado Falls" (GPS: 39 56.4757, -105 18.9658). Return up trail to junction.

1.8 Reach junction with signed Walker Ranch Loop on left (GPS: 39 56.6911, -105 18.9931). Go left on singletrack trail.

2.7 Reach junction. Walker Ranch Loop goes left. Go right on connector trail.

3.3 Arrive at trailhead beside vault toilets (GPS: 39 57.3297, -105 19.3531).

From Eldorado Canyon Trailhead

0.0 Begin at Eldorado Canyon Trailhead and hike north.

2.5 Reach high point of trail. Turn right (west) and descend switchbacks.

3.2 Reach junction with Walker Ranch Loop (GPS: 39 56.5349, -105 18.9151). Turn left toward creek and cross bridge.

3.3 Reach "Eldorado Falls" (GPS: 39 56.4757, -105 18.9658). Return the way you came.

6.6 Arrive back at trailhead (GPS: 39 55.859, -105 17.641).

A year-round cascade slips through the canyon in a tumultuous flourish at "Eldorado Falls."

4 Bridal Veil Falls (Idaho Springs)

Soda Creek slips over a high cliff above I-70 and flows into Clear Creek. A paved trail from downtown Idaho Springs leads to a historic waterwheel and this long, horsetail waterfall.

Start: Harold A. Anderson Park Trailhead
Trail: Charlie Tayler Waterwheel Trail
Difficulty: Easy
Hiking time: About 30 minutes
Distance: 0.2 mile out and back
Elevation trailhead to falls viewpoint: 7,540 to 7,550 feet (+10 feet)
Trail surface: Paved

Restrictions: None posted
Amenities: Picnic table at the trailhead; services in Idaho Springs
Maps: *DeLorme:* Page 39 C7; Trails Illustrated 100: Boulder, Golden; USGS Idaho Springs
County: Clear Creek
Land status/contact: City of Idaho Springs, (303) 567-4421

Finding the trailhead: From I-70 West in Idaho Springs, take exit 241A; from I-70 East take exit 240. Drive to downtown and follow Miner Street in the business district. Turn south on 17th Avenue and park in public lots on Water Street near Harold A. Anderson Park. The trailhead (GPS: 39 44.486, -105 30.883) is by the park and a steam locomotive.

The Hike

Bridal Veil Falls tumbles over 60 feet down a vertical cliff to a boulderfield above Clear Creek on the southern edge of Idaho Springs and I-70. The lacy falls, one of Colorado's most accessible waterfalls, is best seen from Wagon Wheel Park. Afterward, stroll around the town's historic downtown and visit the Idaho Springs Visitor Center and Heritage Museum to discover the area's history.

Begin at the corner of Harold A. Anderson Park, near "Old Smoke and Cinders," a retired narrow-gauge train engine that was built by the Rhode Island Locomotive Works in 1886. The paved trail goes left to Clear Creek and passes under an I-70 bridge. Mine shafts are visible across the creek. Hike west on the paved trail to Wagon Wheel Park, a large plaza with benches that look toward the waterfall and a landmark waterwheel on the south side of the creek. The waterwheel, sitting at the waterfall's base, is a nineteenth-century artifact once used to power a stamp mill. Interpretive signs and a plaque at the plaza describe area history and the wheel, stating that its builder, gold miner Charlie Tayler, attributed his health to the fact that he "never kissed women or took baths."

Bridal Veil Falls (Idaho Springs)

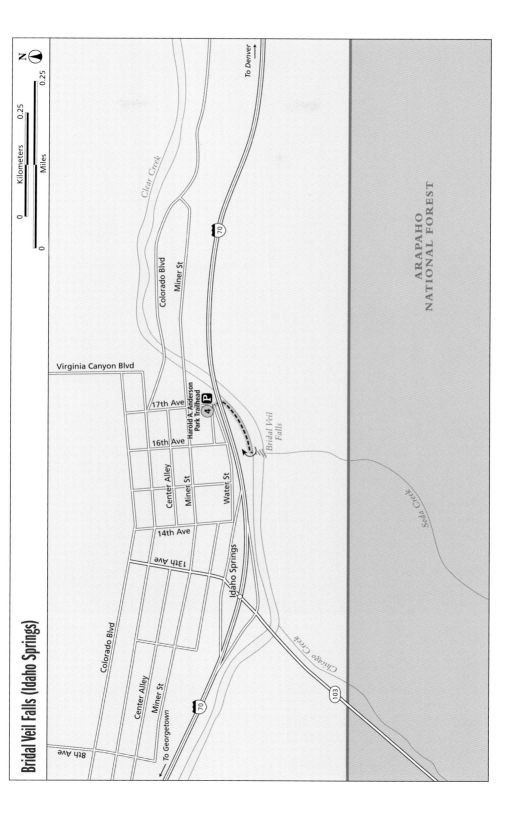

N

0   0.25   0.25
|————————————|————————————| Kilometers
|————————————|————————————| Miles
0   0.25

Clear Creek

Colorado Blvd

Miner St

70

To Denver →

Virginia Canyon Blvd

17th Ave

Harold A. Anderson
Park Trailhead

4 P

16th Ave

Center Alley

Miner St

Water St

Bridal Veil
Falls

14th Ave

13th Ave

Idaho Springs

Colorado Blvd

Center Alley

Miner St

70

To Georgetown →

8th Ave

Chicago Creek

103

Soda Creek

ARAPAHO
NATIONAL FOREST

Reached by a paved trail in Idaho Springs, Bridal Veil Falls slides down a cliff into Clear Creek.

Miles and Directions

0.0 Begin at trailhead by locomotive. Follow paved trail under I-70 bridge and along Clear Creek.

0.1 Reach viewpoint of Bridal Veil Falls (GPS: 39 44.440, -105 30.954). Return under bridge.

0.2 Arrive back at trailhead (GPS: 39 44.486, -105 30.883)

5 Maxwell Falls

Maxwell Creek slides through a trailside defile and slips over granite blocks in shimmery sheets at Maxwell Falls. This up-and-down hike between Evergreen and Conifer is a family favorite.

Start: Upper Maxwell Falls Trailhead; Lower Maxwell Falls Trailhead
Trail: Maxwell Falls Trail #111
Difficulty: Easy from Upper Maxwell Falls Trailhead; easy/moderate from Lower Maxwell Falls Trailhead
Hiking time: Less than 1 hour from upper trailhead; about 3 hours from lower trailhead
Distance: 1.0 mile out and back from upper trailhead to overlook, 1.2 miles out and back from upper trailhead to overlook and base of falls; 3.6 miles out and back from lower trailhead to overlook, 3.8 miles out and back from lower trailhead to base of falls and overlook
Elevation trailheads to falls viewpoints: 8,410 to 8,260 feet (-150 feet) from upper

trailhead to overlook; 7,780 to 8,260 feet (+480 feet) from lower trailhead to overlook
Trail surface: Dirt, rocks
Restrictions: Open sunrise to sunset; dogs must be leashed; no campfires or camping; park in designated lots
Amenities: Services in Conifer and Evergreen
Maps: *DeLorme:* p. 39 E8; Trails Illustrated 100: Boulder, Golden; USGS Meridian Hill, Conifer
County: Jefferson
Land status/contact: Arapaho National Forest, (970) 295-6600; Clear Creek Ranger District, (303) 567-3000

Finding the trailheads: *Upper trailhead:* From US 285 North in Conifer, turn right on CR 73 and immediately go right at a junction on CR 73. Drive 1.8 miles and turn left on Shadow Mountain Drive (CR 78), then drive 3.4 miles to a Y-junction. Keep left on Black Mountain Drive (CR 78). Continue 1.8 miles to the trailhead and parking on the right (GPS: 39 33.7477, -105 22.6039).

Lower trailhead: From the junction of CO 74 and CO 73 in Evergreen, take CR 73 south for 1 mile and turn right on South Brook Forest Road. Drive 3.6 miles west to the trailhead and parking lot on the left side. More parking is past the trailhead. (GPS: 39 34.9436, -105 21.6575).

The Hike

Maxwell Falls is a horsetail waterfall fed by Maxwell Creek, a stream that originates on the north slope of 10,756-foot Black Mountain to the south. The creek usually slows to a trickle by midsummer. The trail and falls, a short distance from Denver's three million people, is being loved to death, especially on summer weekends when cars fill the trailhead parking lots and spill into nearby neighborhoods. To protect the area, campfires, stoves, and camping are prohibited. Plan on hiking on weekdays to avoid crowds.

Turn page: Maxwell Creek trembles through ▷
boulders in shimmery sheets at Maxwell Falls.

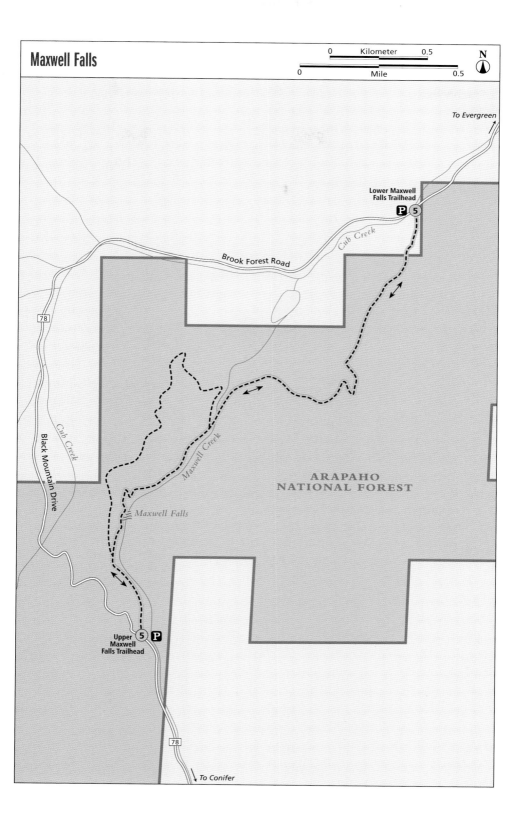

Maxwell Falls

0   Kilometer   0.5

0   Mile   0.5

N

To Evergreen

Lower Maxwell
Falls Trailhead

P 5

Cub Creek

Brook Forest Road

78

Cub Creek

Black Mountain Drive

Maxwell Creek

Maxwell Falls

ARAPAHO
NATIONAL FOREST

Upper
Maxwell
Falls Trailhead

5 P

78

To Conifer

From the upper trailhead, it is a short descent to the falls, with the elevation gain on the hike back to the trailhead. View the falls from a signed overlook or continue down to the base to see the lower leaps. Don't be tempted to descend from the overlook to the waterfall, but rather use the trail to access the base.

From the lower trailhead, it is a longer hike with more elevation gain. Although the net gain from trailhead to falls is 480 feet, the trail rises and falls twice, and hikers have to regain the loss on the way out for a total round-trip gain of over 1,000 feet.

Miles and Directions

Upper Maxwell Falls Trailhead

0.0 Begin at trailhead on left side of parking lot. Follow trail and gravel road, staying left of creek.

0.3 Reach trail junction with Cliff Loop—stay straight toward lower trailhead and falls.

0.4 Follow trail to rock outcrop above falls (GPS: 39 34.086, -105 22.677). Ascend trail to scenic overlook.

0.5 Arrive at overlook above Maxwell Falls (GPS: 39 34.106, -105 22.681). Continue north on main trail.

0.6 Reach junction on right with short trail. Descend to the right to waterfall's base. Arrive at Maxwell Falls (GPS: 39 34.092, -105 22.662). Reverse route to trailhead.

1.2 Arrive back at trailhead (GPS: 39 33.7477, -105 22.6039).

Lower Maxwell Falls Trailhead

0.0 Begin at trailhead on right side of parking lot. Hike southwest on trail.

0.7 Cross Maxwell Creek and switchback right, then left as trail climbs hillside.

0.9 Reach junction—go straight.

1.3 Cross footbridge over creek and take left fork alongside creek. At trail junction with Cliff Loop to right, continue straight along creek.

1.7 Reach junction with short trail and descend left to waterfall base. Arrive at Maxwell Falls (GPS: 39 34.092, -105 22.662). Return to main trail and go left to scenic overlook.

1.8 Arrive at overlook above Maxwell Falls (GPS: 39 34.106, -105 22.681). Return down trail.

3.6 Arrive back at trailhead (GPS: 39 34.9436, -105 21.6575).

6 Elk Falls

North Elk Creek flows southeast through 3,828-acre Staunton State Park, carving a canyon and slipping over a granite cliff at 75-foot Elk Falls. This delightful sheet waterfall is reached by a long hike through the park.

Start: Staunton Ranch Trailhead
Trails: Staunton Ranch Trail, Bugling Elk Trail, Chimney Rock Trail, Elk Falls Trail, Lions Back Trail
Difficulty: Strenuous
Hiking time: 5–6 hours
Distance: 10.8 miles out and back to Elk Falls; 12.3 miles with overlook loop
Elevation trailheads to falls viewpoints:
8,355 feet at trailhead; 8,730 feet at falls; 9,150 feet at Elk Falls Overlook
Trail surface: Gravel, dirt, rocks

Restrictions: Fee area; hikers only on Chimney Rock Trail; leashed dogs allowed; stay on designated trails; mountain bikes only on roads; ground fires prohibited
Amenities: Services in Conifer and Evergreen; walk-in tent campsites
Maps: *DeLorme:* Page 39 E8; Trails Illustrated 100: Boulder, Golden; USGS Meridian Hill, Conifer
Counties: Jefferson, Park
Land status/contact: Staunton State Park, (303) 816-0912

Finding the trailhead: From Denver, drive west on US 285 to Shaffers Crossing, about 6 miles west of Conifer. Turn right (north) on Elk Creek Road (CR 83) and drive 1.3 miles to a signed right turn into the park. Drive 0.4 mile north on the park road to the visitor center. Continue north for 0.5 mile to the upper parking lot and trailhead on the right (GPS: 39 30.0156, -105 22.6766). Park address: 12102 S. Elk Creek Rd.

The Hike

Elk Falls is one of Staunton State Park's crown jewels and the highest waterfall near Denver. The hike, following five trails, crosses easy and moderate terrain with few steep grades and 1,500 feet of elevation gain. The described hike reaches the waterfall's base and a waterfall overlook on Lions Head. The trails and junctions are well marked with park signs.

Begin at the Upper Parking Lot, hub for most of the park's 30 miles of trails, and head northwest on Staunton Ranch Trail (SR) through an open pine forest below mountains studded with cliffs popular with rock climbers. The hike continues on Bugling Elk Trail (BE) to North Elk Creek's wide valley and Elk Falls Pond at 8,846 feet. Past a ranger house, go right on Chimney Rock Trail (CR) to Elk Falls Trail (EF), which switchbacks below Chimney Rock to a viewpoint of Elk Falls spraying down a slab. After admiring the waterfall, return to CR Trail and go left to Lions Back Trail

Turn page: North Elk Creek splashes and sprays down a ▷
granite slab at Elk Falls in Staunton State Park.

Elk Falls

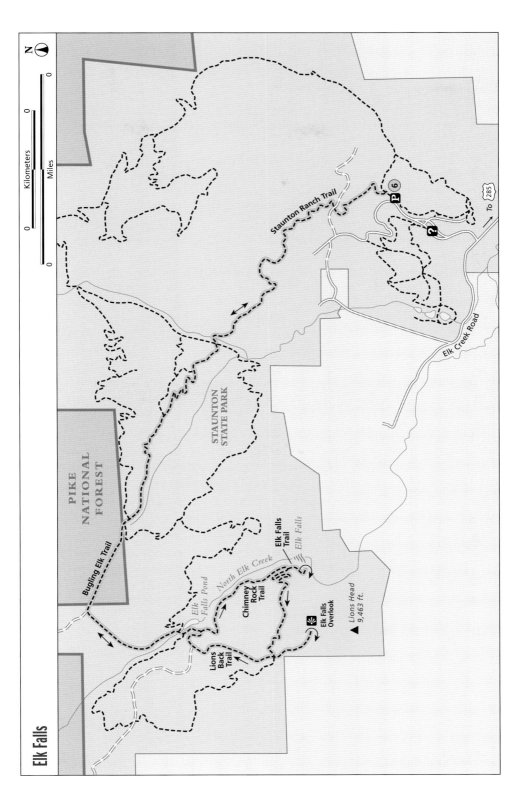

PIKE
NATIONAL
FOREST

STAUNTON
STATE PARK

Bugling Elk Trail

Elk Falls Pond

North Elk Creek

Lions Back Trail

Chimney Rock Trail

Elk Falls Trail

Elk Falls

Elk Falls Overlook

▲ Lions Head
9,463 ft.

Staunton Ranch Trail

Elk Creek Road

To 285

P 6

?

N

Kilometers

Miles

(LB) and 9,150-foot Elk Falls Overlook. Finish by following LB Trail to Elk Falls Pond and then retracing your steps to the trailhead.

Miles and Directions

0.0   Start at Staunton Ranch Trailhead. Hike left for 100 feet to a signed junction. Keep left on Staunton Ranch Trail (SR).

0.5   Reach junction with a park road. Continue straight.

1.7   Pass junction with climbing access trail on right (GPS: 39 30.6908, -105 23.4633). Continue on SR Trail and cross a footbridge.

1.9   Arrive at junction with Old Mill Trail (OM) (GPS: 39 30.7666, -105 23.576). Continue straight on SR Trail.

3.0   Reach a service road and go right on it (SR Trail) (GPS: 39 31.0659, -105 24.326).

3.3   Arrive at junction with Borderline Trail (BL) on right and Marmot Passage Trail (MP) on left (GPS: 39 31.1601, -105 24.6092). This is end of SR Trail. Go west on Bugling Elk Trail (BE) on service road. Descend North Fork of North Elk Creek valley and bend east along North Elk Creek.

4.3   Reach junction with Marmot Passage Trail at Elk Falls Pond (GPS: 39 30.9372, -105 25.2428) and end of BE Trail. Continue past pond on Lions Back Trail (LB), a service road.

4.4   Reach building by pond. Keep right on LB Trail and go uphill.

4.45   Reach junction with Chimney Rock Trail (CR) on left (GPS: 39 30.8372, -105 25.2431). Go left on singletrack CR Trail and contour across north-facing slopes above creek.

5.1   Reach junction with Elk Falls Trail (EF) (GPS: 39 30.4486, -105 24.8785). Go left on EF (hikers only) and descend to overlook.

5.4   Arrive at Elk Falls overlook below Chimney Rock (GPS: 39 30.3784, -105 24.8771).

5.7   Return to junction with CR Trail. Go left and hike uphill.

6.6   Reach junction with wide Lions Back Trail (LB) in aspens (GPS: 39 30.5164, -105 25.3862). Go left up LB Trail and turn left at sign for "Elk Falls Overlook."

6.9   Arrive at 9,150-foot Elk Falls Overlook on slabs (GPS: 39 30.3479, -105 25.2388). After viewing falls, return down LB Trail.

7.2   Return to junction with CR Trail. Continue straight on wide LB Trail.

7.9   Reach junction with start of CR Trail above pond. Continue to pond and hike northwest on LB Trail to junction with Marmot Passage Trail (MP). Continue straight on Bugling Elk Trail (BE) on service road.

9.0   Return to junction with Staunton Ranch Trail (SR) and MP Trail and Borderline Trail. Continue on SR Trail for 0.3 mile. Leave road on left and hike east on signed SR Trail.

12.3   Arrive back at trailhead (GPS: 39 30.0156, -105 22.6766).

7 "Cherry Creek Falls"

Cherry Creek flows northwest through Castlewood Canyon State Park between Denver and Colorado Springs, cutting a deep gorge. Sheer cliffs draw the eye upward, while the sight and sound of rushing waters in the canyon below the trail cast your focus on this scenic cascade.

Start: Falls Spur Trailhead; Inner Canyon Trailhead
Trails: Falls Spur Trail, Canyon View Nature Trail, Inner Canyon Trail, Creek Bottom Trail
Difficulty: Easy from Falls Spur Trailhead; easy/moderate from Inner Canyon Trailhead
Hiking time: Less than 1 hour from Falls Spur Trail; about 3 hours from Inner Canyon Trail
Distance: 0.4 mile out and back from Falls Spur Trailhead; 4.0 miles out and back from Inner Canyon Trailhead
Elevation trailheads to falls viewpoint: 6,340 to 6,300 feet (-40 feet) from Falls Spur Trailhead; 6,610 to 6,300 feet (-310 feet) from Inner Canyon Trailhead

Trail surface: Paved, dirt, rocks
Restrictions: Fee area; day use only; no camping, ground fires, bicycles, or firearms; pets must be leashed; inbound gates locked 1 hour before sunset, all gates locked at sunset
Amenities: Visitor center; picnic areas; restrooms; water at Inner Canyon Trailhead; services in Franktown and Castle Rock
Maps: *DeLorme:* p. 51 B5; Trails Illustrated: none; USGS Castle Rock South, Russellville Gulch
County: Douglas
Land status/contact: Castlewood Canyon State Park, (303) 688-5242

Finding the trailhead: From I-25 in Castle Rock, take exit 184 east to Founders Parkway (CO 86) and drive 4.4 miles. Turn left at the intersection to stay on CO 86.

West entrance: Go 1.6 miles and turn right (south) on Castlewood Canyon Road. Drive 2 miles on this gravel road to the west entrance of Castlewood Canyon State Park. Pay at the gate and follow signs to the Falls Lot (GPS: 39 20.924, -104 45.847).

East (main) entrance: Go 5 miles to Franktown and turn right (south) on CO 83. Drive 5 miles and turn right into Castlewood Canyon State Park. Pay at the gate and follow signs to Inner Canyon Trailhead (GPS: 39 20.016, -104 44.653).

The Hike

"Cherry Creek Falls" is a lovely 20-foot waterfall that plunges off a boulder into a pool in Castlewood Canyon. The canyon was excavated after an upstream dam collapsed in 1933, sending a wall of water down to Denver, claiming seven lives and causing over a million dollars of damage. The waterfall is reached by several routes, but the most scenic trails are described here. Stay on trails to avoid poison ivy and rattlesnakes. Grab a map at the gate or visitor center to choose more hiking adventures.

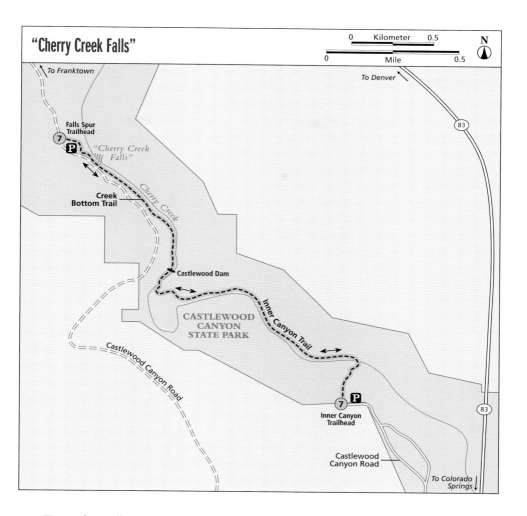

"Cherry Creek Falls"

0   Kilometer   0.5

0   Mile   0.5

N

To Franktown

To Denver

83

Falls Spur
Trailhead

7 P

*"Cherry Creek
Falls"*

Creek
Bottom Trail

Cherry Creek

Castlewood Dam

CASTLEWOOD
CANYON
STATE PARK

Inner Canyon Trail

Castlewood Canyon Road

7 P

Inner Canyon
Trailhead

83

Castlewood
Canyon Road

To Colorado
Springs

From the Falls Lot

Descend the Falls Spur Trail along the canyon's west edge to view the waterfall. No toilets at this trailhead, but there is one at Middle Parking Lot to the north.

From Canyon Point Parking Area near Visitor Center

Take the paved Canyon View Nature Trail to access the Inner Canyon Trail. Descend the steps and follow the trail along the creek to a junction with Rim Rock Trail and Creek Bottom Trail. Go left on Creek Bottom Trail, crossing a meadow then descending to a bridge. Bear right on Creek Bottom Trail, keeping the creek to your right. Pass the Dam Ruins and hike to a fence above the falls. Continue hiking north and look below and to the right for the best view of "Cherry Creek Falls."

◀ *Cherry Creek flows through Castlewood Canyon,
cutting a wide swath at "Cherry Creek Falls."*

Miles and Directions

Easy Hike from Falls Spur Trailhead by West Entrance:

0.0 Begin at trailhead and hike downhill on Falls Spur Trail.

0.1 Turn right on Creek Bottom Trail.

0.2 Reach viewpoint of "Cherry Creek Falls" below (GPS: 39 20.857, -104 45.738). Return the way you came.

0.4 Arrive back at trailhead (GPS: 39 20.924, -104 45.847).

Easy/Moderate Hike from Inner Canyon Trailhead by East Entrance

0.0 From Canyon Point parking lot, hike north on paved Canyon View Nature Trail.

0.1 Reach Inner Canyon Trailhead. Turn left on trail and descend into canyon.

0.2 Cross bridge over Cherry Creek.

0.9 Reach junction with Lake Gulch Trail—stay right on Inner Canyon Trail.

1.1 Reach junction with Rim Rock Trail—go left on Creek Bottom Trail.

1.3 Cross last bridge, bear right, and follow trail past Dam Ruins.

1.9 Arrive at top of "Cherry Creek Falls" (GPS: 39 20.819, -104 45.679). Continue past falls for the best view.

2.0 Enjoy "Cherry Creek Falls" below (GPS: 39 20.857, -104 45.738). Return on trails.

4.0 Arrive back at trailhead (GPS: 39 20.016, -104 44.653).

Tarryall Reservoir provides a segmented ▷
surge of horsetail leaps at "Tarryall Falls.

8 "Tarryall Falls"

North Tarryall Creek flows from 13,000-foot peaks above Boreas Pass, feeding Tarryall Creek and pooling at Tarryall Reservoir. A narrow canyon at the reservoir's southern tip diverts the creek's path, sending waters in a segmented surge of horsetail leaps at "Tarryall Falls."

Start: Turner Gulch Road parking area
Trail: None
Difficulty: Easy
Hiking time: Less than 1 hour
Distance: Roadside
Elevation trailhead to falls viewpoints: Minimal or none for roadside viewing
Trail surface: Dirt, gravel, rocks
Restrictions: Dogs must be leashed.

Amenities: Camping, restrooms, and picnicking at Tarryall Reservoir; services in Lake George and Fairplay
Maps: *DeLorme:* Page 49 C6; Trails Illustrated 105: Tarryall Mountains, Kenosha Pass; USGS Farnum Peak
County: Park
Land status/contact: Tarryall Reservoir State Wildlife Area, Colorado Parks and Wildlife, (303) 291-7227

Finding the trailhead: From Colorado Springs, drive west on US 24 to Florissant. Continue west on US 24 for 5.4 miles past Lake George and turn right on CR 77 (Tarryall Road). Drive 24.1 miles to the east end of Tarryall Reservoir. Turn left on unpaved Turner Gulch Road, then immediately turn right into the parking area. The falls are ahead (GPS: N 39 13.335, -105 36.237).

From Denver, drive west on US 285 to Jefferson. Turn left on CR 77 (Tarryall Road) and drive 17.3 miles to the east end of the dam.

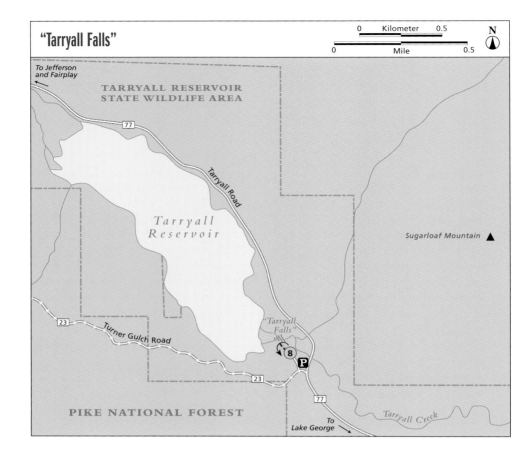

The Hike

After ponding in 175-acre Tarryall Reservoir, Tarryall Creek dashes down a rocky, human-made channel and launches into a frothy 50-foot cascade. The waterfall runs all summer, making it a waterfall stop on South Park's northeastern edge. This popular recreational lake offers camping in summer. To the northwest are views of 13,000-foot summits—Hoosier Ridge, Boreas Mountain, Bald Mountain, and Mount Guyot—on the Continental Divide.

"Tarryall Falls" is seen from the parking lot below the dam off Turner Gulch Road. Walk to the edge of Tarryall Creek and enjoy frothy waterfall views as the creek exits a narrow canyon at the southeast end of Tarryall Reservoir.

Miles and Directions

0.0 View "Tarryall Falls" from the parking area or walk 100 feet toward the creek for a closer look. Return to parking.

Colorado Springs Area

Green Mountain Falls, Manitou Springs, Colorado Springs, Divide, and Guffey

North Cheyenne Creek emerges in a picture-perfect horsetail spray at Helen Hunt Falls.

9 Green Mountain Falls Waterfalls: Crystal Falls and Catamount Falls

North of 14,115-foot Pikes Peak, the town of Green Mountain Falls bills itself as "The Gem of the Rockies." Here, water from three reservoirs—North and South Catamount Reservoirs and Crystal Creek Reservoir—flows northeast to feed Catamount and Crystal Creeks and provide two tumbling cascades and horsetail sprays.

Start: Unnamed trailhead in Green Mountain Falls
Trails: Thomas Trail, Catamount Trail
Difficulty: Very easy for Crystal Falls; easy for Catamount Falls
Hiking time: Less than 1 hour for Crystal Falls; about 2 hours for Catamount Falls
Distance: 1.0 mile out and back for Crystal Falls; 2.8-mile loop for Catamount Falls
Elevation trailhead to falls viewpoints: 7,720 to 7,950 feet (+230 feet) for Crystal Falls; to 8,280 feet (+560 feet) for Catamount Falls
Trail surface: Paved, dirt, rocks

Restrictions: No fires, smoking, camping, or shooting; don't park on town streets by trailheads or trails
Amenities: Restrooms at trailhead; services in Green Mountain Falls
Maps: *DeLorme:* Page 62 A3; Trails Illustrated 137: Pikes Peak, Cañon City; USGS Woodland Park
Counties: El Paso (Crystal Falls) and Teller (Catamount Falls)
Land status/contact: Green Mountain Falls Forest Parkland, (719) 684-9414

Finding the trailhead: From I-25 in Colorado Springs, take Cimarron Street exit 141 and head west on US 24. Drive 13.6 miles and turn left at the second exit for Green Mountain Falls/Chipeta Park. Follow Green Mountain Falls Road (which turns into Ute Pass Avenue) for 0.7 mile and turn left on Lake Street. Park in a public lot. Find the trailhead at the parking lot on the corner of Ute Pass Avenue and Lake Street (GPS: 38 56.032, -105 0.891). *Note:* Do not park on town streets; use only designated parking areas on Ute Pass Avenue.

The Hike

Green Mountain Falls, named for its two falls, offers a 20-mile trail system on seventeen trails, including the Thomas and Catamount Trails. The hike, following these trails, begins at an unnamed trailhead at Gazebo Lake in town since there is no parking at the trailheads. Waterfall hikers need to keep a low profile by parking in designated places and respecting private property along the streets that reach the trailheads. While the falls can be done as separate out-and-back hikes, the clockwise loop is the preferred route.

The hike follows four roads—Ute Pass Avenue, Hotel Road, Park Avenue, and Boulder Street—through a residential area to the Thomas Trailhead at road's end. Crystal Falls is a few steps ahead off Thomas Trail. Following yellow markers, continue

Crystal Creek Reservoir provides a tumbling ▷ cascade in Green Mountain Falls.

Green Mountain Falls Waterfalls

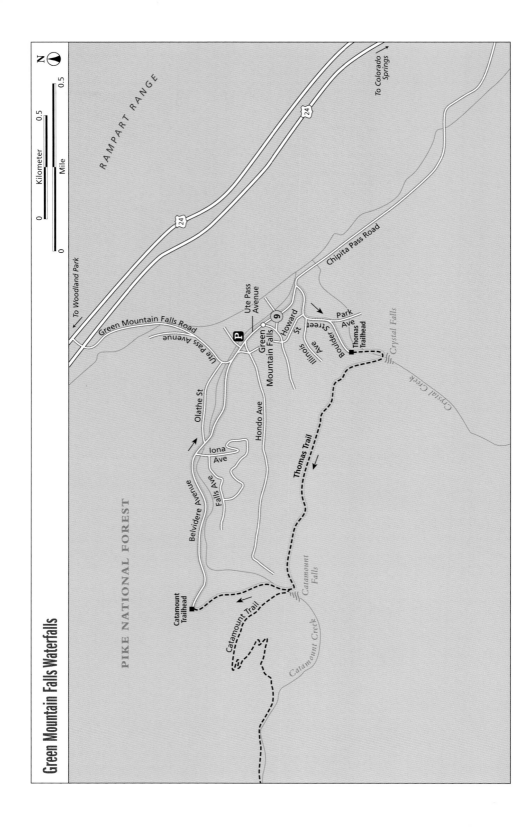

Catamount Falls plunges over giant boulders above the town of Green Mountain Falls.

to Catamount Falls. Finish by descending to Catamount Trailhead and follow Belvidere Avenue to the trailhead and parking.

Miles and Directions

0.0 Begin at trailhead at corner of Ute Pass Avenue and Lake Street. Hike along right side of Gazebo Lake. Cross Ute Pass Avenue and walk up Hotel Street, which turns into Park Avenue.

0.2 Bear left at a Y-junction to stay on Park Avenue.

0.3 Turn right on unpaved Boulder Street.

0.4 Reach Thomas Trailhead at end of Boulder Street. Turn left on trail and hike to creek.

0.5 Reach Lower Crystal Falls (GPS: 38 55.788, -105 01.028). Backtrack to yellow marker at Thomas Trailhead, turn left, and hike up Thomas Trail along right side of creek.

0.6 Reach Upper Crystal Falls (GPS: 38 55.762, -105 01.033). Continue up switchbacks then hike northwest, following yellow markers on Thomas Trail.

1.3 Reach Thomas Trail Memorial. Falls are audible and soon come into view.

1.4 Cut off trail to left and arrive at Catamount Falls (GPS: 38 55.980, -105 01.818). Return to Thomas Trail and hike along creek. Locate yellow markers, cross creek, and pick up trail on north side.

1.5 Reach junction where Catamount Trail goes left. Keep right on Thomas Trail.

1.6 Trail meets road at Catamount Trailhead. View falls to right and hike left down dirt road.

1.8 Pass gate and turn right on Belvidere Avenue. Hike down Belvidere to Ute Pass Avenue.

2.6 Turn right, cross Ute Pass Avenue, and walk south on its east shoulder.

2.8 Arrive back at trailhead (GPS: 38 56.032, -105 0.891).

10 Rainbow Falls

Fountain Creek runs southeast from Woodland Park, following US 24 down Ute Pass. At Manitou Springs, the creek freefalls in a dramatic plunge over red granite at Rainbow Falls Historic Site.

Start: Rainbow Falls Trailhead
Trail: Rainbow Falls Trail
Difficulty: Easy
Hiking time: Less than 1 hour
Distance: 0.26 mile out and back
Elevation trailhead to falls viewpoint: 6,480 to 6,520 feet (+40 feet)
Trail surface: Concrete, dirt
Restrictions: Open 10 a.m.–4 p.m. Sat–Sun Apr–May and Sept–Oct, Fri–Mon June–Aug; limited parking or park in Manitou and hike road to trailhead; no alcohol, glass containers, swimming, fishing, firearms, fireworks, geocaching, or motorized vehicles beyond parking lot; leashed dogs only
Amenities: Creekside picnic tables; services in Manitou Springs
Maps: *DeLorme*: Page 62 B4; Trails Illustrated 139: Pikes Peak, Cañon City; USGS Manitou Springs
County: El Paso
Land status/contact: El Paso County Parks, (719) 520-7529

Finding the trailhead: From I-25 in Colorado Springs, take Cimarron Street exit 141 and go west on US 24. Drive 5.5 miles and turn left at the light (directly across from Cave of the Winds) on Serpentine Drive. Travel 0.3 mile and park at a lot on the road's right side at the first switchback. The trailhead is at the end of the parking lot (GPS: 38 52.1105, -104 55.4667).

The Hike

Rainbow Falls, a 46-foot waterfall, plunges into a shallow pool below the historic 1932 Highway 24 bridge. The famed waterfall appeared in many nineteenth-century photographs taken from the Ute Pass wagon road. Later, Rainbow Falls was defaced with spray-painted graffiti, giving it the moniker "Graffiti Falls." In 2010, El Paso County purchased the property for $10, removed the graffiti, and built a trail to the waterfall. Now Rainbow Falls and several small unnamed waterfalls downstream are part of 5-acre Rainbow Falls Historic Site, which includes a parking lot, interpretive signs, and picnic tables. Park staff and volunteers are at the parking area.

The waterfall trail follows the right side of Fountain Creek, passing a small cascade, to the bridge and falls. The waterfall tucks into a cliff-walled crevice on the northwest side of the creek and bridge. This is a short hike to an impressive waterfall.

Fountain Creek freefalls in a dramatic plunge over a granite cliff at Rainbow Falls. ▷

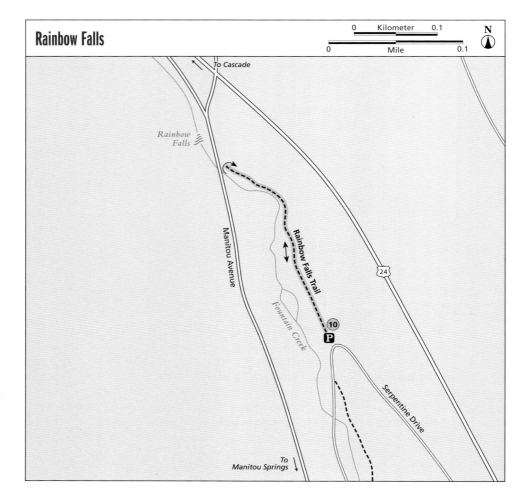

Miles and Directions

0.0 Begin at trailhead at north end of parking area.

0.13 Arrive at base of Rainbow Falls (GPS: 38 52.207, -104 55.551). Return the way you came.

0.26 Arrive back at the trailhead (GPS: 38 52.1105, -104 55.4667).

11 Seven Falls and Midnight Falls

Known as "The Grandest Mile of Scenery in Colorado," a closed road to Seven Falls twists through South Cheyenne Cañon below towering cliffs. The tiered falls, a paid attraction fed by South Cheyenne Creek, provides a spectacle with seven leaps of plunge, cascade, punchbowl, fan, and horsetail spray falls.

Start: Seven Falls Gate
Trails: Seven Falls Trail, Midnight Falls Trail
Difficulty: Easy
Hiking time: About 1 hour
Distance: 0.8 mile to falls base
Elevation trailhead to falls viewpoint: Minimal to falls base
Trail surface: Pavement, metal staircases, dirt
Restrictions: Fee area, walk-in hikers not allowed, purchase tickets at gate, no advance reservations, no online tickets; no parking in South Cheyenne Cañon; tram for accessible users; call for updated hours; dogs must be leashed; no alcoholic beverages or picnicking
Amenities: Toilets; wheelchair access except stairway and hiking trails; restaurant; food truck; elevator and observation platform; services in Colorado Springs
Maps: *DeLorme:* Page 62 C4; Trails Illustrated 137: Pikes Peak, Cañon City; USGS Manitou Springs
County: El Paso
Land status/contact: Broadmoor Hotel, (855) 923-7272

Finding the trailhead: Seven Falls can only be accessed by shuttle service from Norris Penrose Event Center in Colorado Springs. Parking and shuttle are complementary. Reach the shuttle parking lot from exit 141 off I-25. Drive west on US 25 (Cimarron Street) and go left on 8th Street for 0.4 mile to Lower Gold Camp Road. Turn right and drive to shuttle parking at 1045 Lower Gold Camp Road (GPS: 38 49.4302, -104 50.9319).

The Hike

Seven Falls, Colorado's most famous waterfall, drops 181 feet in seven separate waterfalls into a cliff-lined box canyon. The only Colorado waterfall on National Geographic's list of international waterfalls, Seven Falls has long been a privately owned attraction, beginning with James Hull, who bought the property in 1882. After Hull's death in 1890, Seven Falls went through a succession of owners, including oilman Al Hill and his family, who owned the canyon for sixty-eight years. Five days of rain in 2013 erased much of the canyon's infrastructure, leading to the Broadmoor Hotel buying it in 2014.

Seven Falls, the only paid falls in this book, is not a wild waterfall. Hikers take a shuttle to the canyon, pay an entry fee, and hike past a snack bar, food truck, restaurant, and gift shops to the waterfall's base. For full value, climb a metal stairway past the seven leaps—Ramona, Feather, Bridal Veil, Shorty, Hull, Weimer, and Hill. Take rests at platforms along the stairs for views and photo ops.

At the top are more trails. Continue southwest for 0.36 mile on Midnight Falls Trail to its namesake waterfall, a small cascade on Cripple Creek. Inspiration Point

North and South Cheyenne Cañons Waterfalls

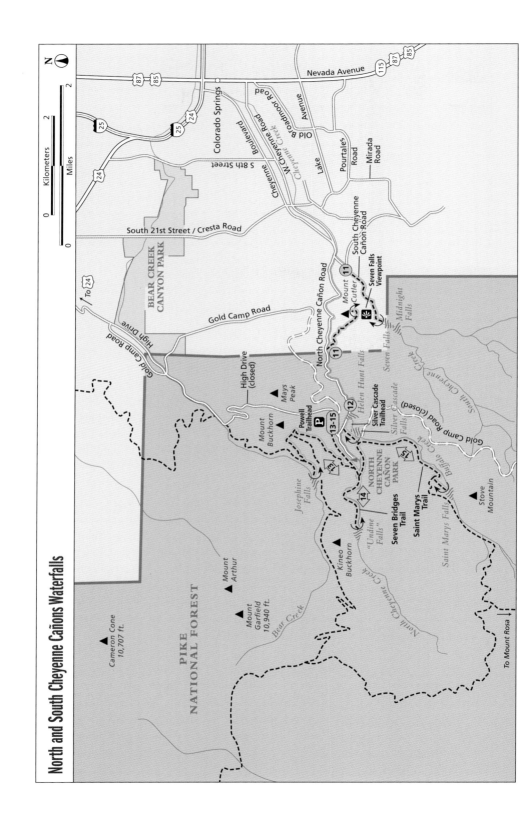

South Cheyenne Creek provides a spectacle in seven leaps at Seven Falls.

Trail, running 0.5 mile from Midnight Falls Trail, threads above cliffs to Inspiration Point, a viewpoint frequented by famed author Helen Hunt Jackson in the 1870s. After her 1885 death, she was buried at the point but relocated to a cemetery in 1892. After hiking, descend the staircase and ride an accessible elevator to Eagle's Nest for another view of Seven Falls.

If you don't want to pay to play, hike up the Mount Cutler Trail from North Cheyenne Cañon Park to the north for free views of Seven Falls in the canyon below. Reach the trailhead by driving west on North Cheyenne Cañon Road for 1.5 miles to parking on the road's left side. Hike almost a mile up the trail to see the falls.

Miles and Directions

0.0 Begin at entrance gate at mouth of canyon. Pay fee and hike Seven Falls Trail to waterfall base.

0.8 Arrive at waterfall (GPS: 38 46.885, -104 52.801). Climb 224 steps to top of waterfall. Hike other trails from here, including Midnight Falls Trail, or descend back to base.

1.6 Arrive back at canyon entrance (GPS: 38 47.1567, -104 52.18). Ride shuttle back to parking area.

12 Silver Cascade Trail Waterfalls: Helen Hunt Falls and Silver Cascade (Spoon) Falls

Two waterfalls in North Cheyenne Cañon offer a short, scenic outing. At the trailhead, North Cheyenne Creek emerges in a picture-perfect horsetail spray at Helen Hunt Falls, while a trail leads to an overlook above the long slide of Silver Cascade Falls.

See map on page 48.
Start: Silver Cascade Trailhead
Trails: Silver Cascade Falls Trail, Buffalo Canyon Trail
Difficulty: Very easy
Hiking time: Less than 1 hour for both falls
Distance: Roadside for Helen Hunt Falls; 0.8 mile out and back for Silver Cascade Falls
Elevation trailhead to falls viewpoints: Minimal for Helen Hunt Falls; 7,190 to 7,460 feet (+270 feet) for Silver Cascade Falls
Trail surface: Dirt, stone steps, gravel

Restrictions: Day use only; no ground fires, camping, or alcoholic beverages; dogs must be leashed
Amenities: Porta-potties; visitor center; benches; services in Colorado Springs
Maps: *DeLorme:* Page 62 C4; Trails Illustrated 137: Pikes Peak, Cañon City; USGS Manitou Springs
County: El Paso
Land status/contact: Colorado Springs Department of Parks & Recreation, (719) 385-5940

Finding the trailhead: From I-25 in Colorado Springs, take Cimarron Street exit 141 and go west on US 24. Drive 1.5 miles and turn left onto South 21st Street, which becomes Cresta Road. Drive 3 miles and turn right on Cheyenne Boulevard. Go 1 mile and bear right on North Cheyenne Cañon Road. Drive 2.5 miles to parking at Helen Hunt Falls Visitor Center. Helen Hunt Falls is visible from the road, and the trailhead for Silver Cascade Falls is right of the falls (GPS: 38 47.326, -104 54.176).

The Hike

North Cheyenne Creek spills over a granite bench, forming 36-foot Helen Hunt Falls. Visible from the road, the falls was named for writer Helen Hunt Jackson, who often visited the waterfall in the 1870s. A visitor center sits near the base of the falls, offering information, hiking tips, and educational programs in the summer. A wheelchair-accessible platform below the falls offers scenic views. For another view and photo op, climb stone steps to a footbridge that crosses above the falls.

Visit Silver Cascade Falls by starting at the trailhead behind the visitor center. The Silver Cascade Falls Trail climbs steps to the top of Helen Hunt Falls and then heads uphill. The trail climbs onto east-facing slopes above slabs and the cascade to the left. Finish at an overlook enclosed by a stone wall. Do not be tempted to climb higher or scramble onto the water-polished slab below the viewpoints. The slick rock is dangerous, and people have lost their lives after falling down the slab.

The long slide of Silver Cascade Falls is visible from the Buffalo Creek overlook.

To see lower Silver Cascade Falls, start at the Buffalo Canyon Trailhead on the south side of the parking strip. Descend steps and cross the creek to the trail, which is used by ice climbers in winter. Follow the trail up the canyon to the base of Silver Cascade Falls. Finish by hiking the trail up slopes north of the falls and then follow Silver Cascade Falls Trail back to the visitor center.

Helen Hunt Falls is named for a famous nineteenth-century writer and poet who lived in early Colorado Springs.

Miles and Directions

0.0 Begin at left side of visitor center. Walk 45 feet to platform below Helen Hunt Falls (GPS: 38 47.332, -104 54.197). Return or continue 20 feet to the Silver Cascade Trailhead (GPS: 38 47.334, -104 54.189). Climb stone steps, cross a bridge, and follow the trail to an overlook.

0.4 Arrive at viewpoint above Silver Cascade Falls (GPS: 38 47.2358, -104 54.3353). Cross a bridge to another overlook on south side of Buffalo Creek. Return the way you came.

0.8 Arrive back at trailhead (GPS: 38 47.326, -104 54.176).

13 Josephine Falls

Bear Creek slides across the western slopes of Mount Garfield and then spills through Bear Creek Canyon, toppling over granite slabs in a combination slide and horsetail waterfall.

See map on page 48.
Start: Powell Trailhead
Trails: Gold Camp Road, Buckhorn Cutoff Trail #776, Bear Creek Trail #666
Difficulty: Moderate
Hiking time: About 3 hours
Distance: 5.4 miles out and back
Elevation trailhead to falls viewpoint: 7,520 to 8,190 feet (+670 feet)
Trail surface: Gravel, dirt
Restrictions: Day use only; leashed dogs only

Amenities: Porta-potties at trailhead; services in Colorado Springs
Maps: *DeLorme:* Page 62 B4 & C4; Trails Illustrated 137: Pikes Peak, Cañon City; USGS Manitou Springs
County: El Paso
Land status/contact: Colorado Springs Department of Parks & Recreation, (719) 385-5940; Pike National Forest, (719) 553-1400; Pikes Peak Ranger District, (719) 636-1602

Finding the trailhead: From I-25 in Colorado Springs, take Cimarron Street exit 141 and go west on US 24. Drive 1.5 miles and turn left onto South 21st Street, which becomes Cresta Road. Drive 3 miles and turn right on Cheyenne Boulevard, then go 1 mile and bear right on North Cheyenne Cañon Road. Drive 3.2 miles and park at the Powell Trailhead where the paved road meets Gold Camp Road. Start at the closed gate on the northwest side of the parking lot (GPS: 38 47.449, -104 54.253).

The Hike

Josephine Falls, riffling 75 feet down granite bedrock, is a secluded waterfall high in Bear Creek Canyon above Colorado Springs. A 3.5-mile stretch of the small creek above the falls is home to an isolated population of the endangered greenback cutthroat trout, the Colorado state fish. The creek has the only known reproducing population of greenbacks in the state.

To protect the trout, trails have been rerouted, including the former trail past the falls. The best way to Josephine Falls is from upper North Cheyenne Cañon. The route, climbing over a high ridge, follows three trails to the falls. An overlook above the falls lies at trail's end. There is no safe way to reach the waterfall's base, but the view from above is splendid. Towering granite walls line the surrounding canyon, while the city sprawls to the northeast.

Miles and Directions

0.0 Begin at trailhead gate at Powell Trailhead. Hike west on closed Gold Camp Road.

Waters spill through Bear Creek Canyon and tumble over granite slabs at Josephine Falls.

0.7   Reach unsigned junction on right with Buckhorn Cutoff Trail (#776) (GPS: 38 47.2092, -104 54.8386) before North Cheyenne Creek. Go right and hike uphill to junction. Go right on trail.

2.0   Reach junction with Captain Jacks Trail (GPS: 38 47.8831, -104 54.3365). Walk left 25 feet and go right on signed Trail 776. Hike down gentle grades on north slope of ridge.

2.5   Reach junction with Bear Creek Trail (#666). Go left on signed Trail 666.

2.7   Arrive at overlook for Josephine Falls below (GPS: 38 47.675, -104 54.917). Return the way you came.

5.4   Arrive back at the trailhead (GPS: 38 47.449, -104 54.253).

14 "Undine Falls"

North Cheyenne Creek drops from Stratton Reservoir high on 12,367-foot Almagre Mountain and meanders east through North Cheyenne Cañon. The creek and a lovely slide waterfall over granite bedrock are enjoyed on the popular Seven Bridges Trail.

See map on page 48.
Start: Powell Trailhead
Trails: Gold Camp Road (FR 370), Seven Bridges Trail #622
Difficulty: Easy
Hiking time: About 2 hours
Distance: 3.4 miles out and back
Elevation trailhead to falls viewpoint: 7,520 to 8,280 feet (+760 feet)
Trail surface: Dirt, stone steps
Restrictions: Day use only; no campfires, camping, or alcoholic beverages; dogs must be leashed

Amenities: Porta-potties at trailhead; services in Colorado Springs
Maps: *DeLorme:* Page 62 C4; Trails Illustrated 137: Pikes Peak, Cañon City; USGS Manitou Springs
County: El Paso
Land status/contact: Colorado Springs Department of Parks & Recreation, (719) 385-5940; Pike National Forest, (719) 553-1400; Pikes Peak Ranger District, (719) 636-1602

Finding the trailhead: From I-25 in Colorado Springs, take Cimarron Street exit 141 and go west on US 24. Drive 1.5 miles and turn left onto South 21st Street, which becomes Cresta Road. Drive 3 miles and turn right on Cheyenne Boulevard, then go 1 mile and bear right on North Cheyenne Cañon Road. Drive 3.2 miles and park at the Powell Trailhead where the paved road meets Gold Camp Road (FR 370). Start at the closed gate on the northwest side of the parking lot (GPS: 38 47.449, -104 54.253).

The Hike

"Undine Falls," riffling down a long slab in upper North Cheyenne Cañon, lies beside the Seven Bridges Trail. The hike initially follows Gold Camp Road, a closed road that was once a railroad bed, before cutting right up the trail alongside North Cheyenne Creek. The trail, ascending through a pine forest, crosses the creek on seven bridges. Look for small waterfalls and cascades along the trail. Past the seventh bridge, look for "Undine Falls" flowing over low-angle bedrock left of the trail. For a longer outing, continue past the falls for 1.5 miles to a meadow at Jones Park. Return east on Captain Jacks Trail #667 and then down Mount Buckhorn Trail to Gold Camp Road and the trailhead.

The lovely slide of "Undine Falls" can be enjoyed via the popular Seven Bridges Trail.

Miles and Directions

0.0 Begin at gate across Gold Camp Road at Powell Trailhead, at northwest side of parking lot. Hike west on road to creek.

0.7 Cross North Cheyenne Creek to a junction with Seven Bridges Trail (#622) on right. Go right and follow trail past a sign, and hike the creekside trail. Cross first bridge to right side of creek and bear left as trail curves past an old sign noting "No Motor Vehicles."

1.6 Cross seventh bridge to right side of creek and follow sign for Trail #622.

1.7 Arrive at "Undine Falls" to left of trail (GPS: 38 47.1984, -104 55.6394). Return the way you came.

3.4 Arrive back at trailhead (GPS: 38 47.449, -104 54.253).

15 Saint Marys Falls

Springs on the eastern slopes of 11,499-foot Mount Rosa feed Buffalo Creek, flowing northeast into steep Buffalo Canyon. The creek sidles around 9,782-foot Stove Mountain and washes down granite slabs in a gleaming slide at Saint Marys Falls.

See map on page 48.
Start: Powell Trailhead
Trails: Gold Camp Road (FR 370), St. Mary's Falls Trail #624
Difficulty: Moderate
Hiking time: About 4 hours
Distance: 6.0 miles out and back
Elevation trailhead to falls viewpoint: 7,520 to 8,870 feet (+1,350 feet)
Trail surface: Gravel, dirt, rocks, timber steps
Restrictions: Day use only; no ground fires, camping, or alcoholic beverages; dogs must be leashed

Amenities: Porta-potties at trailhead; services in Colorado Springs
Maps: *DeLorme:* Page 62 C4; Trails Illustrated 137: Pikes Peak, Cañon City; USGS Manitou Springs
County: El Paso
Land status/contact: Colorado Springs Department of Parks & Recreation, (719) 385-5940; Pike National Forest, (719) 553-1400; Pikes Peak Ranger District, (719) 636-1602

Finding the trailhead: From I-25 in Colorado Springs, take Cimarron Street exit 141 and go west on US 24. Drive 1.5 miles and turn left onto South 21st Street, which becomes Cresta Road. Drive 3 miles and turn right on Cheyenne Boulevard. Go 1 mile and bear right on North Cheyenne Cañon Road. Drive 3.2 miles and park at the Powell Trailhead parking lot where the paved road meets Gold Camp Road (FR 370). Start at the closed gate on the northwest side of the parking lot (GPS: 38 47.449, -104 54.253).

The Hike

Saint Marys Falls, a slide waterfall that tumbles down a steep granite slab, is reached by a popular hike that begins in North Cheyenne Cañon Park. Starting at the Powell Trailhead, the hike follows closed Upper Gold Camp Road across North Cheyenne Creek to a collapsed railroad tunnel. Past the tunnel, the hike goes right on St. Marys Falls Trail, following Buffalo Creek through aspen groves and a ponderosa pine and spruce forest. Go left at a marked junction to the waterfall's base. Enjoy views from the bottom or hike a rocky trail on the right side to a higher viewpoint and a memorial to local hiker Eamon Murphy, who often hiked North Cheyenne Cañon's trails.

Saint Marys Falls is reached by a popular hiking trail up Buffalo Canyon.

Miles and Directions

0.0 Begin at Powell Trailhead at northwest side of parking lot. Hike west up closed Gold Camp Road, cross North Cheyenne Creek, and continue east on road to a closed tunnel.

1.2 Past tunnel, reach a signed junction for Saint Marys Falls Trail on right. Go right and hike along north side of Buffalo Creek.

3.0 Switchback right and uphill at sign "St Marys Falls 0.2" and continue to sign "Base of Falls 500 Ft." Follow social trail and arrive at base of Saint Marys Falls (GPS: 38 46.262, -104 55.105). Return down trail and Gold Camp Road.

6.0 Arrive back at trailhead (GPS: 38 47.449, -104 54.253).

Tumbling over granite slabs and boulders, Horsethief Falls ▷
nestles in thick forest on Pikes Peak's western slope.

16 Horsethief Falls

This slippery slide waterfall nestles among spruce and fir trees west of Pikes Peak. As a primary destination—or a side trip on the way to Pancake Rocks—Horsethief Falls provides peaceful moments on a popular trail.

Start: Horsethief Park Trailhead
Trails: Horsethief Park Trail #704, Horsethief Falls Trail #704B
Difficulty: Moderate
Hiking time: About 2 hours
Distance: 2.8 miles out and back
Elevation trailhead to falls viewpoint: 9,670 to 10,250 feet (+580 feet)
Trail surface: Dirt
Restrictions: Dogs must be leashed

Amenities: Backcountry camping; services in Divide and Cripple Creek
Maps: *DeLorme:* Page 62 B2; Trails Illustrated 137: Pikes Peak, Cañon City; USGS Cripple Creek North, Pikes Peak
County: Teller
Land status/contact: Pike National Forest, (719) 553-1400; Pikes Peak Ranger District, (719) 636-1602

Finding the trailhead: From Divide, turn south on CO 67 and drive 9.3 miles. Watch for an old railroad tunnel on the highway's left side. Past the tunnel the road curves to the left, and there is a paved parking lot and trailhead on the highway's left (east) side (GPS: 38 50.054, -105 08.240).

Horsethief Falls

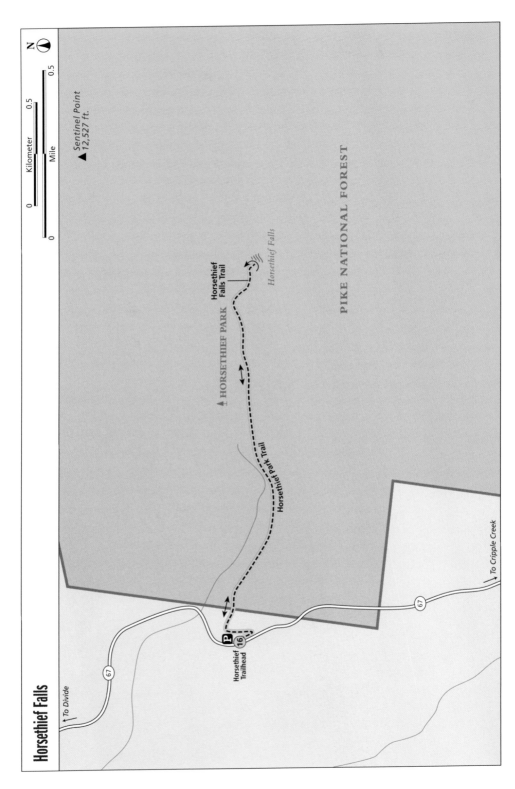

N

0   Kilometer   0.5

0   Mile   0.5

▲ Sentinel Point
   12,527 ft.

To Divide

67

Horsethief
Trailhead

P

16

HORSETHIEF PARK

Horsethief Park Trail

Horsethief
Falls Trail

Horsethief Falls

PIKE NATIONAL FOREST

67

To Cripple Creek

The trail to Horsethief Falls threads along a trickling creek lined with willows.

The Hike

Horsethief Falls, tucked into a wooded valley, is a small waterfall that pours over a boulder and then ripples down a granite slab. It's reached by the popular Horsethief Park Trail and Horsethief Falls Trail. The hike starts right of an abandoned Midland Railroad tunnel on CO 67 and climbs into a broad valley floored with beaver ponds and a trickling creek. Pointed 12,527-foot Sentinel Point towers to the east. Past the junction with the Pancake Rocks Trail, the hike ends at the waterfall's base. For a longer adventure, take the Ring the Peak Trail north through Horsethief Park to Putney Gulch, location of "Harvey Carter Falls," or hike 2.5 miles south up Pancake Rocks Trail to odd rock formations on a ridge.

Miles and Directions

0.0 Begin at Horsethief Park Trailhead on CO 67.

0.7 Reach Ring the Peak Trail junction on left; continue straight.

0.9 Reach signed Pancake Rocks Trail junction on right (GPS: 38 50.037, -105 7.4148); continue straight.

1.3 Cross to left side of creek.

1.4 Arrive at base of Horsethief Falls (GPS: 38 50.030, -105 06.996). Return down trails.

2.8 Arrive back at trailhead (GPS: 38 50.054, -105 08.240).

17 "Guffey Falls"

This two-tiered waterfall gently pours through a slotted crevice amid granite blocks, spilling water into a round punchbowl at Paradise Cove. Tucked off the road in Guffey Gorge, "Guffey Falls" is a diminutive treasure in a magical setting.

Start: Guffey Gorge Trailhead
Trail: Guffey Gorge Trail
Difficulty: Very easy
Hiking time: Less than 1 hour
Distance: 0.8 mile out and back
Elevation trailhead to falls viewpoint: 8,190 to 8,090 feet (-100 feet)
Trail surface: Dirt, rocks
Restrictions: Daily fee; day use only dawn to dusk; no glass bottles; dogs must be leashed; vault toilets and trash cans at parking; no amplified music; no overnight camping or campfires; no parking on county road
Amenities: Services in Guffey and Florissant
Maps: *DeLorme:* Page 61 C8; Trails Illustrated 152: Elevenmile Canyon, South Park; USGS Wrights Reservoir
County: Park
Land status/contact: BLM, Royal Gorge Field Office, (719) 269-8500

Finding the trailhead: From US 24 in Florissant, turn south on CR 1 toward Florissant Fossil Beds National Monument and drive 9.2 miles. Turn right on CR 11 and drive 4.1 miles to a T-intersection with CR 112. Go right on CR 112 for 2.7 miles and park in a lot on the road's right side (GPS: 38 46.1216, -105 20.1576).

The Hike

"Guffey Falls," fed by West Fourmile Creek, is a pretty waterfall that empties into a large plunge pool. The falls area, sometimes called Paradise Cove or Guffey Cove, was once a quiet swimming hole but then, through internet photos, it became a destination for cliff jumpers and partiers, with annual visitation jumping from a few hundred folks to over 24,000 people in 2020. Increased visitation led to litter, trail damage, and diving injuries, resulting in BLM rules and law enforcement.

Diving at the falls is not recommended and is dangerous due to shallow water and rock outcroppings. Injuries regularly occur here. Instead, opt for a safe hike and enjoy the cool water and cooler scenery. You can venture into Guffey Gorge as well, but the trail becomes lost in a boulderfield. Visit during the week to avoid crowds.

Miles and Directions

0.0 Begin at Guffey Gorge Trailhead on west side of parking lot. Hike northeast on trail and descend a twisting canyon, crossing West Fourmile Creek several times. Climb to trail's high point and switchback down until the falls appears to the right.

"Guffey Falls"

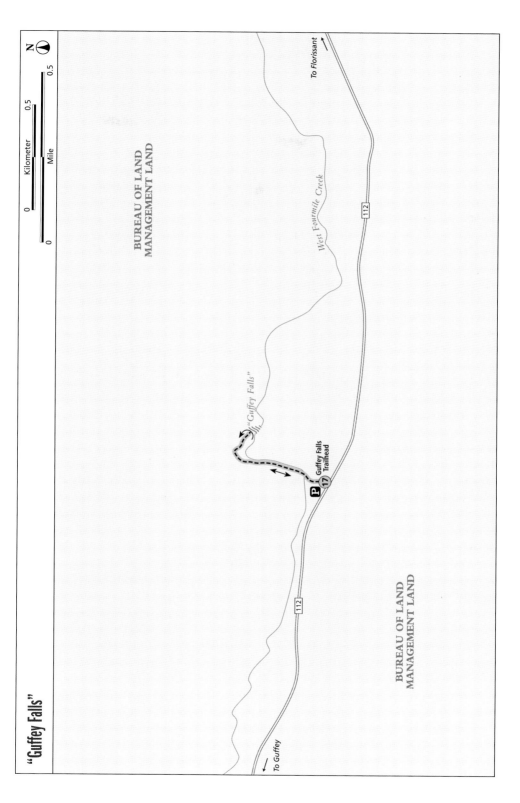

BUREAU OF LAND
MANAGEMENT LAND

BUREAU OF LAND
MANAGEMENT LAND

West Fourmile Creek

"Guffey Falls"

Guffey Falls
Trailhead

17

112

112

To Guffey

To Florissant

N

Kilometer
0   0.5

Mile
0   0.5

Monolithic granite walls surround trickling "Guffey Falls" and a deep pool.

0.4 Reach base of "Guffey Falls" (GPS: 38 46.316, -105 20.03). Continue past falls and look back to see the higher of the waterfall's two tiers. Return the way you came.

0.8 Arrive back at trailhead (GPS: 38 46.1216, -105 20.1576).

Central Colorado

Nathrop, Twin Lakes, and Breckenridge

The best waterfall in the southern Sawatch Range, Browns Creek Falls pours into a cliff-lined canyon.

18 Agnes Vaille Falls

Cascade Creek sweeps down a basin on Mount Princeton's south slopes and bounces off granite cliffs in a dramatic horsetail spray before cascading into a rocky creek. Wedged in Cascade Canyon between towering mountains, Agnes Vaille Falls is one of the Sawatch Range's prettiest waterfalls.

Start: Agnes Vaille Falls Trailhead
Trail: Cascade Creek Trail #1433
Difficulty: Easy
Hiking time: About 1 hour
Distance: 1.1-mile lollipop
Elevation trailhead to falls viewpoint: 8,733 to 9,055 feet (+322 feet)
Trail surface: Dirt, rocks
Restrictions: No motorized vehicles; dogs on leash only; rockfall danger at falls; hiking to base of falls not recommended

Amenities: Interpretive signs; limited services at Mount Princeton Hot Springs; full services at Johnson Village, Buena Vista, and Salida
Maps: *DeLorme:* Page 59 C8; Trails Illustrated 130: Salida, St. Elmo, Mount Shavano; USGS Mount Antero
County: Chaffee
Land status/contact: San Isabel National Forest, (719) 553-1400; Salida Ranger District, (719) 539-3591

Finding the trailhead: From the intersection of US 24 and US 285 in Johnson Village, take US 285 south for 5.4 miles, or from the intersection of US 285 and US 50 in Poncha Springs, drive north on US 285 for 15.5 miles. Turn west on Chalk Creek Drive (CR 162). Drive 8.7 miles to the Agnes Vaille Falls Trailhead sign and parking lot on the right (GPS: 38 42.831, -106 13.971).

The Hike

Agnes Vaille Falls is reached by the Cascade Creek Trail, a loop hike that climbs gently north through a ponderosa pine forest to a cul-de-sac canyon. Take time to read interpretive signs along the trail, detailing the lives of falls namesake Agnes Vaille, and Mount Antero, named for the Uintah Ute chief Antero. Enjoy views south of 14,269-foot Mount Antero, popular with rockhounds for its rich deposits of aquamarine and other gemstones. The trail ends at an elevated platform with a view of the falls in cliffs to the north. The waterfall area and upper canyon were closed after five members of a family were killed by rockfall in 2013. The trail was rerouted to the viewpoint. The US Forest Service recommends that hikers not climb the eroded canyon to the waterfall's base since the area still has active rockfall danger.

The waterfall is named for mountaineer Agnes Vaille, who died on Longs Peak in 1925. Vaille and her climbing partner, Walter Kiener, had just completed the first successful winter ascent of the peak's East Face and were descending the North Face

Agnes Vaille Falls bounces off colorful ▶
granite cliffs in a dramatic horsetail spray.

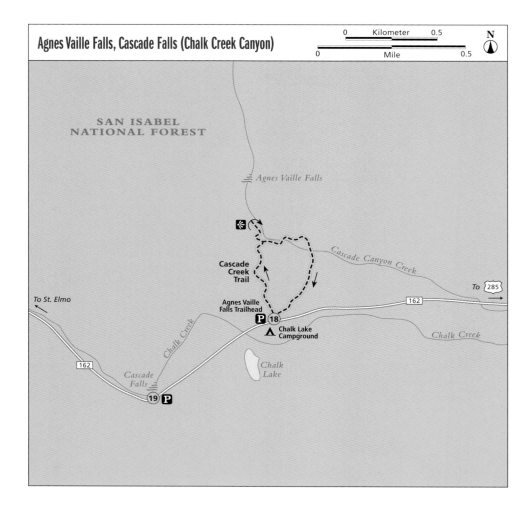

| 0 | Kilometer | 0.5 |
| 0 | Mile | 0.5 |

N

SAN ISABEL
NATIONAL FOREST

Agnes Vaille Falls

Cascade
Creek
Trail

Cascade Canyon Creek

To St. Elmo

Agnes Vaille
Falls Trailhead

P 18

Chalk Lake
Campground

162

To 285

Chalk Creek

162

Cascade
Falls

Chalk Creek

Chalk
Lake

19 P

when she fell during a snowstorm. During a rescue attempt, Kiener suffered serious frostbite and a rescuer, Herbert Sortland, lost his life. Vaille died of exposure.

Miles and Directions

0.0 Begin at Cascade Creek Trailhead. Take left trail of loop and hike north.

0.5 Reach a junction (GPS: 38 43.0416, -106 14.0056). Go left to falls viewpoint platform. Right trail is return loop.

0.65 Arrive at Agnes Vaille Falls viewpoint and geology interpretive sign (GPS: 38 43.1116, -106 14.0574).

0.8 Return to trail junction. Go left on return loop trail, cross Cascade Creek, and hike south on marked trail.

1.1 Arrive back at trailhead (GPS: 38 42.831, -106 13.971).

An ultimate roadside attraction, snowmelt fills ▶
Cascade Falls on a spring afternoon.

19 Cascade Falls (Chalk Creek Canyon)

Chalk Creek meanders east from the Continental Divide to the Arkansas River, passing through Chalk Creek Canyon. White kaolinite cliffs grace the canyon's east entrance, remnants of hot springs that pervade this area. The creek pauses only at Cascade Falls, tumbling over granite blocks in a noisy roadside cascade.

See map on page 68.
Start: Cascade Falls Viewpoint
Trail: None
Difficulty: Easy
Hiking time: Less than 1 hour
Distance: Roadside
Elevation trailhead to falls viewpoint:
Minimal, falls are below the road.
Trail surface: Dirt
Restrictions: None posted

Amenities: Limited services at Mount Princeton Hot Springs; full services in Johnson Village, Buena Vista, and Salida
Maps: *DeLorme:* Page 59 C8; Trails Illustrated 130: Salida, St. Elmo, Mount Shavano; USGS Mount Antero
County: Chaffee
Land status/contact: San Isabel National Forest (719) 553-1400; Salida Ranger District (719) 539-3591

Finding the trailhead: From the intersection of US 24 and US 285 in Johnson Village south of Buena Vista, take US 285 south for 5.4 miles, or from the intersection of US 285 and US 50 in Poncha Springs, drive north on US 285 for 15.5 miles. Turn west on Chalk Creek Drive (CR 162) toward Mount Princeton Hot Springs. Drive 9.2 miles to a pullout on the road's right shoulder and a sign that says "Cascade Falls Viewpoint" (GPS: 38 42.57, -106 14.416).

Chalk Creek riffles and boils over boulders at Cascade Falls near Mount Princeton Hot Springs.

The Hike

Enjoy Cascade Falls, a 500-foot-long stretch of whitewater, from a roadside parking area, or descend a short social trail to the rushing creek for a closer look. Take in the sights and smells of the aspen, fir, and spruce trees that line the rocky banks, and enjoy views of Mount Antero's lower slope to the southwest from bubbling and gurgling Cascade Falls.

Preface your visit to Cascade Falls with a hike to nearby Agnes Vaille Falls, followed by a tour of St. Elmo—one of the Colorado's best-preserved ghost towns. Finish a perfect day with a soak at Mount Princeton Hot Springs. All are located along a 16-mile stretch of CR 162.

Miles and Directions

0.0　Park at Cascade Falls Viewpoint on the right shoulder of CR 162. Enjoy the falls from the parking strip or creekside below the road (GPS: 38 42.57, -106 14.416).

20 "Browns Creek Falls"

Browns Creek splashes down a multi-stepped curtain, while shallow pools—waterfall-fed, yet calm and soothing—tempt the forest bather. The creek, flowing east through the Sawatch Range, provides a hidden treasure at "Browns Creek Falls."

Start: Browns Creek Trailhead
Trails: Wagon Loop Trail, Colorado Trail, Browns Creek Trail #1429
Difficulty: Moderate
Hiking time: About 4 hours
Distance: 5.8 miles out and back
Elevation trailhead to falls viewpoint: 8,980 to 9,830 feet (+850 feet)
Trail surface: Dirt, rocks
Restrictions: No overnight camping or campfires at trailhead; no motorized vehicles; dogs must be leashed

Amenities: Vault toilets at trailhead; services in Johnson Village, Buena Vista, and Salida
Maps: *DeLorme:* Page 60 D1; Trails Illustrated 130: Salida, St. Elmo, Mount Shavano; USGS Mount Antero
County: Chaffee
Land status/contact: San Isabel National Forest, (719) 553-1400; Salida Ranger District, (719) 539-3591

Finding the trailhead: From the intersection of US 24 and US 285 in Johnson Village, take US 285 south toward Nathrop for 8.6 miles and turn right (west) on CR 270. At 1.5 miles the paved road turns to gravel; continue straight to CR 272. Drive 2 more miles and bear left to stay on CR 272. Continue 1.6 miles to Browns Creek Trailhead (GPS: 38 40.3295, -106 9.6964). Park on the road's east side, opposite the trailhead.

The Hike

Rising from the north slope of 13,663-foot Carbonate Mountain, Browns Creek drops down a glaciated valley flanked by high peaks before dashing over a wide notch at Browns Creek Falls. The two-tiered falls roars through a narrow, cliff-lined chasm, offering a noisy spectacle for waterfall lovers. The hike also offers views of surrounding mountains, including 13,604-foot Jones Peak and 13,667-foot Mount White. It's a popular hike, so expect company on weekends.

The falls is reached by three trails. The Wagon Loop Trail runs from the trailhead to a short section of the Colorado Trail. Browns Creek Trail, the last segment, is an easy-to-follow path through an open ponderosa pine woodland to a mixed spruce and fir forest dotted with aspen glades. Several creek crossings are encountered with the final one on a sturdy split-log bridge with a handrail. Look for a sign to the falls on the left past the bridge.

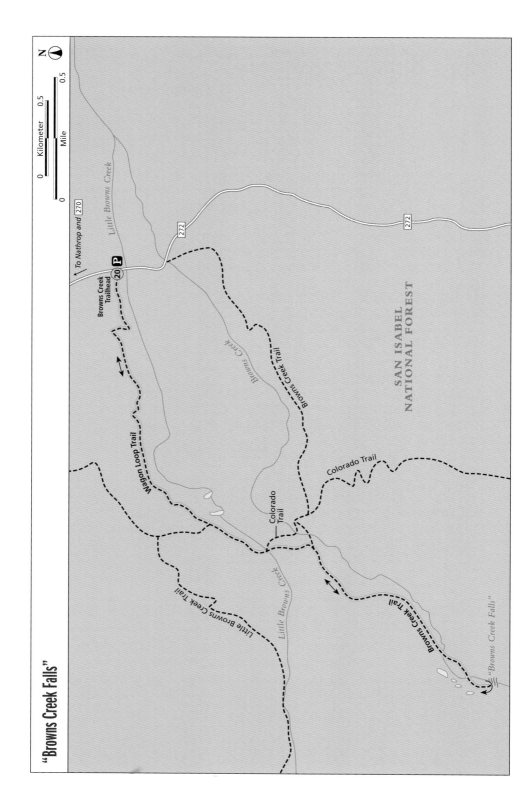

"Browns Creek Falls"

Dazzling waters shimmer and splash in a curtain of liquid brilliance at "Browns Creek Falls."

Miles and Directions

0.0 Begin at Browns Creek Trailhead. Hike west on Wagon Loop Trail past toilets and a sign for Browns Lake, Browns Creek Falls, and Colorado Trail. Pass through a cowboy gate and hike west with Little Browns Creek to the left.

1.4 Reach junction with Colorado Trail—go left on Colorado Trail.

1.6 Reach a trail junction. Bear right and hike west on Browns Creek Trail.

2.8 Reach a sign for the falls left of the trail. Turn left and leave main trail.

2.9 Arrive at base of "Browns Creek Falls" (GPS: 38 39.045, -106 11.544). Return the way you came.

5.8 Arrive back at trailhead (GPS: 38 40.3295, -106 9.6964).

21 Snyder Falls

Lake Creek runs south of Independence Pass, the nation's highest paved road over the Continental Divide, carving a channel through bedrock and driving its waters over a short cliff at Snyder Falls.

Start: Unnamed pullout on south side of CO 82

Trail: Unnamed trail

Difficulty: Very easy

Hiking time: Less than 1 hour

Distance: 0.8 mile out and back

Elevation trailhead to falls viewpoint: 9,815 to 9,765 feet (-50 feet)

Trail surface: Dirt, rocks

Restrictions: None posted

Amenities: Services in Buena Vista and Leadville; limited services in Twin Lakes

Maps: *DeLorme:* Page 47 E7; Trails Illustrated 148: Collegiate Peaks Wilderness Area; USGS Mount Elbert

County: Lake

Land status/contact: San Isabel National Forest, (719) 553-1400; Leadville Ranger District, (719) 486-0749

Finding the trailhead: From Leadville, drive south on US 24 East for 14.3 miles and turn right (west) on CO 82 West, or from Buena Vista, drive north on US 24 West for 19.2 miles and turn left (west) on CO 82 West. Drive 11.5 miles and park at a pullout on the highway's left side, at the trailhead (GPS: 39 4.249, -106 26.989).

The Hike

Lake Creek drops east in a broad valley between Mount Elbert, Colorado's highest mountain, on the north, and La Plata Peak on the south. The creek twists through gravel banks before spurting over a low cliff band at Snyder Falls. The falls, named on the USGS map, is impressive during snowmelt season. It is often jammed with deadfall washed down the creek. Be prepared to thrash a bit through undergrowth and avoid beaver ponds and marshes along the creek's north bank to reach Snyder Falls. To avoid marshy terrain on your return, don't be tempted to follow social trails that lead up to the road from the falls.

Miles and Directions

0.0 Begin at trailhead. Hike south down a trail and bear left on a faint path on creek's north bank. Continue downstream to falls.

0.4 Arrive at Snyder Falls (GPS: 39 4.174, -106 26.67). Return the way you came.

0.8 Arrive back at trailhead (GPS: 39 4.249, -106 26.989).

Lake Creek carves a worn channel ▷
through a short cliff at Snyder Falls.

Snyder Falls, "La Plata Falls"

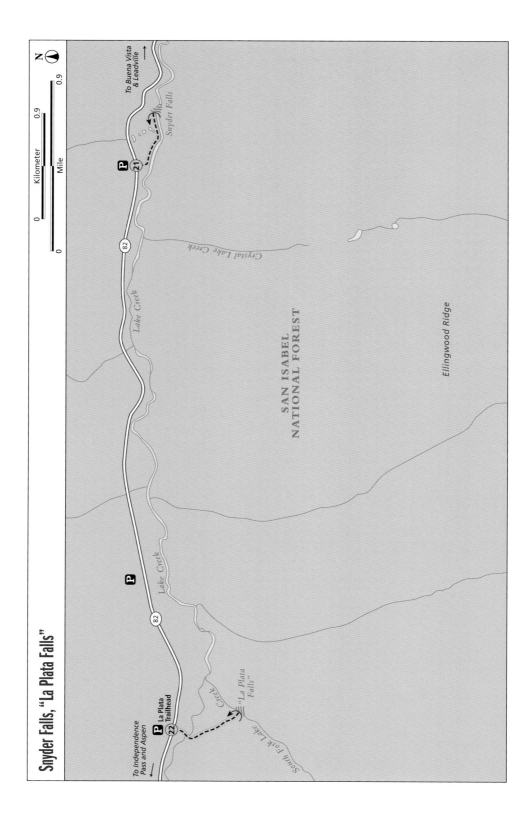

N

Kilometer
0   0.9

Mile
0   0.9

To Buena Vista & Leadville

Snyder Falls

82

21

Crystal Lake Creek

Lake Creek

82

Lake Creek

P

SAN ISABEL NATIONAL FOREST

Ellingwood Ridge

To Independence Pass and Aspen

La Plata Trailhead

22

Creek

"La Plata Falls"

South Fork Lake

22 "La Plata Falls"

Fifteen peaks above 14,000 feet dot the Sawatch Range, the most "14er-rich" mountain range in the state. The trail to one of these mountains—14,360-foot La Plata Peak—crosses South Fork Lake Creek and provides splendid views of a lovely, twisting fan at "La Plata Falls."

See map on page 76.
Start: Unofficial trailhead on highway to La Plata Gulch Trailhead
Trails: FR 291, La Plata Gulch Trail #1474
Difficulty: Very easy
Hiking time: Less than 1 hour
Distance: 0.8 mile out and back
Elevation trailhead to falls viewpoint: 10,150 to 10,130 feet (-20 feet)
Trail surface: Dirt, rocks
Restrictions: Trail crosses private property—stay on trail; do not drink filtered or treated water from creek, it is mineralized and non-potable
Amenities: Services in Aspen, Leadville, and Buena Vista; limited services in Twin Lakes
Maps: *DeLorme:* Page 47 E6; Trails Illustrated 148: Collegiate Peaks Wilderness Area; USGS Independence Pass
County: Lake
Land status/contact: San Isabel National Forest, (719) 553-1400; Leadville Ranger District, (719) 486-0749

Finding the trailhead: From Leadville, drive south on US 24 East for 14.3 miles and turn right (west) on CO 82 West, or from Buena Vista, drive north on US 24 West for 19.2 miles and turn left (west) on CO 82 West. Drive 14.6 miles west to a parking lot on the left side of the highway and the trailhead (GPS: 39 4.068, -106 30.298), signed "South Fork Lake Creek Road." Do not park on FR 391 because of private property.

The Hike

The South Fork of Lake Creek forms "La Plata Falls," a gorgeous waterfall that thunders over boulders into a narrow, cliff-lined chasm. The falls lies along the La Plata Gulch Trail, the normal hiking route up 14,360-foot La Plata Peak. The trail is popular with hikers heading to the summit of La Plata Peak, so expect a full parking lot during the summer.

The hike begins from the parking lot on CO 82 and heads south on South Fork Lake Creek Road/FR 391. Stay on the road to avoid trespassing on private property. When the road crosses a bridge over the North Fork of Lake Creek, pause for views of La Plata Peak and its saw-toothed Ellingwood Ridge. The La Plata Gulch Trail officially begins past the bridge. Look for a sign and go left on it to a footbridge over a chasm. "La Plata Falls" is visible right of the bridge, squeezing around an angular block, twisting into a fan spray, and splashing into a sandstone punchbowl.

A footbridge over South Fork Lake Creek provides splendid views of twisting "La Plata Falls."

Miles and Directions

0.0   Begin at La Plata Peak Trailhead. Hike south on FR 391, crossing bridge over South Fork Lake Creek.

0.3   Continue down road to a signed trail junction. Turn left off gravel road on La Plata Gulch Trail and hike southeast.

0.4   Arrive at footbridge over a small chasm with "La Plata Falls" to right (GPS: 39 3.793, -106 30.182). Return on trail and road.

0.8   Arrive back at trailhead (GPS: 39 4.068, -106 30.298).

23 Continental Falls

On the eastern slopes of the Tenmile Range, Spruce Creek tumbles down a series of marble steps below the Mohawk Lakes at Continental Falls. This airy waterfall affords stunning views east to the Continental Divide and south to 13,822-foot Mount Silverheels.

Start: Spruce Creek Trailhead
Trail: Spruce Creek Trail #58
Difficulty: Moderate
Hiking time: About 4 hours
Distance: 5.0 miles out and back
Elevation trailhead to falls viewpoint: 10,380 to 11,450 feet (+1,070 feet)
Trail surface: Dirt, rocks, duff
Restrictions: Trail closed to motorized vehicles; dogs must be leashed

Amenities: Services in Breckenridge, Alma, and Fairplay
Maps: *DeLorme:* Page 48 A2; Trails Illustrated 606: Breckenridge; USGS Breckenridge
County: Summit
Land status/contact: Arapaho National Forest, (970) 295-6600; Dillon Ranger District, (970) 468-5400

Finding the trailhead: From Fairplay, drive north on CO 9 for 19.3 miles and turn left on unpaved Spruce Creek Road (CR 800). From Breckenridge, drive south on CO 9 for 2.4 miles and turn right on Spruce Creek Road (CR 800). Go 0.1 mile to a T-junction with Crown Drive. Keep left on Spruce Creek Road and drive 1.1 miles to parking on both sides of the road at the trailhead (GPS: 39 26.221, -106 03.035).

The Hike

Beginning in a glaciated cirque below Pacific and Crystal Peaks, Spruce Creek pools in the twin Mohawk Lakes before rushing 225 feet down Continental Falls to a wide valley below. The waterfall, the highest near Breckenridge, drops through a narrow gully over rock steps in a series of cascades and horsetail falls.

The hike follows Spruce Creek Trail through a lodgepole pine forest and open meadows with views of 13,164-foot Mount Helen, and around a large pond. The trail climbs past a closed jeep road, a junction with the trail to Mayflower Lakes, cabin ruins, and remnants of nineteenth-century mining. Finish up a steep trail left of Continental Falls with side trails to views of its many tiers. From the waterfall's top, continue on the trail for another 0.25 mile to Lower Mohawk Lake or 0.75 mile to Mohawk Lake.

Miles and Directions

0.0 Begin at Spruce Creek Trailhead on south side of road. Follow blue diamond-shaped trail markers southwest through forest.
0.4 Cross Spruce Creek on footbridge.

Continental Falls

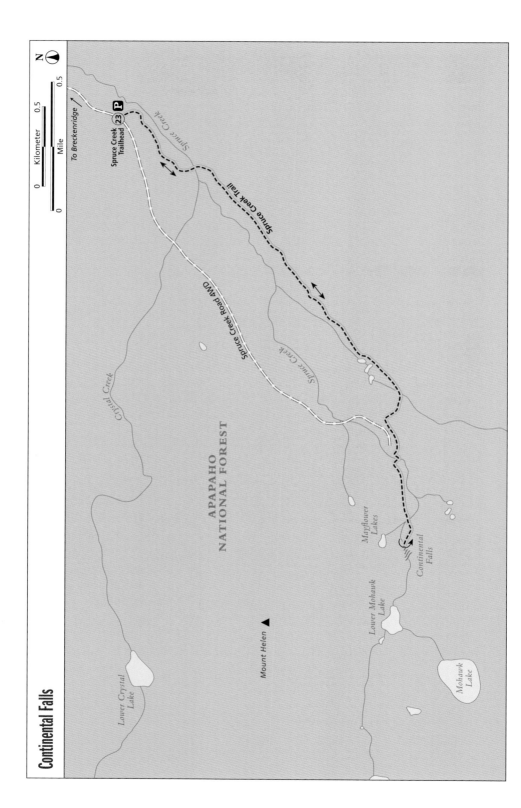

To Breckenridge

Spruce Creek Trailhead

Spruce Creek

Spruce Creek Trail

Spruce Creek Road 4WD

Spruce Creek

Crystal Creek

APAPAHO NATIONAL FOREST

Lower Crystal Lake

Mount Helen

Mayflower Lakes

Lower Mohawk Lake

Continental Falls

Mohawk Lake

N

Kilometer

Mile

0.5

0.5

0

Spruce Creek splashes down a series of spectacular waterfalls and cascades at Continental Falls near Breckenridge.

1.5 Reach junction with Wheeler Trail #39. Go straight on Spruce Creek Trail.

2.0 Pass sign for Spruce Creek Trail and meet Upper Spruce Creek Road, a closed 4WD route (GPS: 39 25.2953, -106 4.4561). Follow road past diversion dam on left.

2.1 Rejoin Spruce Creek Trail past dam (GPS: 39 25.2895, -106 4.50780).

2.3 Reach signed junction with Mayflower Lakes Trail on right (GPS: 39 25.2662, -106 4.7579). Stay left toward Continental Falls and Mohawk Lakes. Hike past cabin ruins on right, cross creek on footbridge, and continue past more ruins.

2.5 Reach top of Continental Falls (GPS: 39 25.2619, -106 5.0772). Return down trail after viewing.

5.0 Arrive back at trailhead (GPS: 39 26.221, -106 03.035).

The South

Westcliffe, Rye, Trinidad, Coaldale, Crestone, Blanca, Jasper, and Antonito

Treasure Creek drops into a shallow gorge at Horsethief Park Falls in the South San Juans.

24 Venable Falls

East of the crest of the Sangre de Cristo Mountains, Venable Creek flows from Venable Lakes to the Wet Mountain Valley. Passing through the Sangre de Cristo Wilderness, its streaming waters plummet down a multi-stepped cascade at Venable Falls, collapsing into a rocky chasm.

Start: Comanche/Venable Trailhead
Trail: Venable Trail #1347
Difficulty: Moderate
Hiking time: About 3 hours
Distance: 4.8 miles out and back
Elevation trailhead to falls viewpoint: 9,055 to 10,335 feet (+1,280 feet)
Trail surface: Dirt, rocks
Restrictions: No bicycles or motorized vehicles in wilderness area; observe wilderness regulations; dogs must be leashed

Amenities: Vault toilets at trailhead; backcountry camping; services in Westcliffe
Maps: *DeLorme:* page 71 E6; Trails Illustrated 138: Sangre de Cristo Mountains [Great Sand Dunes National Park and Preserve]; USGS Horn Peak
County: Custer
Land status/contact: San Isabel National Forest, (719) 553-1400; San Carlos Ranger District, (719) 269-8500

Finding the trailhead: From Westcliffe, take CO 69 south for 3.3 miles, then turn right (west) on CR 140 (Schoolfield Road). Go 4.6 miles and turn left on CR 141 (Schoolfield Road/Willow Lane). Drive 0.2 mile and turn right to get back on CR 140 (Schoolfield Road). Drive 1.6 miles and bear right on CR 148, then go 0.4 mile to parking at the trailhead (GPS: 38 04.950, -105 33.885).

The Hike

Venable Creek dashes east down a glaciated valley to noisy Venable Falls, a stepped waterfall in a cliff-lined gorge. The hike follows the well-traveled Venable Trail, which connects with the Comanche Trail for a 13-mile loop trek. The Venable Trail crosses into the Sangre de Cristo Wilderness and then climbs into a lush valley surrounded by high peaks, including 13,450-foot Horn Peak, 13,277-foot Comanche Peak, 13,244-foot Spring Mountain, and 13,334-foot Venable Peak. As the trail ascends, note the many small cascades in the creek below. At a small wooden sign, step down a side trail to the waterfall. For a longer outing, continue for another 3.0 miles to Venable Lakes, a couple high-elevation lakes below Venable Pass.

Miles and Directions

0.0 Begin at trailhead and follow signs for Venable Trail on right.

0.5 Reach unsigned junction with Comanche Trail. Go right to stay on Venable Trail.

0.6 Reach junction with Rainbow Trail. Go left on Venable Trail toward Venable Lakes.

Venable Falls

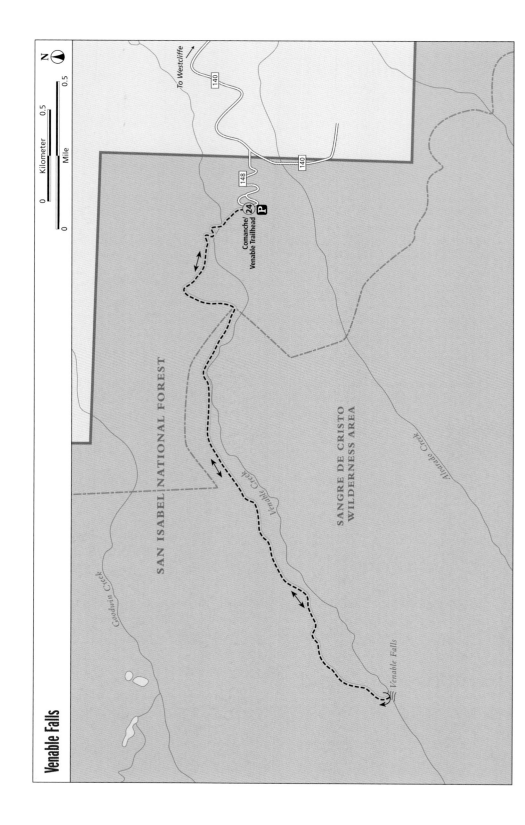

To Westcliffe

140

148

24

P Comanche/
Venable Trailhead

140

SAN ISABEL NATIONAL FOREST

Goodwin Creek

Venable Creek

SANGRE DE CRISTO
WILDERNESS AREA

Alvarado Creek

Venable Falls

N

Kilometer
0   0.5

0   0.5
Mile

Streaming waters plummet and collapse into a rocky trailside chasm at Venable Falls.

2.3 Reach sign for Venable Falls. Take social trail to left that switchbacks down to waterfall.

2.4 Arrive at base of Venable Falls (GPS: 38 04.553, -105 35.690). Return the way you came.

4.8 Arrive back at trailhead (GPS: 38 04.950, -105 33.885).

25 Macey Falls

In high glacial basins below Colony Baldy, the three Macey Lakes drain into Macey Creek. At Macey Falls the creek moves through a steep-walled chasm—splashing water in a cascade and flowing over rock into a chill punchbowl.

Start: Horn Creek Trailhead
Trails: Horn Creek Trail #1342, Rainbow Trail #1336, Macey Trail #1341
Difficulty: Strenuous
Hiking time: About 7 hours
Distance: 11.0 miles out and back
Elevation trailhead to falls viewpoint: 9,140 to 11,160 feet (+2,020 feet)
Trail surface: Dirt, rocks
Restrictions: No bicycles on trail; observe wilderness regulations; dogs must be leashed

Amenities: Vault toilets; backcountry camping; services in Westcliffe
Maps: *DeLorme:* Page 71 E6; Trails Illustrated 138: Sangre de Cristo Mountains [Great Sand Dunes National Park and Preserve]; USGS Horn Peak
County: Custer
Land status/contact: San Isabel National Forest, (719) 553-1400; San Carlos Ranger District, (719) 269-8500

Finding the trailhead: From Westcliffe, take CO 69 south for 3.3 miles, then turn right (west) on CR 140 (Schoolfield Road). Drive 1.8 miles and turn left on CR 129 (Macey Lane). Drive 2 miles and turn right on CR 130 (Horn Creek Road). Go 2.4 miles to Horn Creek Ranch, passing a trailhead for Rainbow Trail (which also accesses the falls, but adds 0.2 mile to the hike in each direction), then turn right and drive 0.5 mile to parking and the trailhead (GPS: 38 03.112, -105 32.159).

The Hike

Remote Macey Falls tumbles down a cliff-lined gorge on the eastern flank of the Sangre de Cristo Mountains. Beginning at Horn Creek Trailhead, the hike is long and arduous, making it a full-day adventure. Most hikers visit the waterfall and then continue to Macey Lakes, a string of three alpine lakes above 11,000 feet.

The hike follows Horn Creek Trail and then heads south on the Rainbow Trail, dipping through shallow, wooded drainages. The hike then leaves the Rainbow Trail at a footbridge and heads west on the Macey Trail. After leaving the trees, spot a thin ribbon falls pouring off Colony Baldy. This unnamed ephemeral falls is a bonus waterfall. Past streaked Copperstain Cliff, look for Macey Falls below the trail to the left.

For more miles, continue up the trail for a mile to Lower Macey Lake, and then climb steeply for another mile to Upper Macey Lake.

Miles and Directions

0.0 Begin at Horn Creek Trailhead on west side of circular road. Following signs for Rainbow Trail, hike southwest on Horn Creek Trail, a rocky 4WD track through forest.

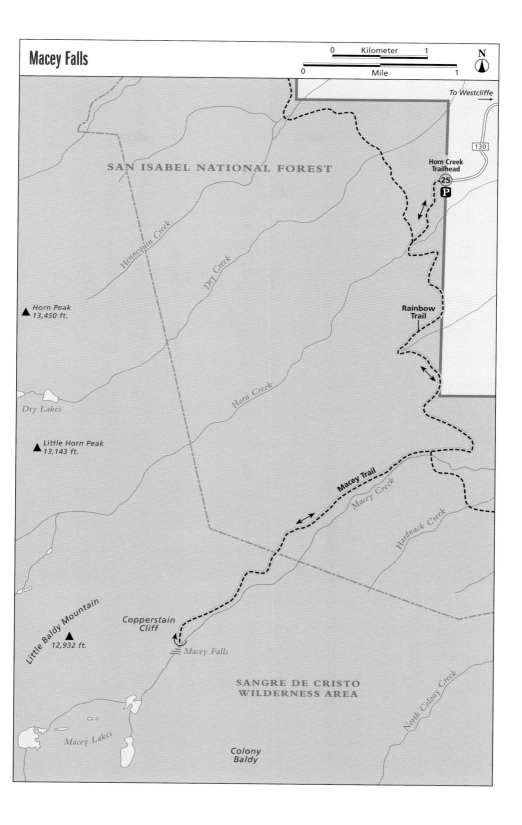

Macey Falls

0   Kilometer   1

0   Mile   1

N

To Westcliffe

130

Horn Creek
Trailhead

25

P

SAN ISABEL NATIONAL FOREST

Hennequin Creek

Dry Creek

▲ Horn Peak
13,450 ft.

Rainbow
Trail

Horn Creek

Dry Lakes

▲ Little Horn Peak
13,143 ft.

Macey Trail

Macey Creek

Hardnack Creek

Little Baldy Mountain

Copperstain
Cliff

▲ 12,932 ft.

Macey Falls

SANGRE DE CRISTO
WILDERNESS AREA

North Colony Creek

Macey Lakes

Colony
Baldy

Macey Creek flows smoothly over rock and drops into a placid punchbowl at Macey Falls.

0.6   Reach junction with Rainbow Trail. Go left on it, heading south toward signed Macey Trail, and cross bridge over Horn Creek.

3.2   Reach junction with Macey Trail, with bridge over Macey Creek and Rainbow Trail continuing to left. Go right on Macey Trail and hike southwest up right side of creek.

5.3   Copperstain Cliff rises to right. Look for a ribbon falls high in cliffs to left on north slopes of Colony Baldy.

5.5   Cut off main trail on side trail to Macey Falls below. Arrive at base of Macey Falls (GPS: 38 00.339, -105 34.002). Return the way you came.

11.0   Arrive back at trailhead (GPS: 38 03.112, -105 32.159).

26 Crystal Falls (Westcliffe)

Rainbow Trail hugs 10,749-foot Beck Mountain to the west, while offering Wet Mountain Valley views to the east. Tucked into an overgrown hideaway off the trail at Crystal Falls Creek, a segmented cascade splashes in a playful show at Crystal Falls.

Start: Grape Creek Trailhead
Trail: Rainbow Trail #1336
Difficulty: Moderate
Hiking time: About 4 hours
Distance: 6.4 miles out and back
Elevation trailhead to falls viewpoint: 9,260 to 9,210 feet (-50 feet)
Trail surface: Dirt, gravel
Restrictions: Dogs must be leashed
Amenities: Trailhead camping and vault toilets; services in Westcliffe

Maps: *DeLorme:* Page 81 A7; Trails Illustrated 139: Sangre de Cristo Mountains [Great Sand Dunes National Park and Preserve]; USGS Beck Mountain
County: Custer
Land status/contact: San Isabel National Forest, (719) 269-8500; San Carlos Ranger District, (719) 269-8500; BLM, Saguache Field Office, (719) 655-2547

Finding the trailhead: From Westcliffe, drive south on CO 69 for 4.5 miles and turn right on Colfax Lane (CR 119). Drive 5.6 miles to a T-intersection. Turn left on South Colony Road (CR 120) and travel 0.7 mile to rejoin CR 119. Continue 4.5 miles south on CR 119 to a parking lot at the Grape Creek Trailhead (GPS: 37 55.825, -105 27.453).

The Hike

Crystal Falls rumbles off a stone bench in a secluded valley on the eastern edge of the Sangre de Cristo Mountains. The hidden falls is reached by hiking north on the Rainbow Trail, a 100-mile path that skirts the eastern flank of the Sangre de Cristos from Salida to Great Sand Dunes National Park. The section of the Rainbow Trail to Crystal Falls is popular with hikers, mountain bikers, dirt bikers, and equestrians, so expect to share the trail.

Follow the trail north through forest and meadows along the edge of Beck Mountain, with views across the Wet Mountain Valley. At Crystal Creek, look for a wooden sign nailed to a tree. This marks the side trail along the creek to the falls. Dense brush and mossy boulders lend a feeling of seclusion to this final section and make for tricky footwork, so tread carefully and enjoy the serene beauty of this remote waterfall.

Miles and Directions

0.0 Begin at Grape Creek Trailhead. Hike north on Rainbow Trail, bending into a canyon and crossing Music Pass Creek.

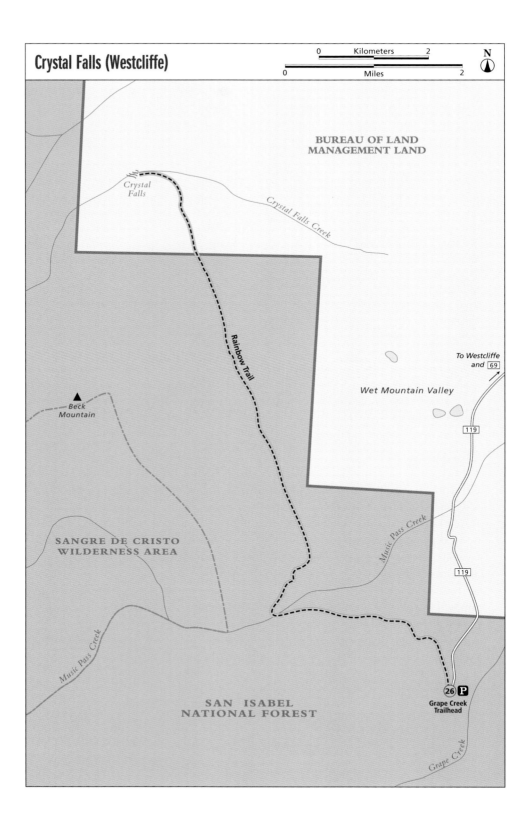

Crystal Falls (Westcliffe)

Kilometers
0 2
Miles
0 2

N

BUREAU OF LAND
MANAGEMENT LAND

Crystal Falls

Crystal Falls Creek

Rainbow Trail

To Westcliffe
and 69

Wet Mountain Valley

119

Beck
Mountain

Music Pass Creek

SANGRE DE CRISTO
WILDERNESS AREA

119

Music Pass Creek

26 P

Grape Creek
Trailhead

SAN ISABEL
NATIONAL FOREST

Grape Creek

A segmented cascade splashes and splays in a playful show of waterfall wonder at Crystal Falls.

3.2 Cross Crystal Falls Creek and note a small sign for the waterfall. Turn left off main trail onto a side trail and hike west along creek. Arrive at base of Crystal Falls (GPS: 37 57.723, -105 28.837). Return south on Rainbow Trail.

6.4 Arrive back at trailhead (GPS: 37 55.825, -105 27.453).

27 Ophir Creek Falls

Ophir Creek, originating on the crest of the Wet Mountains southwest of Pueblo, rumbles down a narrow canyon filled with granite blocks and cliffs to Ophir Creek Falls, a two-leap waterfall over a cliff.

Start: Trailhead at Ophir Creek Campground
Trail: Unnamed trail
Difficulty: Easy
Hiking time: About 1 hour
Distance: 1.0 mile out and back
Elevation trailhead to falls viewpoint: 8,896 to 9,082 feet (+186 feet)
Trail surface: Dirt, rocks
Restrictions: No bicycles or motorized vehicles; dogs must be leashed; ask permission before hiking through campsite #22

Amenities: Limited services in Wetmore and San Isabel; services in Florence and Rye
Maps: *DeLorme:* Page 72 E2; Trails Illustrated: none; USGS St. Charles Peak
County: Custer
Land status/contact: Pike and San Isabel National Forests, (719) 553-1400; San Carlos Ranger District, (719) 269-8500

Finding the trailhead: From East Main Street (CO 115) in Florence, drive south on CO 67 for 11.1 miles to Wetmore. Turn right on CO 96 toward Westcliffe and drive 24.1 miles to Makinzie Junction. Turn left (south) on CO 165 and drive 11.7 miles to a hairpin turn before Bishop Castle. Make a right (west) turn on dirt FR 360 (Ophir Creek Road). Drive 300 feet and turn left into Ophir Creek Campground. Drive 0.6 mile to parking at the end of the campground loop. The trailhead is left of the vault toilets by the parking for campsites 20–22 (GPS: 38 3.5357, -105 6.5199). A sign says, "Parking for Tent Sites 20, 21, 22."

The Hike

Ophir Creek Falls is a gorgeous double waterfall hidden in a rocky canyon above Ophir Creek Campground in the Wet Mountains. The 45-foot-high falls spills over a granite cliff to a hard-rock pool, then cascades down a slick slab to a plunge pool. The waterfall, surrounded by giant boulders and shaggy cliffs, lies a few miles from the famed Bishop Castle, a marvelous fantasy built by Jim Bishop. A Colorado character, Bishop began the project in 1969, calling it "the largest one-man project in the world" and "a tourist attraction without being a tourist trap." After hiking to the falls, stop by the castle (admission is free!) to complete the adventure.

Miles and Directions

0.0   Start at informal trailhead left of vault toilets. Hike straight on trail toward three campsites. Pass through site #22 (ask permission if occupied) and continue along creek, crossing it three times. Use caution if creek is high.

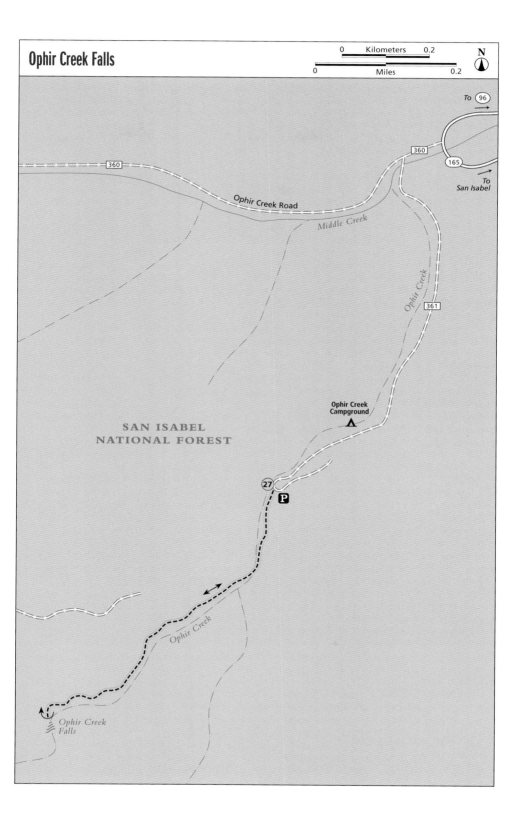

Ophir Creek Falls

0   Kilometers   0.2

0   Miles   0.2

N

To 96

360

165

360

To
San Isabel

Ophir Creek Road

Middle Creek

Ophir Creek

361

Ophir Creek
Campground

SAN ISABEL
NATIONAL FOREST

27

P

Ophir Creek

Ophir Creek
Falls

Ophir Creek Falls hides in a mountain canyon a few miles away from Bishop Castle.

0.5 After last creek crossing, reach base of Ophir Creek Falls (GPS: 38 3.2539, -105 6.8631). Trail reaches pool below lower cascade. Hike around boulders to right and scramble down to base of upper falls. Granite is water-polished so watch your footing. Return on trail.

1.0 Arrive back at trailhead (GPS: 38 3.5357, -105 6.5199).

28 Apache Falls

Nestled in the moist South Apache Creek drainage in the Wet Mountains, Apache Falls pours over 100 feet from a ledge, splashing on boulders in a shimmering horsetail spray.

Start: Bartlett Trailhead
Trails: Bartlett Trail #1310, South Apache Trail #1311, Apache Falls Trail #1357
Difficulty: Very strenuous
Hiking time: About 7 hours
Distance: 11.0 miles out and back
Elevation trailhead to falls viewpoint: 7,650 to 8,550 feet (+900 feet)
Trail surface: Dirt, rocks, scree, duff
Restrictions: No bicycles or motorized vehicles allowed; observe wilderness regulations; dogs must be leashed

Amenities: Backcountry camping; services in Rye
Maps: *DeLorme:* page 82 B3; Trails Illustrated: none; USGS Rye, Hayden Butte
County: Huerfano
Land status/contact: Greenhorn Mountain Wilderness Area; San Isabel National Forest, (719) 553-1400; San Carlos Ranger District, (719) 269-8500

Finding the trailhead: From I-25 south of Pueblo, take exit 74 to CO 165 West (Colorado City/Rye). Turn right on CO 165 and drive 8.4 miles, then turn left on Boulder Avenue in Rye. Go 0.7 mile and turn left on Greenhorn Drive. Go 1.3 miles and bear right on unpaved Baxter Road. Drive 0.5 mile and keep left on Bartlett Trail. This road may be muddy and unsafe after or during rainfall. Drive 2.9 miles on Bartlett Trail to the trailhead (GPS: 37 52.7072, -104 57.4923).

The Hike

Apache Falls, hiding in a cul-de-sac canyon above South Apache Creek, is a dramatic ribbon of water that falls over 100 feet off an overhanging cliff. The unique waterfall, hiding in the Greenhorn Mountain Wilderness, is reached by a strenuous hike on three rough trails. Although the net elevation gain from trailhead to falls is just 900 feet, you first climb 1,685 feet to a saddle, then drop 1,175 feet down to South Apache Creek before climbing 385 feet up to the falls, for a round-trip elevation gain of 3,245 feet.

Miles and Directions

0.0 Begin at Bartlett Trailhead. Hike west up rocky Bartlett Trail through dense scrub oak.

1.1 Reach Greenhorn Mountain Wilderness boundary and cross a saddle. Trail levels and crosses four streams.

3.3 Reach junction with unsigned South Apache Trail to left (east). Follow ridge east and descend steep switchbacks into South Apache Creek's canyon. Trail is faint and overgrown in places. Slow down to stay on course.

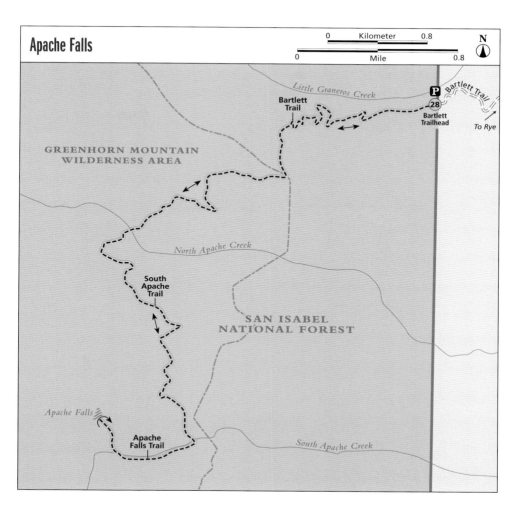

Apache Falls

4.8 Watch for cairned switchback to right and junction with Apache Falls Trail to right. Go right on Apache Falls Trail and hike west up creek, stepping over deadfall.

5.0 Cross creek on branches to left, then follow trail along creek's left bank.

5.2 Pass a backcountry campsite, and cross to right side of creek on branches and boulders. Pick up trail on north bank. Cross creek again and climb up drainage on right to waterfall.

5.5 Arrive at base of Apache Falls (GPS: 37 51.279, -104 59.309). A steep trail climbs left side of falls; use caution and stay clear of polished edge at top. Return the way you came.

11.0 Arrive back at trailhead (GPS: 37 52.7072, -104 57.4923).

Apache Falls splashes and streams over pink and gray boulders in a shimmering horsetail spray.

29 Trinchera Falls

Trinchera Creek slides peacefully north through Trinchera Canyon before settling into the Purgatoire River. At Trinchera Falls, the creek spills through a narrow crevice and emerges in a horsetail spray, dropping into a secret cavern carved in sandstone.

Start: Informal trailhead on CR 127
Trail: Unnamed road and trail
Difficulty: Easy
Hiking time: About 2 hours
Distance: 3.4 miles out and back
Elevation trailhead to falls viewpoint: 5,590 to 5,420 feet (-170 feet)
Trail surface: Dirt road, rocks
Restrictions: Trinchera Cave Archaeological District on Colorado State Land Trust managed by Colorado Division of Wildlife. No restrictions posted. No collecting of archaeological features.
Amenities: Services in Trinidad
Maps: *DeLorme:* Page 100 E2; Trails Illustrated: none; USGS Trementina Canyon, Trinchera Cave
County: Las Animas
Land status/contact: Colorado Parks and Wildlife, (303) 297-1192

Finding the trailhead: From I-25 in Trinidad, take exit 15 to US 160 East and drive 1.1 miles. Turn left and stay on US 160. Continue 5.2 miles and bear right, then turn right on US 160. Drive 25.3 miles and turn left on gravel road CR 127. Drive 2.1 miles and park. Opposite the parking is a road that leads east to a windmill, and an old road on the left that heads west to the falls (GPS: 37 9.855, -103 59.545).

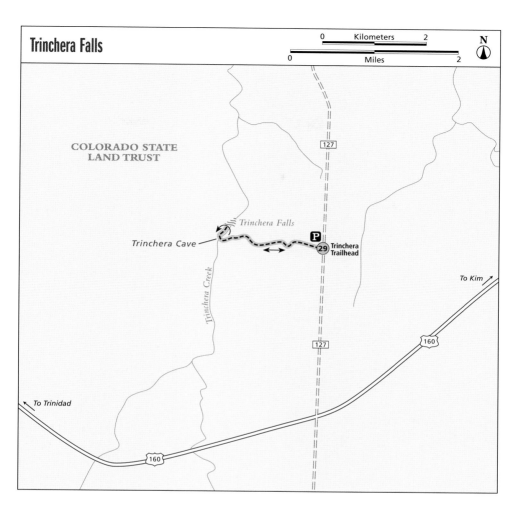

The Hike

Trinchera Falls, one of two known waterfalls on Colorado's plains, tucks into a deep crevice in cliff-lined Trinchera Canyon. The hike follows an unmaintained dirt road through scattered piñon pine, juniper, and cholla cactus, with views of the Culebra Range and the twin Spanish Peaks. When the road fades at the canyon, a rock trail leads past Trinchera Cave, part of 480-acre Trinchera Cave Archaeological District. The shelter cave, a renowned prehistoric site, was discovered by rancher William Louden in 1947. Excavations reveal that Native Americans lived here during the past 4,000 years. Farther north the creek freefalls in a hidden sandstone crevice. Carved into bedrock, the scalloped creek bed is a magnificent sight.

◀ *Trinchera Falls is best viewed from above, but access to the creek below is possible. Take care and step lightly on the delicate rock.*

Trinchera Creek splashes into a secret cavern carved in stone at Trinchera Falls.

Miles and Directions

0.0 Begin at gravel road on left side of CR 127.

1.4 Bear right as road ends and descend rocky trail to Trinchera Creek.

1.5 Cross creek and turn right to follow left (west) side of creek.

1.7 Pass above Trinchera Falls to right of trail (GPS: 37 10.049, -104 0.828). Continue past waterfall for better views at rock outcroppings above canyon. Return the way you came.

3.4 Arrive back at trailhead (GPS: 37 9.855, -103 59.545).

Left: It's a long hike to "Lower Stout Creek Falls," but the area's beauty and solitude is worth the effort.
Right: Stout Creek Falls offers three whitewater leaps below the twin Stout Lakes.

Miles and Directions

0.0 Begin at Rainbow Trailhead across road from parking pullout. Hike northwest on Rainbow Trail along North Prong of Hayden Creek.

0.7 Cross North Prong of Hayden Creek on logs.

0.8 Pass junction with Hayden Creek Campground trail on left. Continue straight (watch for this junction on the way back so you take the correct fork to the trailhead). Cross the creek and its tributaries six more times.

2.8 Reach three-way trail junction at a saddle. Take middle fork to stay on Rainbow Trail. Left trail is Bushnell Lakes Trail.

4.8 Reach junction with Kerr Gulch Trail. Continue straight on Rainbow Trail.

5.0 Reach junction with Stout Creek Trail on left. Leave Rainbow Trail and hike west on Stout Creek Trail.

5.1 Reach Sangre De Cristo Wilderness boundary and sign trail register. Continue up trail, cross creek on log bridge, and pass through deadfall.

7.6 Arrive at "Lower Stout Creek Falls" (GPS: 38 21.451, -105 52.895). Cut off main trail on social trails to view waterfall. Continue west on main trail.

7.7 Arrive at "Middle Stout Creek Falls" (GPS: 38 21.428, -105 52.934). Cut off main trail to view. Continue up main trail to Lower Stout Creek Lake.

7.8 Arrive at Lower Stout Creek Lake and views of the three leaps of Stout Creek Falls.

7.9 Reach base of Stout Creek Falls (GPS: 38 21.347, -105 53.122). Follow creek or take main trail on right to lake.

8.2 Reach trail's end at Stout Creek Lake and top of waterfalls. Descend trail for views of falls from a different vantage point. Reverse trails to hike back to trailhead.

16.4 Arrive back at trailhead (GPS: 38 19.799, -105 49.029).

32 North Crestone Trail Waterfalls: "Lower North Crestone Trail Waterfall" and "Upper North Crestone Trail Waterfall"

North Crestone Lake sits high in the Sangre de Cristo Mountains below 13,554-foot Fluted Peak and 13,931-foot Mount Adams. Icy water spills from the lake down the Lake Fork of North Crestone Creek, gurgling in cascades and horsetail leaps along North Crestone Trail.

Start: North Crestone Trailhead
Trail: North Crestone Trail #744
Difficulty: Strenuous
Hiking time: About 6 hours
Distance: 7.8 miles out and back for "Lower North Crestone Trail Waterfall"; 8.2 miles out and back for "Upper North Crestone Trail Waterfall"
Elevation trailhead to falls viewpoints: 8,545 to 10,555 feet (+2,010 feet) for lower falls; to 10,710 feet (+2,165 feet) for upper falls
Trail surface: Gravel, dirt, rocks
Restrictions: No bicycles or motorized vehicles; observe wilderness regulations; dogs must be leashed in campground

Amenities: Vault toilets; North Crestone Creek Campground; backcountry camping at least 300 feet from lake or 100 feet from stream; services in Crestone
Maps: *DeLorme:* Page 71 E5 and E6; Trails Illustrated 138: Sangre de Cristo Mountains [Great Sand Dunes National Park and Preserve]; USGS Rito Alto Peak
County: Saguache
Land status/contact: Sangre de Cristo Wilderness Area; Rio Grande National Forest, (719) 852-5941; Saguache Ranger District, (719) 480-1402

Finding the trailhead: From Poncha Springs, drive 26.1 miles south on US 285 and turn left on CO 17 South. Go 14.4 miles and turn left on CR T (Russell Street) toward Crestone. Drive 13.6 miles on paved roads through Crestone to a gravel road, the Rio Grande National Forest boundary, and North Crestone Creek Campground. Continue 0.8 mile to the road's end, parking, and the North Crestone Trailhead (GPS: 38 01.125, -105 41.138).

The Hike

The North Crestone Trail, following North Crestone Creek and its Lake Fork, is a strenuous hike, gaining over 2,000 feet in elevation from trailhead to waterfalls. At both waterfalls, the trail runs high above the creek, with the falls dropping from ledges on the creek's far side. The overlooks are exposed, so steer clear of soft or loose edges. Enjoy the waterfalls from the trail or choose a safe route to their bases. If you have the stamina, continue past the falls on North Crestone Trail for an additional 1.5 miles and another 1,100 feet of elevation gain to lovely North Crestone Lake, an alpine lake nestled below the north face of 13,931-foot Mount Adams. This makes for a long trail day, with 11.2 miles of hiking round-trip, and over 3,300 feet of elevation gain.

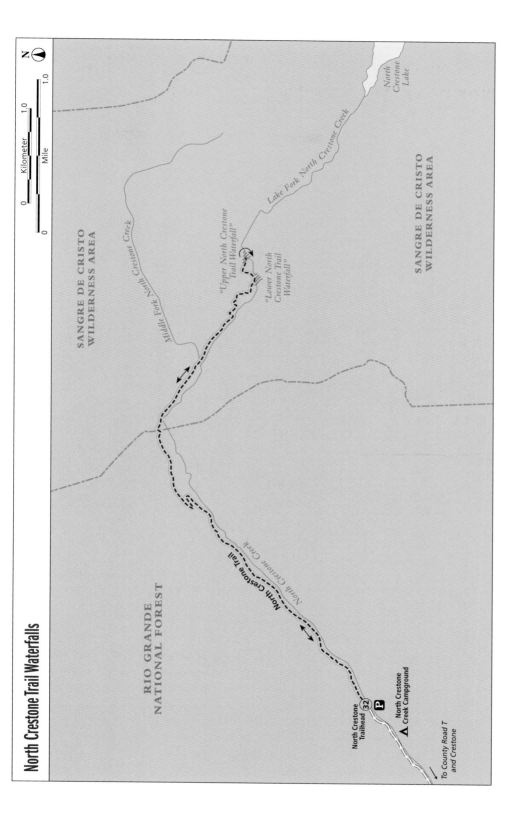

North Crestone Trail Waterfalls

SANGRE DE CRISTO
WILDERNESS AREA

SANGRE DE CRISTO
WILDERNESS AREA

North
Crestone
Lake

Lake Fork North Crestone Creek

Middle Fork North Crestone Creek

"Upper North Crestone
Trail Waterfall"

"Lower North
Crestone Trail
Waterfall"

RIO GRANDE
NATIONAL FOREST

North Crestone Trail

North Crestone Creek

North Crestone
Trailhead 32

North Crestone
Creek Campground

To County Road T
and Crestone

N

Kilometer
0   1.0

Mile
0   1.0

"Lower North Crestone Trail Waterfall" babbles and gurgles in horsetail leaps.

Miles and Directions

0.0   Begin at North Crestone Trailhead. Follow an old gravel road northeast along North Crestone Creek.

0.7   Road turns to trail and rises above creek into forest.

2.5   Reach the marked Sangre de Cristo Wilderness boundary.

2.6   Reach junction with North Fork Crestone Trail and Comanche Trail on left. Keep right toward North Crestone Lake (signed) and hike toward creek through aspens.

3.9   Pass trailside cascades and arrive at viewpoint above "Lower North Crestone Trail Waterfall" (GPS: 38 01.757, -105 38.111).

4.1   Arrive at viewpoint above "Upper North Crestone Trail Waterfall" (GPS: 38 01.809,-105 37.962). Return the way you came.

8.2   Arrive back at trailhead (GPS: 38 01.125, -105 41.138).

33 Willow Lake Trail Waterfalls: "Hiker's Falls," "Lower Willow Creek Falls," "Middle Willow Creek Falls," "Black Slide Falls," "Upper Willow Creek Falls," and "Willow Lake Falls"

Willow Lake Trail is popular with mountaineers climbing 14,081-foot Challenger Point and 14,165-foot Kit Carson Mountain. Willow Creek, fed by snowmelt and springs, fills two alpine lakes and fuels six waterfalls along the trail.

Start: Willow Lake/South Crestone Trailhead
Trail: Willow Lake Trail #860
Difficulty: Strenuous/very strenuous
Hiking time: About 7 hours
Distance: 6.4 miles out and back for "Hiker's Falls"; 6.8 miles out and back for "Lower Willow Creek Falls"; 7.0 miles out and back for "Middle Willow Creek Falls"; 7.4 miles out and back for "Black Slide Falls"; 9.6 miles out and back for "Upper Willow Creek Falls"; 10.8 miles out and back for "Willow Lake Falls"
Elevation trailhead to falls viewpoints: 8,890 to 10,655 feet (+1,765 feet) for "Hiker's Falls"; to 10,810 feet (+1,920 feet) for "Lower Willow Creek Falls"; to 10,880 feet (+1,990 feet) for "Middle Willow Creek Falls"; to 10,960 feet (+2,070 feet) for "Black Slide Falls"; to 11,550 feet (+2,660 feet) for "Upper Willow Creek

Falls"; to 11,790 feet (+2,900 feet) for "Willow Lake Falls"
Trail surface: Sand, dirt, duff, rocks, talus
Restrictions: No bicycles or motorized vehicles; dogs allowed under control; observe wilderness regulations; don't camp within 300 feet of lake or 100 feet of water sources; properly dispose of human waste with wag bag
Amenities: Backcountry camping; services in Crestone
Maps: DeLorme: Page 71 E5 and E6; Trails Illustrated 138: Sangre de Cristo Mountains [Great Sand Dunes National Park and Preserve]; USGS Crestone, Crestone Peak
County: Saguache
Land status/contact: Sangre de Cristo Wilderness Area; Rio Grande National Forest, (719) 852-5941; Saguache Ranger District, (719) 480-1402

Finding the trailhead: From Poncha Springs, drive 26.1 miles south on US 285 and turn left on CO 17 South. Drive 14.4 miles south to a left turn on CR T (Crestone Road), toward Crestone. Alternatively, drive 35.9 miles north on CO 17 from US 160 in Alamosa. Drive east on CR T for 12.5 miles to Crestone and turn right on Galena Avenue, which becomes unpaved after 0.1 mile. Follow signs for South Crestone Trailhead. Follow Galena Avenue to a 2WD parking lot and trailhead at 1.5 miles, or continue another 0.75 mile on rougher road to the 4WD parking and main trailhead. Most vehicles with clearance can drive to the upper trailhead. Find the trailhead at the east side of the parking lot (GPS: 37 59.337,-105 39.749).

*Left: Before crossing Willow Creek, stop and enjoy the lower leaps of "Middle Willow Creek Falls."
Right: Dramatic "Black Slide Falls," fed by springs above, slips down a high-angle conglomerate
slab above the trail.*

The Hike

The Willow Lake Trail climbs up a valley to a picturesque lake fed by plunging Willow Lake Falls. The trail, traversing meadows and a woodland of pine, spruce, and quaking aspen, follows Willow Creek and passes six waterfalls. Plan on a full day to see all the falls, explore Willow Lake, and photograph the stunning scenery. Most of the trail is in the 220,803-acre Sangre de Cristo Wilderness. The road's condition from Crestone to the trailhead varies and may add up to 4 miles of hiking if you can't drive to the upper parking area.

Besides the five lower waterfalls seen from the trail, the highlight of the hike is Willow Lake, a breathtaking lake lined with cliffs in a glacier-carved cirque below Kit Carson Peak. On the lake's east side, "Willow Lake Falls" plunges over 100 feet through deep-cut crevices sliced into a vertical wall, shattering to foam on boulders on the lakeshore below. This majestic spot is a perfect end to the hike. Reach the waterfall's top by following a faint trail that wraps around the lake's north side. Find a sun-warmed seat above the waterfall and enjoy the lake, the pristine alpine valley, and the high peaks that tower above this slice of waterfall heaven.

Willow Lake Trail Waterfalls

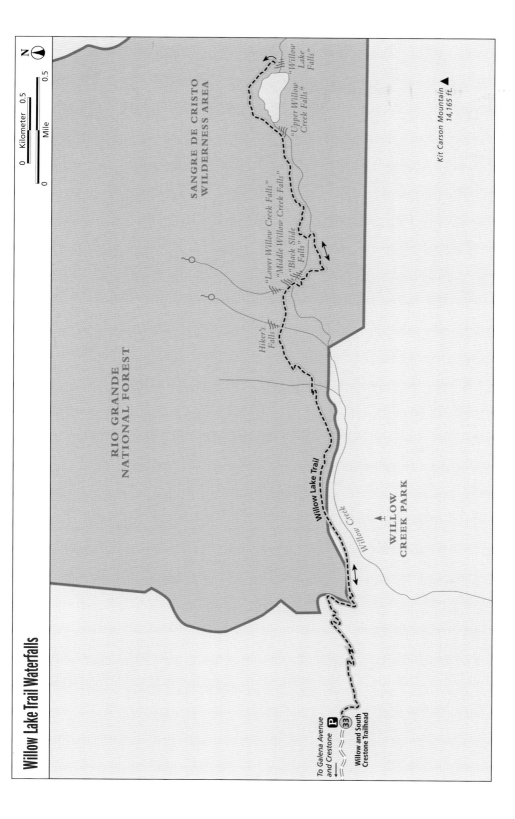

N

0   Kilometer   0.5

0   Mile   0.5

RIO GRANDE
NATIONAL FOREST

SANGRE DE CRISTO
WILDERNESS AREA

"Willow
Lake
Falls"

"Upper Willow
Creek Falls"

"Lower Willow Creek Falls"

"Middle Willow Creek Falls"

"Black Slide
Falls"

Hiker's
Falls

Kit Carson Mountain
14,165 ft.

Willow Lake Trail

Willow Creek

WILLOW
CREEK PARK

To Galena Avenue
and Crestone

P

33

Willow and South
Crestone Trailhead

Willow Lake Falls drops over 100 feet into Willow Lake in the Sangre de Cristo Mountains.

Miles and Directions

0.0 Begin at Willow Lake/South Crestone Trailhead. Hike 500 feet and turn right on Willow Lake Trail.

0.1 Cross South Crestone Creek on rocks and logs and hike to a trail register.

1.0 Enter Sangre de Cristo Wilderness. Trail switches back and forth along wilderness boundary.

1.7 Reenter Sangre de Cristo Wilderness and pass grassy Willow Creek Park.

3.2 Arrive at "Hiker's Falls" (GPS: 37 59.606, -105 37.726), a triple-tiered slide down a rock face, on left.

3.4 Arrive at multiple cascades of "Lower Willow Creek Falls" to right of trail (GPS: 37 59.598, -105 37.578). Upper leaps of "Middle Willow Creek Falls" are visible in cliffs to the east.

3.5 Cross Willow Creek and view lower leaps of "Middle Willow Creek Falls" to left (GPS: 37 59.565, -105 37.487). Continue up trail above creek.

3.7 Arrive at "Black Slide Falls," a slide falls down a high conglomerate slab left of trail (GPS: 37 59.53, -105 37.469). Hike past upper leaps of "Middle Willow Creek Falls," below and left of trail; no safe way to top of these falls.

4.8 Arrive at "Upper Willow Creek Falls" to right of trail (GPS: 37 59.632, -105 36.701). This dramatic horsetail waterfall plummets 50 feet from a rock ledge below Willow Lake.

4.9 Trail scrambles up slabs at west end of 11,564-foot Willow Lake and reaches first view of "Willow Lake Falls." To see waterfall up close, follow a rough trail, marked with cairns, across talus slopes on lake's north side to slabs above falls. Use extreme caution above falls and avoid slick rock.

5.4 Arrive at top of "Willow Lake Falls" (GPS: 37 59.645, -105 36.357). Return down trail.

10.8 Arrive back at trailhead (GPS: 37 59.337, -105 39.749).

34 Zapata Falls

On the northwest ramparts of 14,042-foot Ellingwood Point in the Sangre de Cristo Mountains, snowmelt fills South Zapata Lake, funnels down South Zapata Creek, and flows north to fuel Zapata Falls. This dramatic plunge waterfall—located 8 miles south of Great Sand Dunes National Park—is a family favorite.

Start: Zapata Falls Trailhead
Trail: Zapata Falls Trail
Difficulty: Very easy
Hiking time: Less than 1 hour
Distance: 0.8 mile out and back
Elevation trailhead to falls viewpoint: 9,035 to 9,250 feet (+215 feet)
Trail surface: Talus, rocks, water
Restrictions: No motorized vehicles; dogs must be leashed; no swimming

Amenities: Zapata Falls Campground; vault toilets, interpretive signs, picnic sites, and overlooks at trailhead; services in Blanca, Fort Garland, and Alamosa
Maps: *DeLorme:* Page 81 D6; Trails Illustrated 138: Sangre de Cristo Mountains [Great Sand Dunes National Park and Preserve]; USGS Twin Peaks
County: Alamosa
Land status/contact: BLM, San Luis Valley Field Office, (719) 852-7074

Finding the trailhead: From I-25 in Walsenburg, drive west on US 160 West for 57.3 miles. Turn right on CO 150 North and drive north for 12.5 miles to a sign for Zapata Falls. Turn right on unmarked BLM Road 5415 and drive the steep and winding gravel road for 3.8 miles to a parking lot at the trailhead (GPS: 37 37.295, -105 33.567).

The Hike

Zapata Falls is a 25-foot waterfall tucked into a narrow canyon. The easily accessible falls is a popular spot, so come early on weekends, hike during the week, or stay at the twenty-four-site campground for a moonlit hike. You have to wade up the creek to view the falls, so put on water shoes or sandals and use a trekking pole for balance. Don't attempt it in high water. The final section enters a deep, narrow cleft cut into a cliff. Wade to the base of the falls. You may have to wait for the best views since this is a popular photo spot.

For a longer outing, take the cutoff from Zapata Falls Trail to South Zapata Lake Trail. This steep route is 8.5 miles out and back with 2,800 feet of elevation gain, and climbs to South Zapata Lake, the source of Zapata Falls.

Zapata Falls is a family favorite located near Great Sand Dunes National Park.

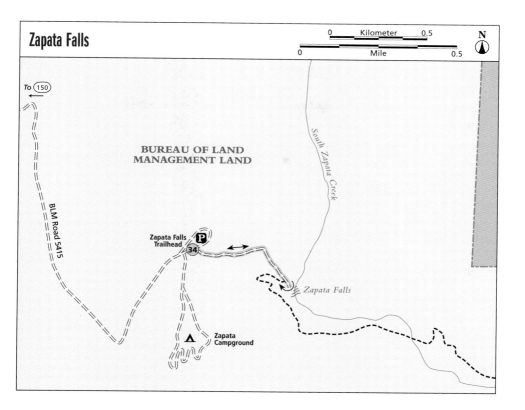

Zapata Falls

Miles and Directions

0.0 Begin at Zapata Falls Trailhead and hike east on a wide, juniper-lined trail to South Zapata Creek. Hike up edge of creek or wade in water to a deep crevice filled by creek.

0.4 Arrive at base of Zapata Falls (GPS: 37 37.185,-105 33.240). Return the way you came.

0.8 Arrive back at trailhead (GPS: 37 37.295, -105 33.567).

35 "Wightman Fork Falls"

Tucked into a narrow, cliff-lined canyon, "Wightman Fork Falls" plunges off a steep cliff into a circular pool above the Alamosa River's broad valley.

Start: Informal trailhead on FR 250
Trail: Unnamed social trails
Difficulty: Easy
Hiking time: About 30 minutes
Distance: 0.4 mile out and back to base; 0.2 mile out and back to overlook
Elevation trailheads to falls viewpoints: 9,395 feet at overlook trailhead; 9,530 feet at falls overlook; 9,395 feet at falls base trailhead; 9,440 feet at pool at base
Trail surface: Dirt, rocks, creek

Restrictions: None posted
Amenities: None; Stunner Campground to west; limited services in Platoro
Maps: *DeLorme:* Page 89 A6; Trails Illustrated 142: South San Juan, Del Norte; USGS Summitville
County: Rio Grande
Land status/contact: Rio Grande National Forest, (719) 852-5941; Conejos Peak Ranger District, (719) 480-9892

Finding the trailhead: From South Fork to the north, drive 7.7 miles west on US 160 and turn left (south) on dirt FR 380 toward Summitville. Continue south to the junction with FR 250. Drive east on FR 250 for 3.1 miles and park on the road shoulder by a bridge.

From Alamosa to the east, drive south on US 285 and turn right on CO 350 to a left turn on CO 15 to a right turn on CR FF. Turn right at its end on dirt FR 250, which leads to Jasper. From a bridge over Burnt Creek in Jasper, drive 3.4 miles and park on the road shoulder by a bridge.

From the junction of CO 17 and FR 250 at Horca to the south, drive north on dirt FR 250 over Stunner Pass to the junction of FR 380 and FR 250. Drive east on FR 250 for 3.1 miles and park on the road shoulder by a bridge.

To hike to the falls base, start at the informal trailhead on the bridge's west side (GPS: 37 24.2978, -106 31.3354). To hike to the overlook, start at informal trailhead on the bridge's east side (GPS: 37 24.2562, -106 31.2875).

The Hike

Dramatic 75-foot "Wightman Fork Falls" slips through a sharp notch and plummets into a rock-rimmed pool. The waterfall, enclosed by cliffs in a cul-de-sac canyon, offers a glimpse of raw nature with the roar of thundering water echoing off volcanic cliffs. The remote falls, reached by short hikes to the waterfall base and a viewpoint, is fed by Wightman Fork, a creek that drains southeast from the Summitville gold mining area to the northwest.

The mining area has leached cyanide and other waste into the Wightman Fork as well as the Alamosa River. In the 1990s the area became a Superfund cleanup site to prevent the release of cyanide and acidic water into area streams. The State of Colorado now manages the Summitville mining area to contain contamination.

Encircled by high cliffs, "Wightman Fork Falls" plunges 70 feet into a deep pool.

When visiting the falls, don't allow your dog to drink creek water. Other dangers include high water, flash flooding, and the unfenced overlook atop a 90-foot cliff. Do not attempt to wade upstream or cross the creek during spring runoff when the creek runs deep and fast. During that time, view the falls from the overlook. When visiting the overlook, control children and dogs. The overlook is atop a high cliff that drops directly to the creek. The unfenced cliff edge is friable, so don't stand on its edge and watch for insecure footing.

There are two ways to view the waterfall. For the overlook, find an informal trailhead on the right side of a pullout east of the bridge. Hike up a steep trail to the overlook, then descend back to the road. To reach the waterfall base, begin left of the bridge and hike up the creek's left bank until boulders force you to cross the creek. Scramble over boulders and wade up the creek to reach the plunge pool.

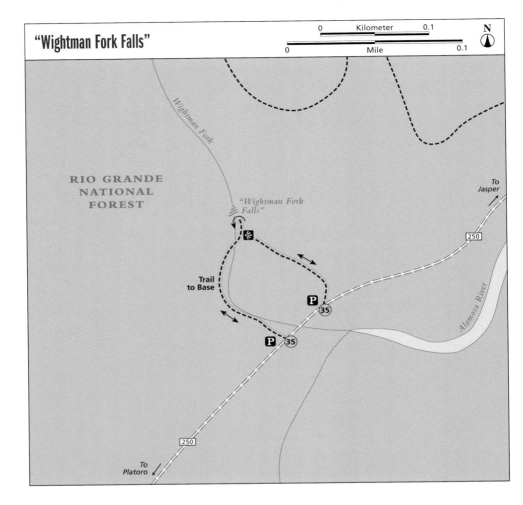

Miles and Directions

Trail to Falls Overlook

0.0 Start at informal trailhead 60 feet right (east) of bridge. Hike steep trail uphill.

0.1 Reach exposed overlook above waterfall (GPS: 37 24.2887, -106 31.3328). Use caution at unfenced overlook. Control children and dogs.

0.2 Arrive back at trailhead (GPS: 37 24.2562, -106 31.2875).

Trail to Waterfall Base

0.0 Start at informal trailhead 90 feet left (west) of bridge. Hike across open area and down-climb rock step to creek bed. Follow trail along creek's west bank to boulders below falls. Wade creek for best views on east bank.

0.2 Arrive at rocks below plunge pool and falls (GPS: 37 24.2978, -106 31.3354).

0.4 Arrive back at trailhead (GPS: 37 24.2345, -106 31.3145).

36 "Prospect Creek Falls"

This lovely horsetail waterfall on the north edge of a wide, glaciated valley in the heart of the South San Juans is the lowest leap of a series of waterfalls tucked into a steep canyon carved by Prospect Creek.

Start: Informal trailhead on FR 243
Trail: Unnamed trail
Difficulty: Very easy
Hiking time: About 30 minutes
Distance: 0.1 mile out and back
Elevation trailhead to falls viewpoint: 10,710 to 10,728 feet (+18 feet)
Trail surface: Dirt
Restrictions: None; dogs must be under control

Amenities: None; Stunner Campground to east; limited services in Platoro
Maps: *DeLorme:* Page 89 B5; Trails Illustrated 142: South San Juan, Del Norte; USGS Summit Peak
County: Conejos
Land status/contact: Rio Grande National Forest, (719) 852-5941; Conejos Peak Ranger District, (719) 480-9892

Finding the trailhead: From South Fork to the north, drive 7.7 miles west on US 160 and turn left on dirt FR 380 toward Summitville. Drive south to the junction of FR 380 and FR 243 by Lake De Nolda (GPS: 37 22.4567, -106 37.4501). Go left on FR 243 and drive 0.7 mile to Prospect Creek.

From Alamosa to the east, drive south on US 285 and turn right on CO 350 to a left turn on CO 15 to a right turn on CR FF, which leads to dirt FR 250. Drive to the junction of FR 380 and FR 250 and continue west for 4.3 miles on FR 380 to a Y-junction with FR 243 past Lake De Nolda (GPS: 37 22.4567, -106 37.4501). Go left on FR 243 and drive 0.7 mile to Prospect Creek.

From the junction of CO 17 and FR 250 at Horca to the south, drive north on dirt FR 250 over Stunner Pass to the junction of FR 380 and FR 250. Turn left on FR 380 and drive west for 4.3 miles to a Y-junction with FR 243 past Lake De Nolda. Go left on FR 243 and drive 0.7 mile to Prospect Creek. Park on the road shoulder.

The informal trailhead is right of the creek on the road's north side (GPS: 37 22.4176, -106 38.1305).

The Hike

"Prospect Creek Falls," a gorgeous 50-foot horsetail waterfall, gushes through a notch and plummets down a volcanic cliff into a boulder-lined pool. The easily accessed waterfall is fed by Prospect Creek, which originates on the east flank of 12,866-foot Long Trek Mountain in the South San Juan Wilderness. Below the falls, the creek drops into Horsethief Park and empties into Treasure Creek.

At least five more waterfalls hide in the cliff-lined drainage above "Prospect Creek Falls." The lower ones can be reached by scrambling up steep social trails on the right side of the falls. Use caution and do not tumble boulders onto hikers below. After

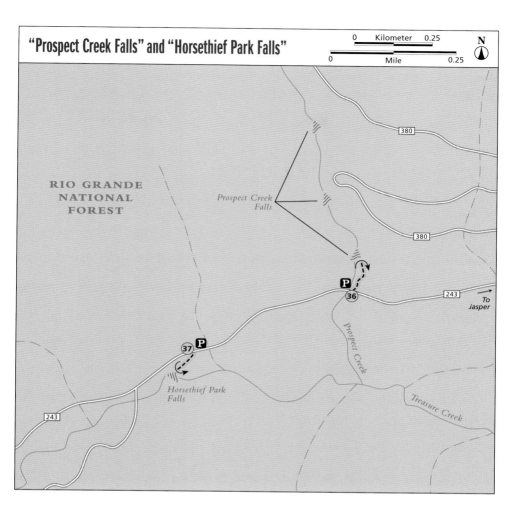

RIO GRANDE
NATIONAL
FOREST

Prospect Creek
Falls

380

380

243
To
Jasper

Horsethief Park
Falls

243

Prospect Creek

Treasure Creek

enjoying the falls, continue west on FR 242 to see "Horsethief Park Falls," "Treasure Creek Falls," "Treasure Ribbon Falls," and others.

Miles and Directions

0.00 Start at informal trailhead on north side of road. Hike north on trail along creek's east bank.

0.05 Reach viewpoint on rocks below falls (GPS: 37 22.4468, -106 38.1217).

0.1 Return to trailhead (GPS 37 22.4176, -106 38.1305).

Top left: Fed by snows on the Continental Divide, Prospect Creek dashes down a steep canyon to Prospect Creek Falls.
Top right: Prospect Creek Falls is the lowest of a string of waterfalls in a rock-walled canyon.
Bottom: Prospect Creek Falls pours over a volcanic cliff in the South San Juan Mountains.

37 "Horsethief Park Falls"

After thundering down "Treasure Creek Falls," Treasure Creek runs east down a glaciated valley before dashing over "Horsethief Park Falls" and a couple frothy cascades in a short, cliff-lined canyon, then meanders across Horsethief Park.

See map on page 123.
Start: Informal trailhead on FR 242
Trail: Unnamed social trail
Difficulty: Very easy
Hiking time: About 30 minutes
Distance: 0.06 mile out and back
Elevation trailhead to falls viewpoint: 10,735 to 11,715 feet (+980 feet)
Trail surface: Dirt
Restrictions: None posted

Amenities: None; Stunner Campground to east; limited services in Platoro
Maps: *DeLorme:* Page 89 B5; Trails Illustrated 142: South San Juan, Del Norte; USGS Summit Peak
County: Conejos
Land status/contact: Rio Grande National Forest, (719) 852-5941; Conejos Peak Ranger District, (719) 480-9892

Finding the trailhead: From South Fork to the north, drive 7.7 miles west on US 160 and turn left on dirt FR 380 toward Summitville. Drive south to the junction of FR 380 and FR 243 by Lake De Nolda (GPS: 37 22.4567, -106 37.4501). Go left on FR 243 for 1.1 miles and park on the road shoulder.

From Alamosa to the east, drive south on US 285 and turn right on CO 350 to a left turn on CO 15 to a right turn on CR FF, which leads to dirt FR 250. Drive west to the junction of FR 380 and FR 250 and continue 4.3 miles west on FR 380 to a Y-junction with FR 243 by Lake De Nolda. Go left on FR 242 for 1.1 miles and park on the road shoulder.

From the junction of CO 17 and FR 250 at Horca to the south, drive north on dirt FR 250 over Stunner Pass to the junction of FR 380 and FR 250. Go left on FR 380 and drive 4.3 miles to a Y-junction with FR 243 by Lake De Nolda. Go left on FR 243 for 1.1 miles and park on the road shoulder.

Start at the informal roadside trailhead (GPS: 37 22.2884, -106 38.5131).

The Hike

A fork of the Alamosa River, Treasure Creek originates on 13,300-foot Summit Peak before cascading down a steep drainage to a valley. Before entering Horsethief Park, the creek drops through a notch in dark cliffs, forming "Horsethief Park Falls," and then runs down a sharp canyon to the open park. The plunge falls is easily seen from a viewpoint that's a short walk from a rough road that runs up the valley.

The Treasure Creek drainage offers plenty of other waterfall diversions, including nearby "Prospect Creek Falls," as well as "Treasure Creek Falls," "Treasure Ribbon Falls," cascades and falls on Cataract Creek, and other unnamed waterfalls, including five on Treasure Creek below Horsethief Park.

Summit Peak towers above a glacier-scraped valley and Horsethief Park Falls.

Miles and Directions

0.0 Begin at informal trailhead on south shoulder of road. Hike east on social trail across meadows. Look for faint trail that goes right to edge of gorge.

0.03 Reach falls viewpoint above gorge (GPS: 37 22.2789, -106 38.4971).

0.06 Arrive back at trailhead (GPS: 37 22.2884, -106 38.5131).

38 Treasure Creek Waterfalls: "Treasure Creek Falls," "Treasure Ribbon Falls," Unnamed Falls, and "Cataract Creek Falls"

The Summit Peak Trailhead area on the eastern edge of the South San Juan Wilderness offers rugged terrain, hanging glaciated valleys, and steep creeks bursting with whitewater and waterfalls, including "Treasure Creek Falls."

Start: Summit Peak Trailhead
Trail: No named trails
Difficulty: Moderate
Hiking time: About 1 hour
Distance: 0.4 mile out and back
Elevation trailhead to falls viewpoint: 10,950 to 11,155 feet (+205 feet)
Trail surface: Dirt
Restrictions: Wilderness restrictions apply; no motorized vehicles; dogs must be under control

Amenities: None; Stunner Campground to east; limited services in Platoro
Maps: *DeLorme:* Page 89 B5; Trails Illustrated 142: South San Juan, Del Norte; USGS Summit Peak
County: Conejos
Land status/contact: Rio Grande National Forest, (719) 852-5941; Conejos Peak Ranger District, (719) 480-9892

Finding the trailhead: From South Fork to the north, drive 7.7 miles west on US 160 and turn left on dirt FR 380 toward Summitville. Drive south to the junction of FR 380 and FR 243 by Lake De Nolda (GPS: 37 22.4567, -106 37.4501). Go left on narrow FR 243 and drive 1.9 miles to Summit Peak Trailhead at road's end (GPS: 37 21.7738, -106 40.2077).

From Alamosa to the east, drive south on US 285 and turn right on CO 350 to a left turn on CO 15 to a right turn on CR FF, which leads to dirt FR 250. Continue west to the junction of FR 380 and FR 250. Go right on FR 380 and drive 4.3 miles to a Y-junction with FR 243 by Lake De Nolda. Go left on narrow FR 243 and drive 1.9 miles to Summit Peak Trailhead at road's end.

From the junction of CO 17 and FR 250 at Horca to the south, drive north on dirt FR 250 over Stunner Pass to the junction of FR 380 and FR 250. Go left on FR 380 and drive 4.3 miles west to a Y-junction with FR 243 by Lake De Nolda. Go left on FR 243 and drive 1.9 miles to Summit Peak Trailhead at road's end.

The Hike

Treasure Creek, beginning from a lake at 12,419 feet, below the Continental Divide, drops 2.1 miles and 1,500 feet in a continuous cataract of frothy cascades and at least half a dozen waterfalls. "Treasure Creek Falls," a horsetail waterfall, is the most glorious torrent, plunging over 100 feet off a sheer volcanic cliff. Below the falls, the creek dashes over smaller cliffs before reaching a broad valley.

A bonus waterfall, "Treasure Ribbon Falls" is a spectacular 200-foot waterfall that rushes down a steep rock groove east of the road. This ribbon falls, fed by snowmelt

Treasure Creek Waterfalls

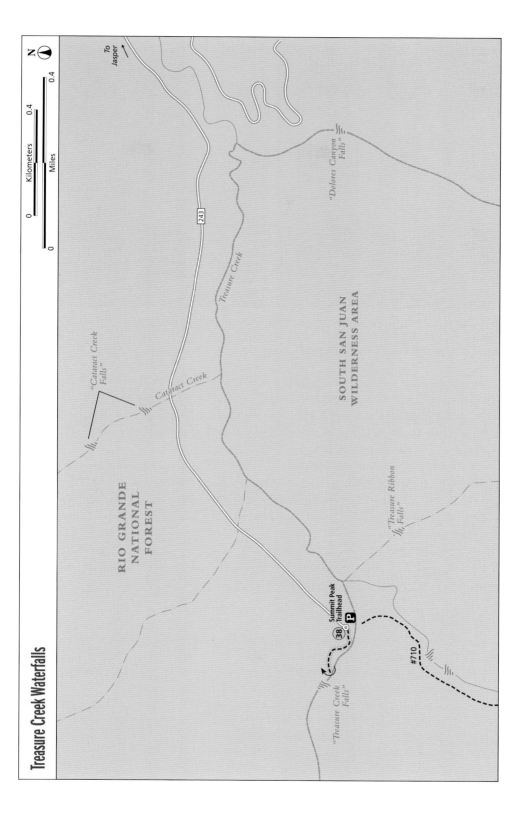

N

Kilometers
0   0.4

Miles
0   0.4

To
Jasper

RIO GRANDE
NATIONAL
FOREST

"Cataract Creek
Falls"

Cataract Creek

243

Treasure Creek

"Dolores Canyon
Falls"

SOUTH SAN JUAN
WILDERNESS AREA

"Treasure Ribbon
Falls"

38 Summit Peak
    Trailhead
    P

"Treasure Creek
Falls"

#710

Left: Treasure Creek, emptying into a basin below Summit Peak, forms a gorgeous horsetail at "Treasure Creek Falls."
Right: "Treasure Ribbon Falls" gushes down a steep chute from a hanging valley.

and springs, is best seen from the road near the trailhead. Two more unnamed waterfalls flush down a tight canyon 0.3 mile south of the trailhead along Treasure Creek Trail. Lastly, northeast of the trailhead, Cataract Creek drops down a steep ravine, forming several waterfalls and cascades. These are hard to see from the road and cannot be accessed except by bushwhacking.

"Treasure Creek Falls," the highlight waterfall in the Alamosa River drainage, is reached by a short, steep hike that gains 260 feet in less than a quarter mile. The last section of trail to the base of the waterfall traverses a rocky slope with loose footholds and dirt. Use extreme caution crossing this slope, since a slip would result in a 100-foot fall down the slope to the creek. Children and anyone with vertigo or poor balance should view the falls from a viewpoint by a large tree before the traverse. If hikers insist on traversing, it would be prudent to bring a safety rope that can be clipped to trees at both ends of the traverse.

Miles and Directions

0.0 Start at west end of Summit Peak Trailhead. Look for an informal trail on right and head up it on steep wooded slopes right of roaring creek.

0.15 Reach overlook on cliff of "Lower Treasure Creek Falls," a 25-foot gusher squeezed between boulders. Continue up path to unobvious left turn that goes to a large tree.

0.2 Arrive at viewpoint by tree of "Treasure Creek Falls" (GPS: 37 21.8037, -106 40.3173).
If conditions are dry, scramble 100 feet across steep, broken rock to base of falls. *Use extreme caution* traversing this section—a fall could be fatal.

0.4 Return to trailhead (GPS: 37 21.7738, -106 40.2077).

39 "Rough Creek Falls"

North of Cumbres Pass in the South San Juan Wilderness, two lakes—Alverjones and Hourglass—combine forces to fuel Rough Creek and send it tumbling over a cliff in a powerful plunge at "Rough Creek Falls."

Start: Ruybalid Trailhead
Trail: Ruybalid Trail #855
Difficulty: Easy
Hiking time: About 1 hour
Distance: 2.0 miles out and back
Elevation trailhead to falls viewpoint: 8,830 to 9,140 feet (+310 feet)
Trail surface: Dirt, rocks
Restrictions: No bicycles or motorized vehicles; dogs must be leashed; observe wilderness regulations

Amenities: Services in Antonito
Maps: *DeLorme:* Page 89 C7; Trails Illustrated 142: South San Juan, Del Norte; USGS Spectacle Lake
County: Conejos
Land status/contact: Rio Grande National Forest, (719) 852-5941; Conejos Peak Ranger District, (719) 274-8971

Finding the trailhead: From Alamosa, take US 285 South for 28 miles to Antonito, then follow CO 17 South for 23 miles and turn right at Horca on unpaved FR 250.

From Pagosa Springs, take US 84 East for 47 miles to Chama, then follow NM 17 North for 8 miles to CO 17. Drive 26 miles on CO 17 North and turn left at Horca on unpaved FR 250.

From the intersection of CO 17 and FR 250 at Horca, drive 7.6 miles on FR 250 and turn left on Record Bridge Road. Drive 0.2 mile over a bridge, turn left on South Riverview Road, and park on the road's right side before the trailhead (GPS: 37 11.224, -106 26.967).

The Hike

"Rough Creek Falls," tucked in a canyon on the eastern edge of the South San Juan Wilderness, is out of the way, but the waterfall is lovely, unique, and worth the long drive. The access highway—CO/NM 17 from Antonito to Chama—is part of the Los Caminos Antiguos Scenic Byway. The trailhead is reached on a forest road that follows the Conejos River up a gorgeous valley, passing several campgrounds. The falls is reached by the first mile of Ruybalid Trail, which continues onto an alpine plateau, climbing 5.1 miles and over 2,400 feet to glistening Ruybalid Lake, No Name Lake, and Alverjones Lake, the headwaters of Rough Creek.

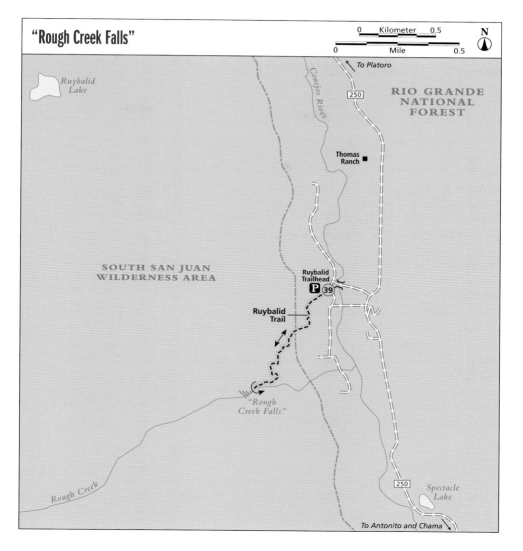

Miles and Directions

0.0 Begin at Ruybalid Trailhead and hike southwest up grassy slopes and aspen groves.

0.2 Cross South San Juan Wilderness boundary and enter forest.

0.7 Reach a signed trail junction. Go left on side trail and descend to Rough Creek. Hike west along right side of creek to falls viewpoint.

1.0 Arrive at "Rough Creek Falls" (GPS: 37 10.71, -106 27.442). Return the way you came.

2.0 Arrive back at trailhead (GPS: 37 11.224, -106 26.967).

◀ *Near Cumbres Pass, Rough Creek tumbles off a cliff in a powerful plunge at "Rough Creek Falls."*

40 "Trujillo Meadows Falls"

This lovely waterfall tucks into a secluded canyon on the edge of a campground sandwiched between Cumbres Pass and the South San Juan Wilderness.

Start: Informal trailhead in Trujillo Meadows Campground
Trail: Unnamed trail
Difficulty: Very easy
Hiking time: About 30 minutes
Distance: 0.08 mile out and back
Elevation trailhead to falls viewpoint: 10,130 to 10,103 feet (-27 feet)
Trail surface: Dirt, wooden steps, wooden observation deck
Restrictions: None posted; campground open Memorial Day through Labor Day weekend or second week of Sept (if closed, hike campground road to overlook)
Amenities: Services in Antonito and Chama, NM; vault toilets; drinking water
Maps: *DeLorme:* Page 89 E7; Trails Illustrated 142: South San Juan, Del Norte; USGS Cumbres
County: Conejos
Land status/contact: Rio Grande National Forest, (719) 852-5941; Conejos Peak Ranger District, (719) 274-8971

Finding the trailhead: From Alamosa, follow US 285 South for 28 miles to Antonito and a junction with CO 17 on the town's south side. Drive 35.2 miles on CO 17 South to a "Trujillo Meadows Reservoir" sign on Cumbres Pass. Turn right on dirt FR 118 and drive 2.2 miles north to Trujillo Meadows Campground. Turn right into campground and, keeping right, drive 0.6 mile to a parking area that's opposite campsites 40 and 41. An informal trailhead is on the west side of the parking strip (GPS: 37 2.7856, -106 26.8939).

The Hike

"Trujillo Meadows Falls," hiding in a canyon at Trujillo Meadows Campground, lies north of Cumbres Pass and a scant 3.6 miles from the New Mexico border. The 40-foot plunge waterfall, fed by a perennial creek, is easily reached by a short trail in the campground that leads to an observation deck perched above the falls. The campground is only open in summer, so if you visit in the shoulder seasons, plan on walking from the campground gate to the overlook, making a 1.2-mile round-trip hike.

Combine a quick visit to this waterfall with a hike to "Rough Creek Falls" farther north. For a closer falls adventure, head north from the campground on rough FR 118.2 to its end and then hike north on Los Pinos Trail (#736) about a half mile to "Rio de los Pinos Falls" (GPS: 37 5.5009, -106 29.7532), a 35-foot horsetail pouring over a cliff, and another fall on an unnamed creek to its left.

"Trujillo Meadows Falls" sprays off a verdant cliff into ▶
a cul-de-sac canyon near the New Mexico border.

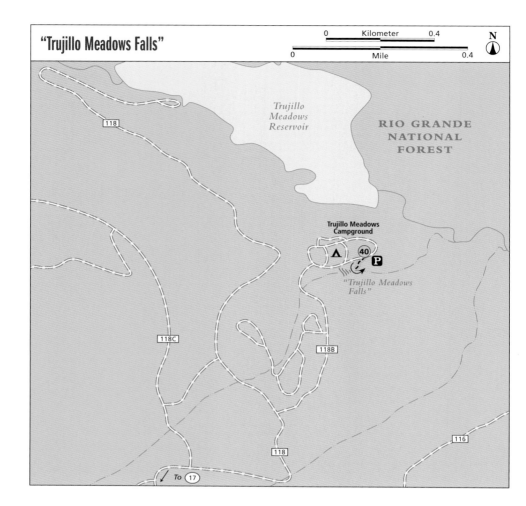

"Trujillo Meadows Falls"

0   Kilometer   0.4

0   Mile   0.4

N

Trujillo
Meadows
Reservoir

RIO GRANDE
NATIONAL
FOREST

Trujillo Meadows
Campground

40   P

"Trujillo Meadows
Falls"

118

118C

118B

118

116

To 17

Miles and Directions

0.0 Start at informal trailhead at parking area in campground's lower loop. Hike 200 feet down trail to wooden steps to observation deck on canyon edge or walk down sloped ramp to deck.

0.04 Reach fenced deck with waterfall view (GPS: 37 2.764, -106 26.9099).

0.08 Arrive back at trailhead (GPS: 37 2.7856, -106 26.8939).

The Southwest

Pagosa Springs, Creede, Lake City, Ouray, Silverton, Durango, Telluride, Ames, and Dolores

Waterfall Creek spreads its waters in a shimmering veil of translucent wonder at Silver Falls.

41 Silver Falls

Waterfall Creek flows south from the Continental Divide to the East Fork of the San Juan River, south of Wolf Creek Pass. At Silver Falls, the creek springs over a shelf and spreads its waters in a shimmering bridal veil waterfall.

Start: Silver Falls Trailhead
Trail: Silver Falls Trail
Difficulty: Very easy
Hiking time: Less than 1 hour
Distance: 0.4 mile out and back
Elevation trailhead to falls viewpoint: 8,210 to 8,440 feet (+230 feet)
Trail surface: Dirt, rocks
Restrictions: Dogs must be leashed

Amenities: Dispersed, primitive camping along road to trailhead
Maps: *DeLorme:* Page 88 A4; Trails Illustrated 140: Weminuche Wilderness; USGS Wolf Creek Pass
County: Mineral
Land status/contact: San Juan National Forest, (970) 247-4874; Pagosa Ranger District, (970) 264-2268

Finding the trailhead: From Pagosa Springs, take US 160 East for 10.4 miles and turn right on unpaved East Fork Road (FR 667). Drive 8 miles on rough East Fork Road, taking care over dips and washed-out areas. Park at a signed lot on the road's left side and the trailhead at a gate (GPS: 37 25.195, -106 46.876).

Originating on the Continental Divide, aptly named Waterfall Creek rumbles over two leaps at Silver Falls.

Silver Falls

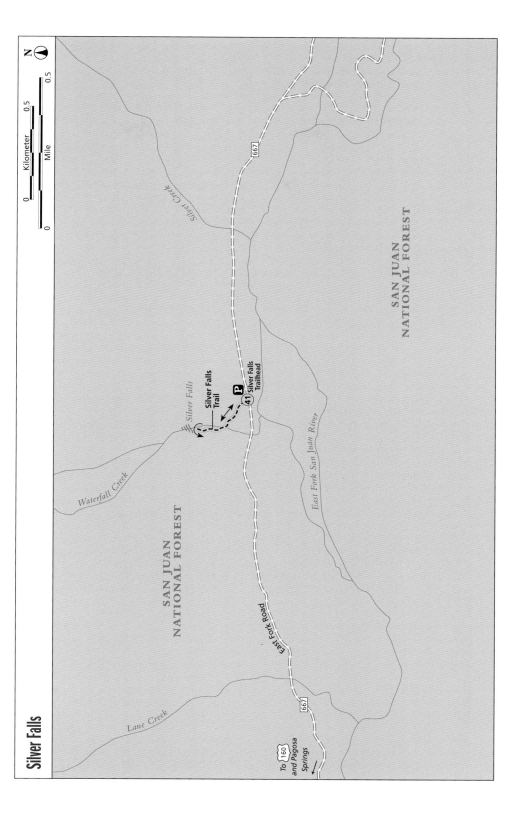

The Hike

Several waterfalls scatter along Wolf Creek Pass and on the creeks spilling south across East Fork Road, but Silver Falls is by far the loveliest. The south-facing falls, fed by Waterfall Creek, dashes over a cliff band and then rollicks and roars down a long cascade.

Use caution when driving East Fork Road to the trailhead as the road is rough and washboarded. Treasury Creek, Lane Creek, and Waterfall Creek all flow across the road, so take care over dips or find a pullout and walk to the trailhead if conditions are bad. The wooded banks of the East Fork of the San Juan River are popular with campers and anglers, so camp away from the road to avoid traffic noise and dust.

Miles and Directions

0.0   Begin at Silver Falls Trailhead on north side of road. Pass through a gate and hike up the steep trail. Avoid social trails and keep right of creek.

0.2   Arrive at Silver Falls (GPS: 37 25.319, -106 46.963). Return down trail.

0.4   Arrive back at trailhead (GPS: 37 25.195, -106 46.876).

42 Treasure Falls (Wolf Creek Pass)

Treasure Falls is a roadside spectacle above US 160, east of Pagosa Springs. Fall Creek plunges over a cliff and freefalls 105 feet—then flows beneath the highway—providing passersby with a dazzling display that's worth a stop and a hike.

Start: Treasure Falls Trailhead
Trail: Treasure Falls Trail #563
Difficulty: Very easy
Hiking time: Less than 1 hour to Blowout Overlook and Misty Deck
Distance: Roadside; 0.7 mile out and back to Blowout Overlook; 0.8 mile out and back to Misty Deck; 0.9 mile out and back to combine both hikes
Elevation trailhead to falls viewpoints: 8,125 to 8,275 feet (+150 feet) for Blowout Overlook; to 8,310 feet (+185 feet) for Misty Deck

Trail surface: Dirt, rocks
Restrictions: Dogs must be leashed
Amenities: Vault toilets; interpretive signs; trailside benches
Maps: *DeLorme:* Page 88 A3; Trails Illustrated 140: Weminuche Wilderness; USGS Saddle Mountain, Wolf Creek Pass
County: Mineral
Land status/contact: San Juan National Forest, (970) 247-4874; Pagosa Ranger District, (970) 264-2268

Finding the trailhead: From Pagosa Springs, take US 160 East for 15.1 miles and park in a signed and paved lot on the highway's right side. The trailhead is right of the restrooms (GPS: 37 26.563, -106 52.64). The trailhead and parking is also available from westbound US 160 below Wolf Creek Pass. Use caution turning left across highway traffic.

The Hike

Treasure Falls, one of Colorado's best roadside waterfalls, plummets through a notch in a vertical cliff above US 160, the famed Wolf Creek Pass highway, and shatters to mist on boulders below. According to legend, the falls was named for a cache of gold left by a group of prospecting French fur trappers in the mid-1700s. After being attacked by Native Americans and Spaniards, the trappers hid their pot of gold in three locations near a "great water fountain." Beginning in the 1800s, seekers have searched in vain for the yellow stash around what was called Treasure Falls but have returned empty-handed.

Called Treasure Falls Observation Site, the paved parking lot and sidewalk at Treasure Falls make this waterfall easily accessible. While the waterfall can be seen from the parking lot, the short hike is ideal for kids or travelers ready to stretch their legs after the drive over Wolf Creek Pass. Enjoy the signs and stories along the interpretive trail, and the viewpoints of the waterfall along the trail to Blowout Overlook. If you make it up to Misty Deck below the falls, expect to get wet!

Turn page: Treasure Falls is a roadside spectacle ▶
that provides passersby with a dazzling display.

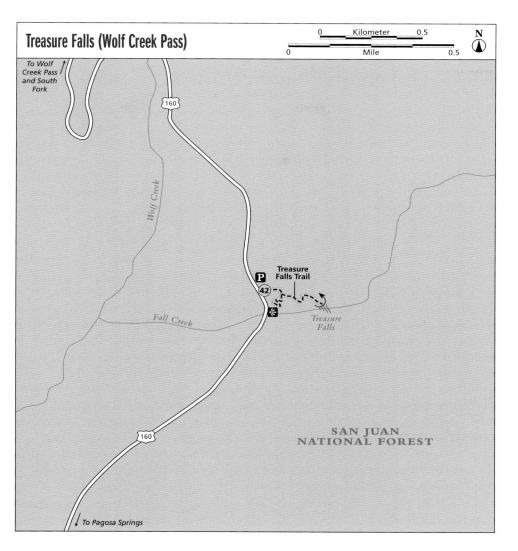

Treasure Falls (Wolf Creek Pass)

Miles and Directions

0.0 Begin at Treasure Falls Trailhead by an interpretive sign near restrooms at north end of parking lot.

0.1 At trail junction, bear right toward Blowout Overlook.

0.3 Bear right again at next trail junction, cross a bridge, and descend to Blowout Overlook below Treasure Falls (GPS: 37 26.55, -106 52.481). Return to main trail and follow signs to Misty Deck.

0.5 Arrive at Misty Deck below Treasure Falls (GPS: 37 26.555, -106 52.469). Return to main trail and descend west to trailhead.

0.9 Arrive back at trailhead (GPS: 37 26.563, -106 52.64).

43 Fourmile Trail Waterfalls: Falls Creek Falls and Fourmile Creek Falls

Two fairy-tale waterfalls highlight a storybook setting north of Pagosa Springs. Falls Creek and Fourmile Creek lend liquid pleasure to a plunge falls and a tiered falls, while the scenery is provided courtesy of Colorado wildflowers and the San Juan Mountains.

Start: Fourmile Trailhead
Trail: Fourmile Stock Drive Trail #569
Difficulty: Moderate
Hiking time: About 4 hours
Distance: 6.0 miles out and back for Falls Creek Falls; 6.0 miles out and back for Fourmile Creek Falls; 6.2 miles out and back for both waterfalls
Elevation trailhead to falls viewpoints: 9,195 to 9,645 feet (+450 feet) for Falls Creek Falls; to 9,825 feet (+630 feet) for Fourmile Creek Falls

Trail surface: Dirt, rocks
Restrictions: Observe wilderness regulations
Amenities: Vault toilet; backcountry camping; services in Pagosa Springs
Maps: *DeLorme:* Page 88 A2; Trails Illustrated 140: Weminuche Wilderness; USGS Pagosa Peak
County: Mineral
Land status/contact: Weminuche Wilderness Area; San Juan National Forest, (970) 247-4874; Pagosa Ranger District, (970) 264-2268

Finding the trailhead: From US 160 in Pagosa Springs, go north on Lewis Street and immediately bear left on 5th Street, which turns into unpaved Fourmile Road (CR 400). Drive 8.7 miles and take the right fork to stay on Fourmile Road (CR 645). Bear right at a sign for Fourmile Trailhead, then take the road's right fork and drive 4.4 miles. Pass a parking lot and vault toilet at the stock trailhead and continue to a second parking lot and vault toilet at the road's end and the hiker's trailhead (GPS: 37 24.562, -107 3.162).

The Hike

This lovely hike offers plenty of wow scenery with soaring volcanic cliffs, old-growth spruce and fir forests, and two spectacular waterfalls on the southern edge of the 499,771-acre Weminuche Wilderness, a huge swath of pristine mountains almost the size of Rhode Island. The misty attractions at the hike's end are Falls Creek Falls, plunging almost 250 feet in two drops, and Fourmile Creek Falls, a dramatic 200-foot freefall over a cliff. The hike follows the Fourmile Stock Drive Trail north up a wide valley floored by rushing Fourmile Creek, which originates among 12,000-foot peaks at the twin Fourmile Lakes.

A fairy-tale waterfall highlights the ▶
storybook setting at Falls Creek Falls.

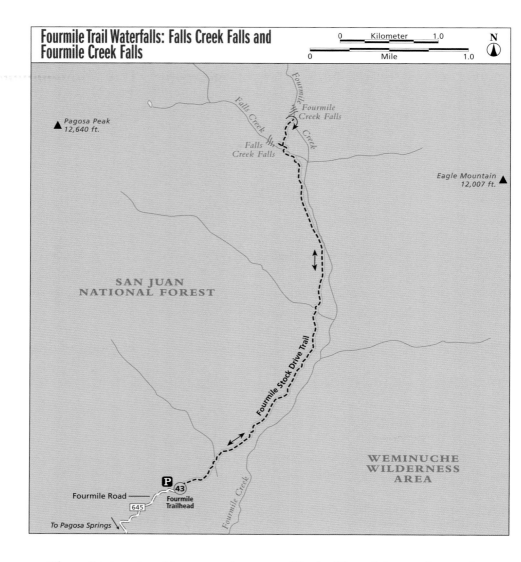

Fourmile Trail Waterfalls: Falls Creek Falls and Fourmile Creek Falls

The trail is best in midsummer when water fills the falls and flowers festoon the meadows. The popular trail is easy to follow and the trail junctions are obvious, so there's no chance of getting lost. The first section descends from the trailhead to meadows by the creek, a steep haul that has to be reversed on the way back. The trail's last segment also requires an uphill ascent to viewpoints of both waterfalls.

The trail reaches the base of Falls Creek Falls, a spectacular plunge off a cliff. Early in summer, icicles sometimes dangle from crumbling rock beneath the waterfall. It's difficult to reach the base of Fourmile Creek Falls since a trail that once climbed to the falls is now closed and covered by thick deadfall. It's best to admire the froth from the trail.

Left: Falls Creek Falls pours almost 250 feet off an overhanging cliff into Fourmile Creek's glaciated valley.
Right: Fourmile Creek Falls plunges over a towering volcanic cliff into an enchanted forest.

Miles and Directions

0.0 Begin at Fourmile Trailhead and hike northeast on Fourmile Stock Drive Trail. Don't go left on Anderson Trail.

0.3 Hike through spruce and fir forest and cross an unnamed creek.

0.5 Enter Weminuche Wilderness. Continue on trail.

1.7 Cross an unnamed creek that drains east from Pagosa Peak (GPS: 37 25.5986, -107 2.2239).

2.8 Reach junction with old trail closed by deadfall at 9,502 feet (GPS: 37 26.465, -107 2.3976). Go left on main trail and climb uphill toward Falls Creek Falls.

2.9 Arrive at viewpoint by Falls Creek of Falls Creek Falls to west (GPS: 37 26.4917, -107 2.4509). Dip down and cross creek on rocks. This is the trail's only major creek crossing, and poles may be handy. Do not cross if creek is high, especially May to mid-June.

3.0 Reach junction with spur trail to falls (GPS: 37 26.5179, -107 2.4708). Go left and hike 200 feet to a spectacular viewpoint below Falls Creek Falls (GPS: 37 26.532, -107 2.501). Return to junction and go left on main trail.

3.1 Reach viewpoint on trail that looks east to Fourmile Creek Falls pouring over cliff (GPS: 37 26.5844, -107 2.445). Turn around here to return to trailhead. Alternatively, continue up the trail to the waterfall's top. To see "Upper Fourmile Creek Falls," hike another 0.15 mile north (GPS: 26.6693, -107 2.3974). Return down trail.

6.2 Arrive back at trailhead (GPS: 37 24.562, -107 3.162).

44 Piedra Falls

The East Fork of the Piedra River pours from an unnamed lake at 11,000 feet in the San Juan Mountains and heads southwest for 11 miles to the Piedra River. At Piedra Falls, the river surges through a narrow cleft, plunges over volcanic rock, and explodes in a thundering mist.

Start: Piedra Falls Trailhead
Trail: Piedra Falls Trail #671
Difficulty: Very easy
Hiking time: Less than 1 hour
Distance: 1.0 mile out and back
Elevation trailhead to falls viewpoint: 8,260 to 8,340 feet (+80 feet)
Trail surface: Dirt, rocks
Restrictions: No motorized vehicles

Amenities: Primitive camping at trailhead; services in Pagosa Springs
Maps: *DeLorme:* Page 78 E1; Trails Illustrated 140: Weminuche Wilderness; USGS Pagosa Peak
County: Mineral
Land status/contact: San Juan National Forest, (970) 247-4874; Pagosa Ranger District, (970) 264-2268

Finding the trailhead: From Pagosa Springs, drive west on US 160 for 2.7 miles and turn right on Piedra Road (CR 600). Piedra Road becomes unpaved CR 631. Drive 17.7 miles on Piedra Road and FR 631 to Sportsman's Campground. Turn right here on FR 636, signed "Piedra Falls." Drive 1.8 miles and turn right on FR 637. Drive 7.6 miles on FR 637 to the trailhead and parking lot (GPS: 37 28.7404, -107 6.1024).

Flowing water and solid rock form an elemental landscape at Piedra Falls.

Piedra Falls

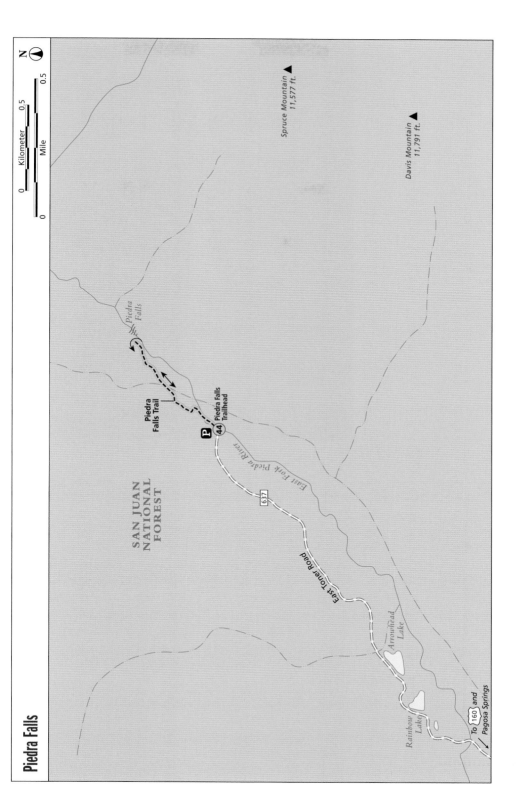

Piedra Falls surges through a narrow cleft and explodes in a thundering mist.

The Hike

Piedra Falls Trailhead is the most difficult trailhead to find in this book, but the hike is short and the waterfall spectacular. Piedra Falls Trail begins on a gravel road at the eastern edge of the parking area and follows the river's west bank upstream. The trail veers left, travels through open forest, and then curves right to again meet the river. The narrow trail traverses a steep slope and enters a canyon walled with volcanic cliffs. Large boulders obstruct a direct view of 65-foot Piedra Falls but won't shield you from its powerful spray. The water squeezes through a V-shaped slot and tumbles down two tiers with pounding force. Several perches near the river afford good views, but you will get wet. Whitewater rushing over black rock provides a dynamic display, but keep your camera dry and your footing steady to avoid falling into the spume.

Miles and Directions

0.0 Begin at Piedra Falls Trailhead. Follow an old road along river's north bank. Bear left to a narrow trail that rises away from river, passes through woods, and returns to river.

0.5 Arrive at Piedra Falls viewpoint (GPS: 37 29.001, -107 5.733). Return southwest on trail.

1.0 Arrive back at trailhead (GPS: 37 28.7404, -107 6.1024).

45 Lower Clear Creek Waterfalls: "Lower North Clear Creek Falls" and "Lower South Clear Creek Falls"

These two waterfalls, lying north of CO 149, plunge into tight canyons just upstream of the junction of North and South Clear Creeks, two fast-flowing streams that originate on high plateaus to the northwest.

Start: Trailhead at Bristol Head Campground
Trail: Lower South Clear Creek Falls Nature Trail #904
Difficulty: Very easy
Hiking time: Less than 1 hour
Distance: 0.5 mile out and back for both waterfalls
Elevation trailhead to falls viewpoints: 9,500 to 9,420 feet (-80 feet) for "Lower North Clear Creek Falls"; to 9,425 feet (-75 feet) for "Lower South Clear Creek Falls"
Trail surface: Dirt, rocks

Restrictions: Fee area; no horses or motor vehicles
Amenities: Vault toilets at campground; services in Lake City and Creede
Maps: *DeLorme:* Page 78 B1; Trails Illustrated 139: La Garita, Cochetopa Hills; USGS Hermit Lakes
County: Hinsdale
Land status/contact: Rio Grande National Forest, (719) 852-5941; Divide Ranger District, (719) 859-2374; Creede Office, (719) 239-1150

Finding the trailhead: From Lake City, take CO 149 south for 28.3 miles; from Creede take CO 149 north for 21.7 miles. Turn east (left from Lake City, right from Creede) on unpaved FR 510. Continue 0.3 mile and turn right into Bristol Head Campground. Go 0.6 mile and park at a pullout on the left, then walk to a loop at road's end and the trailhead (GPS: 37 49.018, -107 8.226).

The Hike

Between South Fork and Lake City, the Silver Thread Scenic Byway offers four waterfalls in a 5-mile stretch of highway south of Spring Creek Pass. Below North Clear Creek Falls and South Clear Creek Falls are two lower falls—"Lower North Clear Creek Falls" and "Lower South Clear Creek Falls"—near the confluence of the creeks. Both waterfalls, easily reached from Bristol Head Campground, plummet through deep-cut gorges.

Bristol Head Campground is open seasonally and gated in the off-season, so plan accordingly. Use extreme caution when viewing the waterfalls and walking on the edge of high cliffs above the gorges. Control dogs and children, since a fall would be fatal. "Lower North Clear Creek Falls" is multitiered and located in a deep canyon below the trail. "Lower South Clear Creek Falls" is a long, multitiered, horsetail falls in a broad chute. There is no safe way to reach the base of either waterfall. The creeks join below the two falls.

"Lower North Clear Creek Falls" plummets through deep-cut gorges at Clear Creek Canyons.

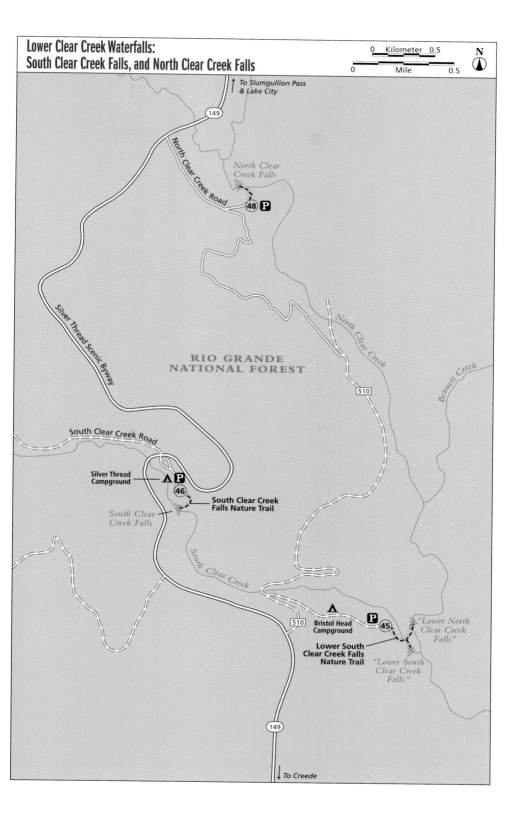

Lower Clear Creek Waterfalls:
South Clear Creek Falls, and North Clear Creek Falls

0   Kilometer   0.5

0   Mile   0.5

N

To Slumgullion Pass
& Lake City

149

North Clear Creek Road

North Clear
Creek Falls

48 P

Silver Thread Scenic Byway

RIO GRANDE
NATIONAL FOREST

North Clear Creek

Bennett Creek

510

South Clear Creek Road

Silver Thread
Campground

46 P

South Clear Creek
Falls Nature Trail

South Clear
Creek Falls

South Clear Creek

510

Bristol Head
Campground

P 45

Lower South
Clear Creek Falls
Nature Trail

"Lower North
Clear Creek
Falls"

"Lower South
Clear Creek
Falls"

149

To Creede

"Lower South Clear Creek Falls" tumbles away below your feet and disappears into the canyon.

Miles and Directions

0.0   Begin at trailhead at east end of campground. Hike down a wooded hillside to South Clear Creek.

0.1   Cross log over creek.

0.2   Reach a trail fork. Go left and hike east over a slight hill.

0.3   Arrive at viewpoint above "Lower North Clear Creek Falls" (N 37 49.03, -107 8.085). Use caution at vertical drop-offs on cliff edge. Control children and dogs. Return to junction and go left. (It's also possible to follow a trail along cliff edge to next falls.)

0.4   Arrive at viewpoint above "Lower South Clear Creek Falls" (37 48.93, -107 8.096). Again, exercise caution above vertical cliffs. Return to trail fork and bear left to creek crossing.

0.5   Arrive back at trailhead (GPS: 37 49.018, -107 8.226).

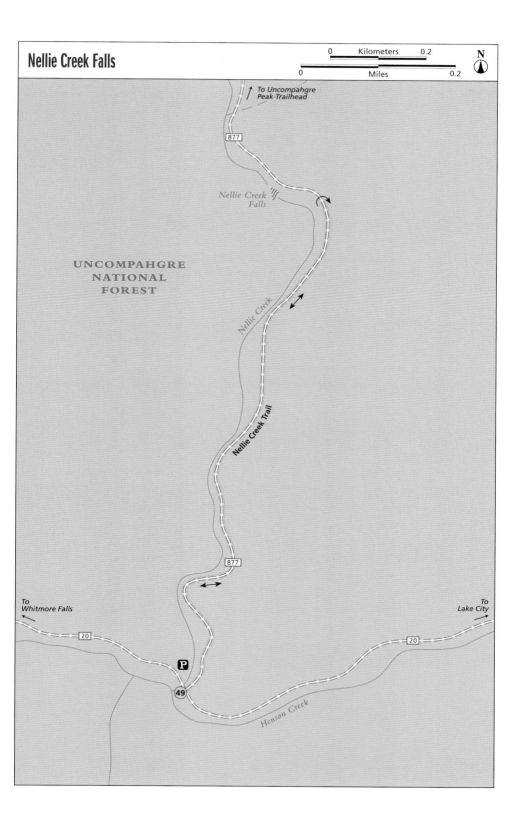

Nellie Creek Falls

0   Kilometers   0.2

0   Miles   0.2

N

To Uncompahgre
Peak Trailhead

877

Nellie Creek
Falls

UNCOMPAHGRE
NATIONAL
FOREST

Nellie Creek

Nellie Creek Trail

877

To
Whitmore Falls

To
Lake City

20

20

P

49

Henson Creek

50 Whitmore Falls

Henson Creek runs east from Engineer Pass and enters Lake City to join the Lake Fork of the Gunnison River. The Alpine Loop Backcountry Byway follows the creek to water springing from the mountainside in a glorious plunge at Whitmore Falls.

Start: Whitmore Falls Trailhead
Trail: Unnamed trail
Difficulty: Easy
Hiking time: Less than 1 hour
Distance: 0.2 mile out and back
Elevation trailhead to falls viewpoint: 9,970 to 9,920 feet (-50 feet)
Trail surface: Wooden steps, dirt, scree

Restrictions: None posted
Amenities: Services in Lake City
Maps: *DeLorme:* Page 67 E6; Trails Illustrated 141: Telluride, Silverton, Ouray, Lake City; USGS Redcloud Peak
County: Hinsdale
Land status/contact: BLM, Gunnison Field Office, (970) 642-4940

Finding the trailhead: In Lake City, take CO 149 South (Gunnison Avenue) and turn right (west) on 2nd Street. Go 0.1 mile and turn left on Bluff Street, which becomes unpaved at 0.1 mile and turns into Alpine Loop Backcountry Byway. Drive 9.1 miles on the unpaved road and turn left to cross a bridge. Continue another 1.9 miles, past the Capitol City townsite, to a pullout on the road's right side and the falls overlook and trailhead on the left (GPS: 37 59.209, -107 29.003).

The Hike

Located on the Silver Thread Scenic Byway and the Alpine Loop Backcountry Byway, Lake City, the only town in Hinsdale County, is a popular town for mountaineers who come to climb five 14,000-foot peaks. Whitmore Falls and Nellie Creek Falls are the only waterfalls near Lake City that can be seen without trespassing on private property, like Crooke and Argenta Falls on the Lake Fork.

The short hike to Whitmore Falls from the road is steep, and a trekking pole is handy for balance on the rough path. The waterfall is stunning and worth the trip. After seeing the falls, hikers with a 4WD vehicle and skilled at four-wheeling can continue west on the 64-mile Alpine Loop. This spectacular drive descends from Engineer Pass to Ouray and Silverton, then climbs east over Cinnamon Pass and back to Lake City. The rugged road is as unforgiving as it is scenic, so know your limits and do your homework before traveling it.

Henson Creek appears to spring from high cliffs ▶
in a glorious plunge at Whitmore Falls.

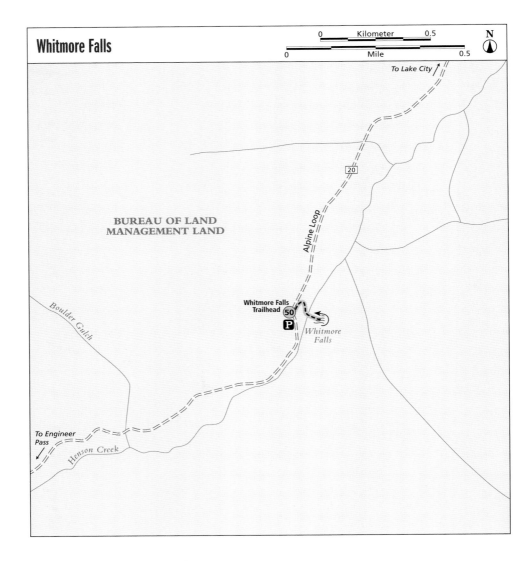

Miles and Directions

0.0 Begin at trailhead at Whitmore Falls Overlook. Go down steps and bear right to descend steep, loose trail.

0.1 Arrive at Whitmore Falls (GPS: 37 59.174, -107 29.002). Return the way you came.

0.2 Arrive back at trailhead (GPS: 37 59.209, -107 29.003).

51 Lower Cascade Falls (Ouray)

Cascade Creek slips through a drainage south of 12,368-foot Cascade Mountain and pours 160 feet down a vertical cliff into Ouray. The final leap shoots over a lip of sandstone in a frothy, white spray and splashes over boulders at Lower Cascade Falls Park.

Start: Lower Cascade Falls Trailhead
Trail: Lower Cascade Falls Trail
Difficulty: Easy
Hiking time: Less than 1 hour
Distance: 0.3 mile out and back
Elevation trailhead to falls viewpoint: 7,960 to 8,060 feet (+100 feet)
Trail surface: Dirt, rocks
Restrictions: No bicycles, horses, or motor vehicles

Amenities: Restrooms at trailhead; services in Ouray
Maps: *DeLorme:* Page 66 E4; Trails Illustrated 141: Telluride, Silverton, Ouray, Lake City; USGS Ouray
County: Ouray
Land status/contact: City of Ouray Parks and Recreation, (970) 325-7065

Finding the trailhead: Enter Ouray on Main Street (US 550) and turn east on 8th Avenue. Drive uphill on 8th for 0.3 mile to a parking lot at the trailhead (GPS: 38 1.492, -107 39.995).

The Hike

Lower Cascade Falls Trail, the lowest of seven waterfalls that stairstep up the canyon above, is one of Ouray's iconic watery wonders. The trailhead is within walking distance of downtown Ouray's restaurants and shops, and the hike up Lower Cascade Falls Trail to the waterfall is even shorter, and steeper. Partway up, the trail meets the 6.5-mile Ouray Perimeter Trail, which circumnavigates Ouray. Pick up a trail map at the Ouray Visitor Center to hike the trail and enjoy views of skyscraping peaks, rushing creeks, Uncompahgre Gorge, and Box Canyon Falls. The trail is a great introduction to Ouray, "The Switzerland of America."

Miles and Directions

0.0 Begin at Lower Cascade Falls Trailhead at end of parking lot. Walk up dirt trail with the creek and concrete flume to left. Pass junction with Ouray Perimeter Trail on right and reach a shelter with bench and info signs. Cross footbridge over creek on left.

0.1 Continue up stone steps to the waterfall base. Arrive at Lower Cascade Falls (GPS: 38 1.539, -107 39.892). Return down trail.

0.3 Arrive back at trailhead (GPS: 38 1.492, -107 39.995).

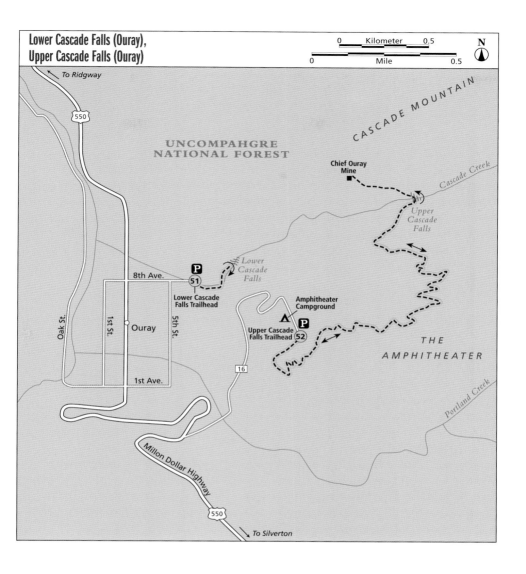

Lower Cascade Falls (Ouray),
Upper Cascade Falls (Ouray)

0 — Kilometer — 0.5

0 — Mile — 0.5

N

To Ridgway

550

UNCOMPAHGRE
NATIONAL FOREST

CASCADE MOUNTAIN

Chief Ouray
Mine

Cascade Creek

Upper
Cascade
Falls

8th Ave.

P
51

Lower Cascade
Falls Trailhead

*Lower
Cascade
Falls*

Amphitheater
Campground

Oak St.

1st St.

Ouray

5th St.

Upper Cascade
Falls Trailhead **52**

P

THE
AMPHITHEATER

1st Ave.

16

Portland Creek

Million Dollar Highway

550

To Silverton

*Lower Cascade Falls shoots over
pink cliffs in a frothy, white spray.*

52 Upper Cascade Falls (Ouray)

The trail to the leaps of Upper Cascade Falls climbs a hillside at the northwest arc of the Amphitheater, a horseshoe-shaped drainage formed by a volcanic explosion millions of years ago. The falls filters over bedrock in tiered horsetails above the trail, then freefalls in a dramatic plunge below.

See map on page 167.
Start: Upper Cascade Falls Trailhead
Trails: Cascade Amphitheater Tie Trail #213.1A, Upper Cascade Falls Trail #213
Difficulty: Moderate
Hiking time: About 3 hours
Distance: 4.2 miles out and back
Elevation trailhead to falls viewpoint: 8,480 to 9,980 feet (+1,500 feet)
Trail surface: Dirt, rocks

Restrictions: No horses, bicycles, or motor vehicles
Amenities: Services in Ouray
Maps: *DeLorme:* Page 66 E4; Trails Illustrated 141: Telluride, Silverton, Ouray, Lake City; USGS Ouray
County: Ouray
Land status/contact: Uncompahgre National Forest, (970) 874-6600; Ouray Ranger District, (970) 240-5300

Finding the trailhead: From downtown Ouray, drive US 550 South (Main Street) and turn left on CR 16 at the sign for Amphitheater Campground. Drive 1.1 miles on CR 16 (which turns into Amphitheater Campground Road after 0.1 mile), past the campground to a parking area at the trailhead (GPS: 38 1.311, -107 39.632).

The Hike

Cascade Creek, originating high in Cascade Canyon, slides through a deep notch to form Upper Cascade Falls, a 60-foot horsetail waterfall. The falls is reached by the Upper Cascade Falls Trail, which crosses southwest-facing slopes above Ouray. The trail is recommended for experienced hikers.

The hike, beginning at Amphitheater Campground, ascends switchbacks up steep slopes, gaining 1,100 feet in a mile, with 360-degree views of surrounding peaks including 12,801-foot Abrams Mountain. The town lies far below as the steep, dirt path crosses rugged slopes. Colorful, broken chips of pink, blue, and gray rock line the trail. After the grade relents, the trail rounds a buttress to stunning views of the Sneffels Range. The waterfall lies below the trail, while more falls are seen in the canyon above. The historic Chief Ouray Mine and the trail's end is another 0.2 mile up the mountain.

Miles and Directions

0.0 Begin at Upper Cascade Falls Trailhead at a parking lot in the campground. Hike south on Cascade Amphitheater Tie Trail.

0.2 Reach junction with Upper Cascade Falls Trail (begins in Ouray) to right. Go left on it toward Chief Ouray Mine.

Upper Cascade Falls filters through rock above the trail, then freefalls in a plunge below.

0.5 Reach junction with Lower Cascade Falls Trail to left. Continue straight on Upper Cascade Falls Trail.

0.8 Reach junction with Portland Trail on right. Keep left toward Chief Ouray Mine and switch-back up steep mountainside.

2.1 Arrive at top of Upper Cascade Falls (GPS: 38 1.758, -107 39.192). If conditions permit, cross creek for views from other side, but stay clear of edge, and don't cross if water is high. For extra credit, continue 0.2 mile to Chief Ouray Mine. Return on trail.

4.2 Arrive back at trailhead (GPS: 38 1.311, -107 39.632).

53 Million Dollar Highway Waterfalls: Bear Creek Falls, "Ralston Creek Falls," and "Uncompahgre River Falls"

The Million Dollar Highway runs from Ouray to Silverton. The highway section up Uncompahgre Gorge and Red Mountain Pass is especially exciting with hairpin turns above drop-offs, pavement edges that fall away into the abyss—and no guardrails. Three roadside waterfalls, including Bear Creek Falls, offer relaxing relief for travelers.

Start: Roadside; Sutton Mine Trailhead
Trails: Roadside; unnamed trail, Sutton Mine Trail #197
Difficulty: Very easy for roadside; moderate for hike to hillside overlook
Hiking time: Less than 1 hour for roadside; about 3 hours for hike to hillside overlook
Distance: 0.1 mile for roadside viewing; 4.2 miles out and back for hillside hike
Elevation trailheads to falls viewpoints: 8,120 to 8,810 feet (+690 feet) for hillside hike
Trail surface: Paved, dirt, rocks roadside; dirt, rocks on hike

Restrictions: No bicycles, horses, or motor vehicles
Amenities: Interpretive roadside signs; services in Ouray
Maps: *DeLorme:* Pages 66 E4; Trails Illustrated 141: Telluride, Silverton, Ouray, Lake City; USGS Ouray, Ironton
County: Ouray
Land status/contact: Uncompahgre National Forest, (970) 874-6600; Ouray Ranger District, (970) 240-5300; City of Ouray Parks and Recreation, (970) 325-7065

Finding the trailhead: *Roadside:* From Ouray, take US 550 South (Million Dollar Highway), past Camp Bird Road (CR 361). Continue 1.5 miles to a pullout for an overlook on the highway's right side, before a bridge over Bear Creek Falls (GPS: 37 59.988, -107 39.658). The overlook is only accessible to uphill traffic.

For "Uncompahgre River Falls": Continue south on the highway for 1.1 miles to unmarked parking on the right side, directly across the highway from the 4WD Engineer Mountain Trail to Engineer Pass (GPS: 37 59.313, -107 38.986).

The hike: From Ouray, take US 550 South and turn right on unpaved Camp Bird Road (CR 361) at the first hairpin turn above Ouray. Drive 0.4 mile on dirt Camp Bird Road and park on the right side, across from the Sutton Mine Trailhead (GPS: 38 0.934, -107 40.568).

The Drive

The Million Dollar Highway is treacherous, so observe the speed limits and drive slow as conditions require. From Ouray, drive south on twisting US 550 with the Uncompahgre Gorge to your right and Abrams Mountain straight ahead. Pull off

Bear Creek passes under the Million Dollar Highway before ▶
freefalling at Bear Creek Falls into the Uncompahgre Gorge.

to the right on a highway bend to Bear Creek Falls Overlook, a 125-foot sidewalk above a high cliff. The overlook, fenced for safety, includes waterfall views and a 25-foot-long metal skywalk above the abyss. The 200-foot waterfall, fed by snowmelt from a basin above, passes under the highway and freefalls to rocks below. Interpretive signs relate the story of Otto Mears, a pioneer road builder, who—along with Fred Walsen—built the original road here in 1881, at a cost of about $10,000 per mile. From the viewpoint, look west across the gorge to "Ralston Creek Falls," also called "Horsetail Falls." The falls is a thin ribbon splashing down a crevice in the cliffs.

Continue south on the highway to a roadside pullout on the right opposite the Engineer Pass 4WD track. Hike west down a social trail for 230 feet to the top of "Uncompahgre River Falls." Another trail goes right from the parking lot to the waterfall's north side. Be extremely cautious of slick rock at the top of the 195-foot falls. The waterfall was created when the highway was built; the river's water is diverted through a culvert and channeled down a cliff.

Left: The Uncompahgre River cascades down a rocky slab below the Million Dollar Highway. Right: Abrams Mountain towers above Uncompahgre River Falls.

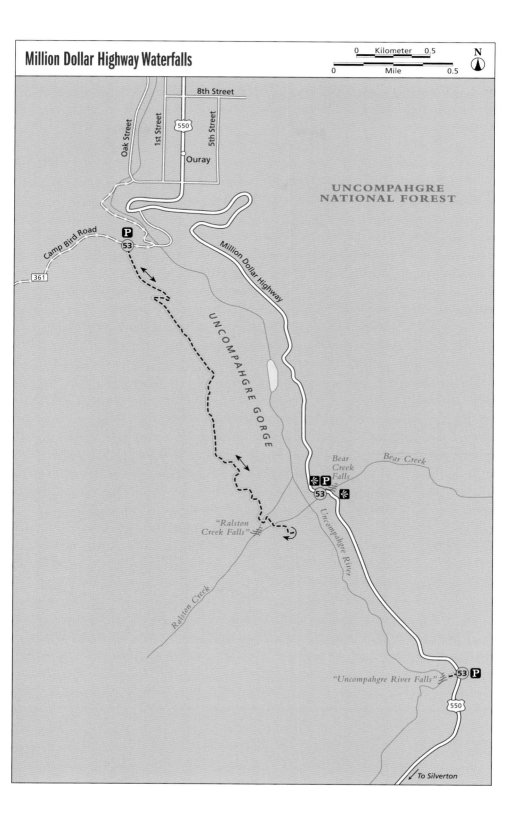

Million Dollar Highway Waterfalls

0 — Kilometer — 0.5
0 — Mile — 0.5

N

8th Street

Oak Street

1st Street

550

5th Street

Ouray

Camp Bird Road

P

53

361

Million Dollar Highway

UNCOMPAHGRE
NATIONAL FOREST

U N C O M P A H G R E   G O R G E

Bear
Creek
Falls

Bear Creek

P

53

Uncompahgre River

"Ralston
Creek Falls"

Ralston Creek

"Uncompahgre River Falls"

53

P

550

To Silverton

The long, thin ribbon of "Ralston Creek Falls" is best viewed from the Bear Creek Falls viewpoint.

The Hike

For more waterfall views, hike the Sutton Mine Trail off Camp Bird Road. At the trailhead, do not turn left onto a gravel service road, but look up and right for the trailhead sign. This trail is used in winter to access Ouray Ice Park. Avoid stepping on

Gorgeous Bear Creek Falls freefalls off a cliff into a rock-walled amphitheater.

exposed PVC pipe that's used to farm the ice falls below in winter. The trail heads south to Ouray Overlook, Bear Creek Overlook, and "Ralston Creek Falls." Past the falls is a fabulous view of Bear Creek Falls below. For a longer outing, continue to the preserved remains of the Neosho Mine.

Miles and Directions

Roadside Overlooks

0.0 Start at junction of US 550 and Camp Bird Road (CR 361). Drive south on US 550 for 2.2 miles to parking lot for Bear Creek Falls Overlook on right (GPS: 37 59.99, -107 39.644). If traveling north on highway, don't turn left into parking lot on blind turn.

2.2 At overlook, "Ralston Creek Falls" is in cliffs across the gorge. View Bear Creek Falls from metal skywalk.

3.3 Drive south on highway and park at pullout on right across from Engineer Pass Road. From pullout, hike a short trail either left or right to top of "Uncompahgre River Falls" (GPS: 37 59.309, -107 39.022). Return north on US 550 to first junction.

6.6 Arrive back at junction with Camp Bird Road (GPS: 38 1.0637, -107 40.4764).

"Ralston Creek Falls" and Bear Creek Falls Hike

0.0 Begin at Sutton Mine Trailhead on Camp Bird Road. Hike south up steep trail.

0.6 Arrive at Ouray Overlook with dizzying views of town. Follow trail southeast and switchback up hillside. Cross wooded slopes and rock slabs with views of Abrams Mountain.

1.7 Pass a pond on right and arrive at signed Bear Creek Overlook, with highway below. Continue on trail.

2.0 Cross Ralston Creek and middle leaps of "Ralston Creek Falls" (GPS: 37 59.871, -107 39.844). Continue on trail across hillside.

2.1 Arrive at best viewpoint of highway and Bear Creek Falls (GPS: 37 59.844, -107 39.75). Turn around and return north on trail.

4.2 Arrive back at trailhead (GPS: 38 0.934, -107 40.568).

54 Box Canyon Falls

Canyon Creek roars through the Ouray Fault and plunges into a narrow canyon at Box Canyon Falls, one of Colorado's most dramatic waterfalls. The creek thunders through the narrow slot canyon in a bubbling cauldron of cold, dark water, filling the air with a turbulent mist.

Start: Box Canyon Falls Trailhead
Trail: Falls Trail
Difficulty: Easy
Hiking time: Less than 1 hour
Distance: 0.2 mile out and back
Elevation trailhead to falls viewpoint: 7,830 to 7,860 feet (+30 feet)
Trail surface: Paved, dirt, metal grate walkway
Restrictions: Entrance fee May to Oct; no smoking; no dogs allowed

Amenities: Open year-round 8 a.m. to 8 p.m. daily; trailside benches, picnic tables, interpretive signs, visitor center; services in Ouray
Maps: *DeLorme:* Page 66 E4; Trails Illustrated 141: Telluride, Silverton, Ouray, Lake City; USGS Ouray
County: Ouray
Land status/contact: Box Cañon Park, City of Ouray Parks and Recreation, (970) 325-7080 or (970) 325-7065

Finding the trailhead: From Ouray, drive south on Main Street (US 550 South) onto the Million Dollar Highway. At the first hairpin turn above town, turn right on unpaved Camp Bird Road (CR 361). Drive 300 feet and turn right on unpaved one-way Box Canyon Road, then continue 0.3 mile to a small parking lot at the trailhead and visitor center (GPS: 38 1.067, -107 40.726). In the off-season or if the lot is full, park at a large lot on the north side of US 550 opposite the turn onto Camp Bird Road and hike the closed road for 0.3 mile to the trailhead.

The Hike

Box Canyon Falls, hidden in a deep slot canyon on the southwestern edge of Ouray, is the town's most famous natural attraction. The roaring waterfall plummets more than 125 feet in a tiered series of horsetail falls that are mostly hidden within the twisted gash. The sheer slot canyon was carved by Canyon Creek, a rushing stream fed by melting snow and springs in high mountain basins, which ensures consistent flows. The waterfall is spectacular in winter, with icicle draperies adorning the canyon walls. Bring microspikes for foot traction on the icy path and metal catwalk. The best time to visit is May and June when the creek plunges down, filling the air with a fine mist.

The slot canyon is reached by the Falls Trail, which clings to the canyon walls above the racing creek. Inside the canyon the trail follows a steel walkway attached to a cliff. At its end is a viewpoint of the lower 70 feet of roiling Box Canyon Falls tucked into a narrow crevice. Three flights of stairs descend to the canyon floor. Do not wade in the creek, especially if the water level is high. Afterward, hike the park's two other trails. The scenic High Bridge Trail climbs 200 feet in 0.25 mile to a hanging bridge poised above the falls, and the easy 0.2-mile Native Plants Loop explores area plants.

Canyon Creek exits Box Canyon Falls' narrow canyon through a keyhole slot.

Box Canyon Falls, Twin Falls and Camp Bird Road Waterfalls

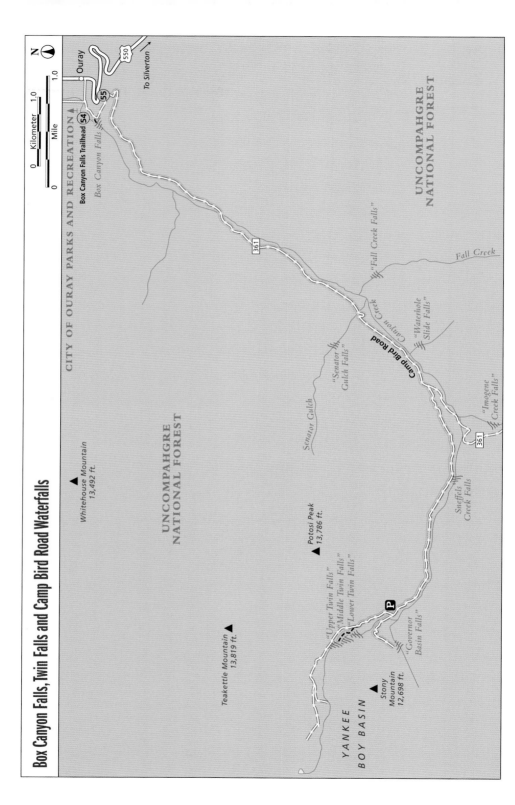

N

0   Kilometer   1.0
0   Mile   1.0

CITY OF OURAY PARKS AND RECREATION

Ouray

550

To Silverton

55

Box Canyon Falls Trailhead **54**

Box Canyon Falls

Whitehouse Mountain
13,492 ft.

UNCOMPAHGRE
NATIONAL FOREST

361

"Fall Creek Falls"

Fall Creek

Canyon Creek

Camp Bird Road

"Waterhole
Slide Falls"

"Senator
Gulch Falls"

Senator Gulch

"Imogene
Creek Falls"

361

UNCOMPAHGRE
NATIONAL FOREST

Teakettle Mountain
13,819 ft.

Potosi Peak
13,786 ft.

"Upper Twin Falls"
"Middle Twin Falls"
"Lower Twin Falls"

Sneffels
Creek Falls

P

"Governor
Basin Falls"

Stony
Mountain
12,698 ft.

YANKEE
BOY BASIN

Top left: A metal catwalk hugs the wall of a deep slot canyon at Box Canyon Falls.
Top right: Box Canyon Falls leaps and roars into a mist-filled corridor.
Bottom: Box Canyon Falls roars through a quartzite canyon and fills a dark, cold, bubbling cauldron.

Miles and Directions

0.0 Begin at Box Canyon Falls Trailhead at visitor center. Hike up gravel path and follow signs to falls. Descend concrete steps to an elevated metal-grate walkway that leads into slot canyon.

0.1 Arrive at Box Canyon Falls at end of walkway (GPS: 38 1.082, -107 40.714). Descend stairs to creek level. Return on trail.

0.2 Arrive back at trailhead (GPS: 38 1.067, -107 40.726).

55 Twin Falls and Camp Bird Road Waterfalls: "Fall Creek Falls," "Senator Gulch Falls," "Waterhole Slide Falls," "Imogene Creek Falls," Sneffels Creek Falls, "Governor Basin Falls," "Lower Twin Falls," "Middle Twin Falls," and "Upper Twin Falls"

The narrow Camp Bird Road west of Ouray offers six scenic waterfalls on rugged mountain slopes. At road's end, Sneffels Creek slips down from Yankee Boy Basin and tumbles in three glorious whitewater leaps at Twin Falls that are reached by a leg-stretching hike beside a 4WD road.

See map on page 178.
Start: Camp Bird Road and Yankee Boy Basin Road
Trails: Yankee Boy Basin Road (FR 853 1B), unnamed side trails
Difficulty: Easy for Twin Falls; very easy for roadside falls
Hiking and travel time: About 1 hour for Twin Falls; 3 hours for Camp Bird Road falls
Distance: 1.3 miles out and back for Twin Falls; 14.4-mile round-trip drive to see Camp Bird Road falls
Elevation trailhead to falls viewpoints: 10,740 to 11,160 feet (+420 feet) for Twin Falls

Trail surface: Dirt, rocks
Restrictions: None posted; keep off roadside private and mining property, which may not be posted; uphill traffic has right-of-way
Amenities: Vault toilet 0.2 mile past upper falls; services in Ouray
Maps: *DeLorme:* Page 66 E4 and Page 76 A4; Trails Illustrated 141: Telluride, Silverton, Ouray, Lake City; USGS Ironton, Telluride
County: Ouray
Land status/contact: Uncompahgre National Forest, (970) 874-6600; Ouray Ranger District, (970) 240-5300

Finding the trailhead: In Ouray, take US 550 South (Million Dollar Highway) and turn right at the first switchback on unpaved Camp Bird Road (CR 361). Drive 7 miles, making six waterfall stops, and park at a flat area off the road at 10,705 feet (GPS: 37 58.648, -107 45.4298). Alternatively, drive another 0.1 mile to limited parking at a fork in the road. The right fork continues up 4WD Yankee Boy Basin Road past the falls. This fork is the informal Twin Falls trailhead (GPS: 37 58.76, -107 45.538).

The Drive

Six roadside waterfalls along the Camp Bird Road make a pleasant drive with wet views all around. This narrow, dirt road is passable in a passenger car in dry conditions. Some falls are near the road, while others fall down inaccessible slopes and gullies. For

Left: The hike to Twin Falls is a good leg-stretcher after the long drive up Camp Bird Road.
Right: "Senator Gulch Falls" flows south from Senator Gulch and pours over a roadside cliff.

safety, pull completely off the road to view each waterfall. Plan a few hours to drive the road and avoid driving out in the dark. If you aren't comfortable driving, hire an outfitter in Ouray for a 4WD tour to Yankee Boy Basin.

The Hike

Rising from a glacial tarn in Yankee Boy Basin below 14,150-foot Mount Sneffels, Sneffels Creek runs through alpine meadows before dashing over the three leaps of Twin Falls. These beautiful falls, surrounded by rugged mountains, are not to be missed, especially in June when snowmelt fills the creek. This short hike, climbing to the triple waterfalls at timberline, might easily be missed if you are driving a Jeep up Yankee Boy Basin Road, a rough and stony track. Instead, leave the car at a parking area below the silvered ruins of the Atlas Mine and Mill. Hike up the road to a junction and keep right at a sign pointing toward Yankee Boy Basin. Follow the 4WD road north to the waterfalls (watch for traffic).

"Lower Twin Falls," showering over black volcanic rock, is a gorgeous dual-segmented horsetail waterfall. Farther up is "Middle Twin Falls," a short block waterfall that drops over a rock step. A couple hundred feet higher is "Upper Twin Falls," a segmented horsetail waterfall with twin channels. The waterfall's brilliant white water tumbles over dark rock, making a stark and enchanting contrast with Mount Sneffels beyond. This is a place to linger and enjoy views across Sidney Basin, ragged St. Sophia Ridge, and 12,698-foot Stony Mountain. On the hike down, look up left for "Potosi Falls," a ribbon waterfall tucked in a deep gully on 13,786-foot Potosi Peak.

Drive Miles and Directions

0.0 Turn off US 550 and drive west up Camp Bird Road (CR 361). Reset your odometer and use these mileages to find the falls.

3.3 Arrive at viewpoint for "Fall Creek Falls" on road's left side to south (GPS: 37 59.202, -107 42.409). Continue up road.

3.6 Arrive at viewpoint for "Senator Gulch Falls" on right side to northwest (GPS: 37 59.089, -107 42.597). Continue up road.

4.8 Arrive at viewpoint for "Waterhole Slide Falls" and "Imogene Creek Falls" on road's left side to east and south, respectively (GPS: 37 58.495, -107 43.428). Continue up road.

5.7 Arrive at viewpoint for Sneffels Creek Falls, below and left of road to south (GPS: 37 58.388, 107 44.302). Continue to junction with 4WD Yankee Boy Basin Road (Twin Falls trailhead) at 7 miles. Bear left on Governor Basin Road (CR 26A).

7.2 Arrive at "Governor Basin Falls" on road's right to west (GPS: 37 58.887, -107 45.672). Return down roads (or continue to Twin Falls hike).

14.4 Arrive back at junction with US 550.

Miles and Directions

0.0 Begin at informal trailhead at fork on Camp Bird Road. Bear right on 4WD Yankee Boy Basin Road (FR 853 1B). Hike up steep road. Look left to "Governor Basin Falls," a series of white cascades and falls in a wooded ravine. Above are St. Sophia Ridge and more falls tumbling down gullies.

0.4 Leave road on unmarked side trail to left and contour toward base of obvious falls.

0.5 Arrive at "Lower Twin Falls" (GPS: 37 59.154, -107 45.753). Follow social trail up slopes east of falls and hike northwest to next falls.

0.6 Arrive at "Middle Twin Falls" (GPS: 37 59.189, -107 45.807), a short waterfall over a ledge. Continue up social trail for 220 feet to higher leap.

0.65 Arrive at gorgeous "Upper Twin Falls" (GPS: 37 59.202, -107 45.842). Return to road and hike back down.

1.3 Arrive back at parking area (GPS: 37 58.76, -107 45.538).

56 Ice Lake Trail Waterfalls: "Clear Creek Falls," Unnamed Waterfalls, "Lower Ice Lake Basin Falls," "Island Lake Falls," "Ice Lake Falls," "Fuller Lake Falls," "Ice Lake Basin Falls," and "Upper Ice Lake Falls"

Azure pools and lavender–hued peaks offer an otherworldly vision at Ice Lake Basin, attracting hikers who glimpse many waterfalls sprinkled along the trail.

Start: Ice Lakes Trailhead

Trail: Ice Lakes Trail #505

Difficulty: Easy for "Clear Creek Falls"; moderate/strenuous for "Island Lake Falls," "Ice Lake Falls," "Fuller Lake Falls," and "Ice Lake Basin Falls"; strenuous for "Upper Ice Lake Falls"

Hiking time: About 2 hours for "Clear Creek Falls"; 4 hours for "Island Lake Falls," "Ice Lake Falls," "Fuller Lake Falls," and "Ice Lake Basin Falls"

Distance: 1.2 miles out and back for "Clear Creek Falls"; 6.4 miles out and back for "Island Lake Falls" and "Ice Lake Falls"; 6.6 miles out and back for "Fuller Lake Falls"; 6.8 miles out and back for "Ice Lake Basin Falls"; 7.8 miles out and back for all waterfalls including "Upper Ice Lake Falls"

Elevation trailhead to falls viewpoints: 9,930 to 10,220 feet (+290 feet) for "Clear Creek Falls"; to 10,510 feet (+580 feet) for Unnamed Falls; to 11,460 feet (+1,530 feet) for "Island Lake Falls"; to 11,480 feet (+1,550 feet) for "Ice Lake Falls"; to 11,600 feet (+1,670 feet) for "Fuller Lake Falls"; to 11,710 feet (+1,780 feet) for "Ice Lake Basin Falls"; to 12,240 feet (+2,310 feet) for "Upper Ice Lake Falls"

Trail surface: Dirt, rocks

Restrictions: Limited parking; citations issued for illegal parking; practice Leave No Trace ethic; use wag bags for human waste; pack out trash; follow existing trails only; check for possible permit system

Amenities: Backcountry camping; trailhead vault toilets; services in Silverton

Maps: *DeLorme:* Page 76 B3; Trails Illustrated 141: Telluride, Silverton, Ouray, Lake City; USGS Ophir

County: San Juan

Land status/contact: San Juan National Forest, (970) 247-4874; Columbine Ranger District, (970) 884-2512

Finding the trailhead: From Ridgway, take US 550 South toward Silverton. Drive 59.6 miles and turn right on unpaved CR 7/FR 585 toward South Mineral Campground. From Silverton, drive 2 miles northwest on US 550 and turn left on CR 7. Continue 4.4 miles to the campground and parking lot on the right at the trailhead (GPS: 37 48.4, -107 46.438).

The Hike

Ice Lake Basin, in the heart of the San Juan Mountains, is a breathtaking alpine area. The basin is reached by the Ice Lakes Trail, a popular hike lined with many waterfalls. Plan on a full day to see all the falls and the basin lakes.

Ice Lakes Trail is one of the most heavily used footpaths in the San Juans, with crowds of people jamming it on weekends. This has led to resource damage, including deterioration of fragile tundra caused by social trails that fan across the high-elevation landscape, campers making fires above treeline, human waste and toilet tissue, and trash. To protect the trail and upper basins, the US Forest Service plans to establish a permit system to limit overuse of the area. Call the ranger station before arriving to see what restrictions are in place.

The trail starts steep and strenuous, passing through meadows and forest, some burned in the Ice Fire in October 2020. The fire torched almost 600 acres on lower Ice Lakes Trail, leaving exposed soil and dead trees that fall across the trail. As the trail climbs, it passes many waterfalls. "Clear Creek Falls," the first encountered, is one of the best. Higher are a couple of unnamed waterfalls before the trail reaches "Lower Ice Lake Basin Falls," tucked in a deep defile in Lower Ice Lake Basin.

Lakes in the upper basin feed waterfalls that rumble down cliffs encircling the lower basin, including "Island Lake Falls" streaming through a notch to the north and "Ice Lake Falls" in cliffs to the northwest. The trail climbs out of the basin, passing views of "Fuller Lake Falls" and "Ice Lake Basin Falls" in a crevice below the trail. The hike's toughest section climbs to Ice Lake Basin and turquoise-colored Ice Lake. Enjoy views of cascading "Upper Ice Lake Falls" and a ragged ring of high peaks, including Beattie, Fuller, and Vermilion Peaks, pointed Golden Horn, and Pilot Knob's rocky fin.

Miles and Directions

0.0 Begin at Ice Lakes Trailhead and hike up switchbacks. Cross dramatic Clear Creek at 0.5 mile and hike to waterfall's base.

0.6 Arrive at base of "Clear Creek Falls" (GPS: 37 48.6842, -107 46.6868). Return to main trail and continue up switchbacks to short spur on right overlooking waterfall.

1.1 Arrive at upper leaps of "Clear Creek Falls." Return to main trail and continue up.

1.4 Leave main trail for social trail on left. Cross hillside and loose talus to base of unnamed waterfall.

1.5 Arrive at unnamed waterfall (GPS: 37 48.726, -107 47.071), a tiered falls with lovely plunge pool. Return to main trail and hike up.

1.7 Leave main trail for social trail on left.

1.8 Arrive at viewpoint above unnamed waterfall (GPS: 37 48.7286, -107 47.122). Return to main trail and continue uphill.

2.1 Arrive at viewpoint for "Lower Ice Lake Basin Falls" (GPS: 37 48.642, -107 47.263). Terrain between trail and waterfall is steep, so view from trail. Continue up main trail. More

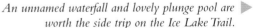

An unnamed waterfall and lovely plunge pool are worth the side trip on the Ice Lake Trail.

Ice Lake Trail Waterfalls

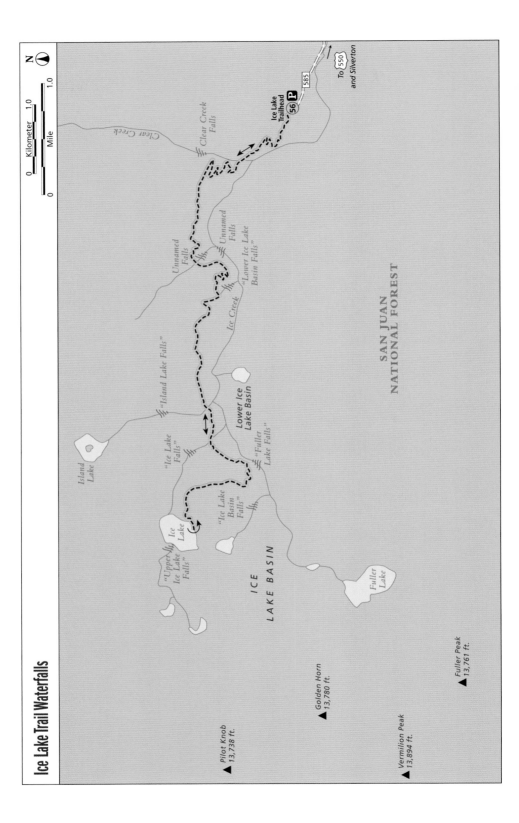

Left: "Clear Creek Falls" is your first waterfall on the hike up to Ice Lake, near Silverton.
Center: "Clear Creek Falls" stair-steps down cliffs and boulders above Ice Lake Trail.
Right: "Fuller Lake Falls" flows from Fuller Lake, southwest of Ice Lake Basin.

waterfalls come into view in Lower Ice Lake Basin. Hike past Lower Ice Lake on left.

3.2 Reach viewpoint of "Island Lake Falls" in cliffs 0.3 mile to right (north) of trail (GPS: 37 48.710, -107 47.930). "Ice Lake Falls" and "Ice Lake Basin Falls" are also seen ahead. Hike another 100 feet to viewpoint for "Ice Lake Falls," 0.2 mile ahead to northwest (GPS: 37 48.695, -107 48.007). Hike to base or continue on trail. Cross the creek.

3.3 Reach viewpoint of "Fuller Lake Falls" 0.3 mile to southwest (GPS: 37 48.651, -107 48.165). Continue up steep, loose trail.

3.4 Arrive at "Ice Lake Basin Falls" to left of trail (GPS: 37 48.586, -107 48.189). Continue up trail. Enjoy views of upper cascades of "Fuller Lake Falls" and "Ice Lake Basin Falls" along hillside to southwest. Social trail on left leads up to Fuller Lake, and more social trails lead to hillside cascades. Stay right on main trail. Reach Ice Lake and continue around left side of lake.

4.1 Arrive at viewpoint on Ice Lake's southeast edge for "Upper Ice Lake Falls" across lake to northwest (GPS: 37 48.7691, -107 48.5192). Return the way you came, minus the waterfall spur trails.

7.8 Arrive back at trailhead (GPS: -37 48.4, -107 46.438).

"Ice Lake Basin Falls" tumbles into a deep crevice beside the trail.

57 South Mineral Creek Falls

This gorgeous two-tiered waterfall drops over cliffs into clear pools in a valley south of the Ice Lakes Trailhead.

Start: Ice Lakes Trailhead
Trail: Road, unnamed trail
Difficulty: Easy
Hiking time: About 1 hour
Distance: 0.8 mile
Elevation trailhead to falls viewpoint: 9,842 to 9,910 feet (+68 feet)
Trail surface: Dirt, rocks
Restrictions: Limited parking; citations issued for illegal parking; practice Leave No Trace ethic

Amenities: Trailhead vault toilets; services in Silverton
Maps: *DeLorme:* Page 76 B3; Trails Illustrated 141: Telluride, Silverton, Ouray, Lake City; USGS Ophir
County: San Juan
Land status/contact: San Juan National Forest, (970) 247-4874; Columbine Ranger District, (970) 884-2512

Finding the trailhead: From Ridgway, take US 550 South toward Silverton. Drive 59.6 miles and turn right on unpaved CR 7/FR 585 toward South Mineral Campground. From Silverton, drive 2 miles northwest on US 550 and turn left on FR 585. Continue 4.4 miles to the campground and Ice Lakes Trailhead parking area on the right. Begin at the southwest side of the parking lot (GPS: 37 48.3892, -107 46.4514).

The Hike

The South Fork of Mineral Creek, springing from rugged peaks in a high basin, dashes northeast down a glaciated valley over many cascades and small waterfalls before dropping 55 feet at South Mineral Creek Falls. This waterfall features two drops, an upper 35-foot plunge into a deep pool and a 20-foot dive into a rock-walled gorge. The falls is easy to reach from the Ice Lakes Trailhead and parking lot.

From the trailhead, walk up the shoulder of a dirt road to the west side of a bridge. Dip left on an informal trail. Follow the well-used trail along the right bank of Clear Creek and then bend right and continue up the right bank of South Fork of Mineral Creek to the lower falls. Traverse a rock shelf to reach the edge of the plunge pool below the lower falls. Return to the main path and finish by hiking to the upper falls.

South Mineral Creek Falls offers double waterfalls ▶
and plunge pools near the Ice Lake Trailhead.

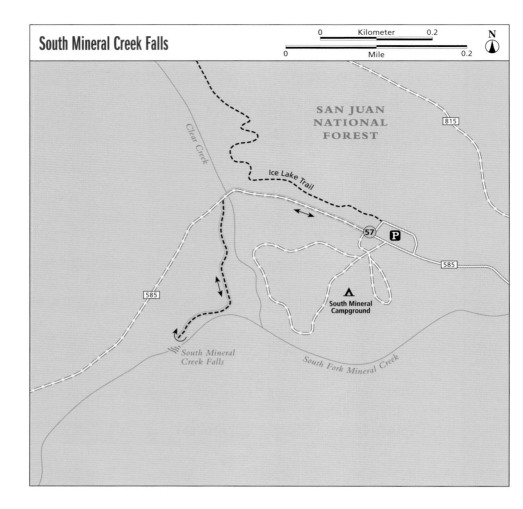

South Mineral Creek Falls

Miles and Directions

0.0 Start at Ice Lakes Trailhead parking lot. Walk west on FR 585 and cross bridge over Clear Creek.

0.2 Go left on unmarked trail at west side of bridge (GPS: 37 48.4231, -107 46.6313). Follow trail on right side of creek to confluence with South Mineral Creek.

0.3 Continue along west bank to view lower falls (GPS: 37 48.285, -107 46.6795).

0.4 Reach viewpoint of upper falls. Return the way you came.

0.8 Arrive back at parking lot (GPS: 37 48.3892, -107 46.4514).

58 Cascade Creek Waterfalls: "Engine Creek Falls," "50-Foot Falls," "Behind the Falls," "Two-Tier Falls," "Ice Cream Scoop Falls," "Endless Cascade," "Cascade Creek Falls," and "150-Foot Falls"

Following Cascade Creek north of Durango, Cascade Creek Trail twists up a wide mountain valley, passing eight spectacular waterfalls on the creek and two of its tributaries.

Start: Cascade Creek Trailhead
Trail: Cascade Creek Trail #510
Difficulty: Moderate
Hiking time: About 6 hours to "Two-Tier Falls"; 8 hours to "150-Foot Falls"
Distance: 10.8 miles out and back to "Two-Tier Falls"; 12.6 miles out and back to "150-Foot Falls"
Elevation trailhead to falls viewpoints: 8,885 to 9,925 feet (+1,040 feet) for "Two Tier Falls"; to 10,210 feet (+1,325 feet) for "150-Foot Falls"

Trail surface: Dirt, rocks
Restrictions: No motorized vehicles past red gate; pack out trash; wilderness rules apply
Amenities: Services in Durango
Maps: *DeLorme:* Page 76 D3 and C3; Trails Illustrated 144: Durango, Cortez; USGS Engineer Mountain
County: San Juan
Land status/contact: San Juan National Forest, (970) 247-4874; Columbine Ranger District, (970) 884-2512

Finding the trailhead: From Durango, drive 30 miles north on US 550 to a hairpin turn past Purgatory Resort and south of Coal Bank Pass. Turn left on unmarked, dirt Cascade Road (FR 783) at the hairpin. Follow the rough road west for 0.7 mile to a marked trailhead on the left before the road crosses Cascade Flume (GPS: 37 39.9919; -107 49.1547). High-clearance 4WD vehicles can continue for 0.9 mile to the trailhead at a red gate.

The Hike

Cascade Creek, rising from a ring of peaks in the San Juan Mountains, rushes down a glaciated valley, tumbling over six waterfalls. Two more are in tributary creeks. The lightly used trail, gaining over 1,500 feet of elevation, is easy to follow but requires creek crossings. These may be high in snowmelt season, so use caution and trekking poles. The faint spur trails to the waterfalls are not signed, so do as locals advise— listen for the sound of falling water. The hike's turnaround point is before the trail crosses a swampy meadow. If you do the "Extra Credit Hike," plan on wet feet or carry sandals to cross the mire.

Cascade Creek spills over a limestone cliff in a gorgeous plunge and horsetail falls at "Behind the Falls."

Start at the Cascade Flume, an elevated wooden flume built in 1923 to divert water to the Tacoma Hydroelectric Project and Electra Lake. The trail follows a 4WD road and then gently climbs through aspen, fir, and spruce woods, crossing flower-filled meadows and passing four waterfalls. After you view these falls, the described

"Engine Creek Falls," a two-step wonder, drops into a cliff-lined pool off the Cascade Creek Trail.

Lower "Two-Tier Falls" at the hike's end is a noisy waterfall tucked into an amphitheater.

hike turns around, with an extra credit extension continuing to an overlook of "150-Foot Falls." The trail then continues another mile to the Colorado Trail.

The first falls, "Engine Creek Falls," lies off the trail at a footbridge. The noisy two-drop waterfall squeezes between overhanging cliffs. Almost half a mile later is "50-Foot Falls," a gusher seen from a clifftop overlook. Roaring like a runaway train, the falls is misnamed since it has an 85-foot drop. Continue to "Behind the Falls," a

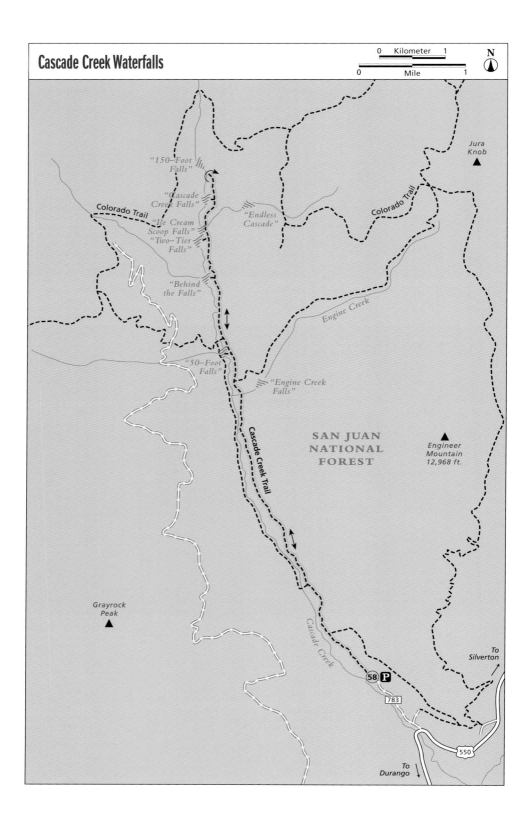

Cascade Creek Waterfalls

0   Kilometer   1

0   Mile   1

N

Jura Knob ▲

"150–Foot Falls"

Colorado Trail

"Cascade Creek Falls"

"Endless Cascade"

Colorado Trail

"Ice Cream Scoop Falls"

"Two–Tier Falls"

"Behind the Falls"

Engine Creek

"50–Foot Falls"

"Engine Creek Falls"

SAN JUAN NATIONAL FOREST

▲ *Engineer Mountain 12,968 ft.*

Cascade Creek Trail

Grayrock Peak ▲

Cascade Creek

58 **P**

783

To Silverton

To Durango

550

Cascade Creek forms a gigantic horsetail waterfall at "50-Foot Falls."

hidden 100-foot waterfall that freefalls off a cliff in a spreading horsetail. See the falls from a viewpoint beneath an overhanging cliff. At the end of the described hike is "Two-Tier Falls," with a 10-foot upper drop and a 20-foot lower horsetail falls that fills a deep pool. With time and energy, hike north to more wonderful waterfalls. "Ice Cream Scoop Falls" is a 70-foot waterfall that pours through a gap in a cliff; "Endless Cascade" offers several falls in a side creek; 70-foot "Cascade Creek Falls" hides in a cliffed gorge; and lastly, "150-Foot Falls" is a three-tiered monster that's considerably higher than 150 feet.

Miles and Directions

0.0   Start at Cascade Creek Trailhead near Cascade Flume. Hike northwest up 4WD road past cabins and dispersed campsites.

0.9   Reach end of road and trailhead at red gate (GPS: 37 40.5206, -107 49.6784). Pass gate and hike northwest to first creek crossing.

1.7   Cross meadow and arrive at base of switchbacks. Hike uphill through aspens and gain 300 feet to bench. Continue on trail through forest and meadows, dipping across drainages.

3.4   Reach footbridge over creek and view of "Engine Creek Falls" (GPS: 37 42.3104, -107 50.4695). Follow side trail on right for 110 feet to pool below falls. Hike north from bridge.

3.65   Reach junction with Engine Creek Trail on right (GPS: 37 42.4064, -107 50.5265). Continue straight across wide meadow and cross wooded hillside with glimpse left of next falls.

3.9   Reach indistinct Y-junction (GPS: 37 42.647, -107 50.6107). Take path on left and hike 125 feet to top of "50-Foot Falls" (GPS: 37 42.6485, -107 50.6324). Use caution—exposed cliff edges and loose rock. Return to main trail and go left through woods and meadows.

4.2   Reach marked junction on left with alternate Cascade Creek Trail (returns on south side of creek) and Graysill Trail, which crosses creek and climbs south to Colorado Trail. Continue straight on main trail across meadow.

4.6   Reach indistinct junction at thin cliff band near ridgetop (GPS: 37 43.2676, -107 50.7497). Go left for 300 feet on steep, loose trail down to viewpoint under cliff of spectacular "Behind the Falls." Return to main trail and go left.

5.1   Arrive at hike's end on rounded bedrock ridge before wide meadow (GPS: 37 43.6061, -107 50.7999). Go left on faint trail along ridge for 0.05 mile (600 feet) to viewpoint above upper "Two-Tier Falls." Descend left on rough path to base of lower falls (GPS: 37 43.5672, -107 50.8806). Return to main trail.

5.4   Reach turnaround point on main trail. Go right to return to trailhead.

10.8   Arrive back at trailhead (GPS: 37 39.9919; -107 49.1547).

Extra Credit Hike

To continue to more waterfalls: Walk north from hike's turnaround point and cross a marshy meadow for 0.3 mile. Plan to squish through mud and 2 to 4 inches of water. After 5.9 miles from trailhead, cross a side creek and reach a junction on left (GPS: 37 43.9214, –107 50.7485). Hike 0.05 mile to spectacular "Ice Cream Scoop Falls." Return to main trail at 6.0 miles and continue to view of "Endless Cascade," with several falls rushing down a chute on right. Partway up, bushwhack left to "Cascade Creek Falls" in a creek bend. Continue hiking the steep trail to an overlook for "150-Foot Falls" at 6.3 miles (GPS: 37 44.1313, –107 50.8061). The overlook may be hard to find.

59 Cornet Falls

Cornet Creek, flowing south to Telluride from high on Greenback Mountain, jumps a cliff in a single leap at Cornet Falls. Ruddy rock cliffs provide a unique backdrop for this lovely waterfall that's a short hike from town.

Start: Jud Weibe Memorial Trailhead
Trail: Cornet Falls Trail
Difficulty: Moderate
Hiking time: Less than 1 hour
Distance: 0.5 mile out and back
Elevation trailhead to falls viewpoint: 8,910 to 9,130 feet (+220 feet)
Trail surface: Dirt, scree, sand, talus

Restrictions: None posted; observe parking limits
Amenities: Services in Telluride
Maps: *DeLorme:* Page 76 A3; Trails Illustrated 603: Telluride [Local Trails]; USGS Telluride
County: San Miguel
Land status/contact: Uncompahgre National Forest, (970) 874-6600; Ouray Ranger District, (970) 240-5300

Finding the trailhead: In Telluride, drive east on CO 145 (West Colorado Avenue) to Aspen Street. Turn left (north) and drive up the steep street for 0.2 mile; park along the road. Walk about 200 feet to the pavement's end and up a dirt road to the trailhead (GPS: 37 56.456, -107 48.75).

The Hike

Cornet Falls, hiding above Telluride in a cul-de-sac canyon, pours through a sharp notch and freefalls 85 feet down an overhanging sandstone cliff. The dramatic falls, a plunge ribbon waterfall, is easily accessed by a short, steep trail. Use caution since it is narrow, crosses hardpan slopes, steeply drops to the creek, and is slippery when wet. Take your time—a trekking pole is handy.

Begin at the top of Aspen Street and walk up the steep, narrow road past houses to the Jud Weibe Memorial Trailhead; the trail goes left across a bridge. Continue north on the unmarked Cornet Falls Trail on the right side of Cornet Creek. Hike north to the pink cliffs and brilliant spray of Cornet Falls. For a longer outing, return to the bridge and hike west on the Jud Wiebe Trail (#432), following signs for a 2.9-mile loop hike over mountainsides northwest of Telluride.

Miles and Directions

0.0 Begin at Jud Weibe Memorial Trailhead at footbridge on left. Continue north up unmarked trail along creek's right side.
0.25 Arrive at Cornet Falls (GPS: 37 56.594, -107 48.619). Return the way you came.
0.5 Arrive back at trailhead (GPS: 37 56.456, -107 48.75).

Turn page: Candy-colored cliffs provide a bright ▷
and whimsical backdrop at Cornet Falls.

Cornet Falls, Bear Creek Trail Waterfalls, and Bridal Veil Falls Trail Waterfalls

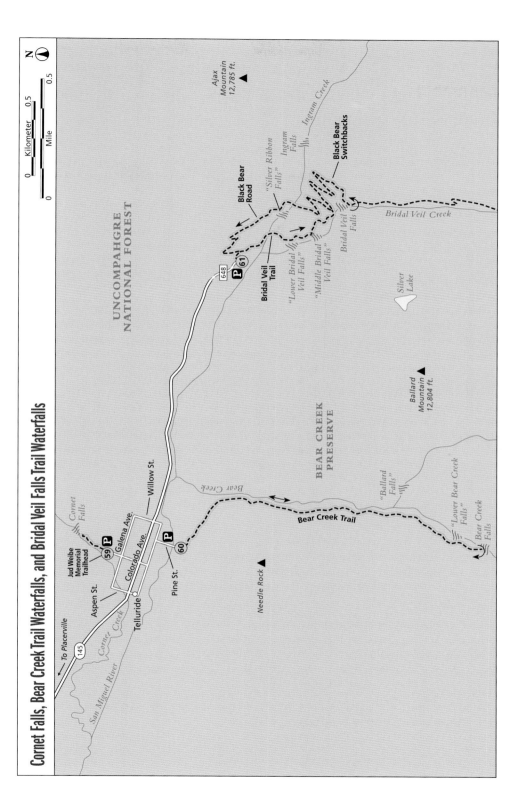

60 Bear Creek Trail Waterfalls: Bear Creek Falls, "Lower Bear Creek Falls," and "Ballard Falls" (Telluride)

The Bear Creek Trail climbs a wooded valley south of Telluride, passing two waterfalls before reaching Bear Creek Falls. Here, cold water splashes over a water-stained cliff in a translucent sheet of light and mist.

See map on page 199.
Start: Bear Creek Trailhead
Trail: Bear Creek Trail #635
Difficulty: Moderate
Hiking time: About 3 hours
Distance: 4.6 miles out and back
Elevation trailhead to falls viewpoint: 8,800 to 9,800 feet (+1,000 feet)
Trail surface: Gravel, dirt

Restrictions: No motor vehicles
Amenities: Services in Telluride
Maps: *DeLorme:* Page 76 A3; Trails Illustrated 603: Telluride [Local Trails]; USGS Telluride
County: San Miguel
Land status/contact: Uncompahgre National Forest, (970) 874-6600; Ouray Ranger District, (970) 240-5300; Telluride Parks and Recreation, (970) 728-2173

Finding the trailhead: In Telluride, drive east on CO 145 (West Colorado Avenue) and turn right (south) on South Pine Street. Park on the street north of the trailhead. Parking is metered with a pay kiosk every block. Buy up to 3 hours of time and place the receipt on the driver's side dashboard. Parking at the trailhead is reserved for condo residents. The gated trailhead is 0.2 mile from CO 145 at the end of South Pine Street and on the south side of a bridge (GPS: 37 56.061,-107 48.716).

The Hike

The 2.3-mile hike to Bear Creek Falls, a local favorite, follows the Bear Creek Trail up an old mining road into a valley south of Telluride, passing "Ballard Falls" and "Lower Bear Creek Falls" before reaching the main event—Bear Creek Falls. This four-tiered, horsetail falls drops more than 80 feet, breaking on ledges creasing a cliff. "Lower Bear Creek Falls," east of Bear Creek Falls, is a two-tiered waterfall that dashes through trees before plunging over a cliff. Both are fed by Bear Creek, which originates high in Lena Basin below 13,470-foot Silver Mountain and runs north down glaciated Bear Creek Valley. "Ballard Falls," tucked in a water-worn crevice below 12,804-foot Ballard Mountain, offers six leaps when spring snowmelt fills its unnamed creek. The falls is above the debris field of an avalanche that occurred in 2019. The avalanche swept down slopes right of the falls, tossing trees like toothpicks in a 500-foot-wide swath.

Left: Bear Creek splashes over ledges in a misty sheet at Bear Creek Falls.
Top right: Ribbons of water plunge over six leaps at "Ballard Falls" in a crevice canyon above Bear Creek Trail.
Bottom right: Bear Creek tumbles over a cliff into a clear pool at "Lower Bear Creek Falls."

The hike's first section lies in 325-acre Bear Creek Preserve, a Telluride–owned natural area that was donated to town citizens in 1995, while the upper trail is in Uncompahgre National Forest.

Miles and Directions

0.0   Begin at Bear Creek Trailhead. Walk up closed, aspen-lined road that bends west and heads up a broad valley. Bear Creek roars through gorge below trail.

1.5   Reach viewpoint of "Ballard Falls" to left on east side of avalanche area (GPS: 37 54.9143, -107 48.4697).

1.8   Reach three-way junction with old road (GPS: 37 54.6523, -107 48.5604). Continue straight on Bear Creek Trail, climbing the rocky road.

1.9   Reach junction with Wasatch Trail (#508) on right. Keep straight on main trail and reach social trail on left that leads 400 feet to "Lower Bear Creek Falls" (GPS: 37 54.5163, -107 48.6245). Return to main trail and continue west toward waterfall.

2.1   Reach huge boulder on left at flat area above lower falls. Go right on first social trail and traverse slopes up left on singletrack trail to base of falls.

2.3   Reach Bear Creek Falls (GPS: 37 54.363, -107 48.72). Return on trail.

4.6   Arrive back at trailhead (GPS: 37 56.061, -107 48.716).

61 Bridal Veil Falls Trail Waterfalls: Bridal Veil Falls, "Lower Bridal Veil Falls," "Middle Bridal Veil Falls," Ingram Falls, and "Silver Ribbon Falls" (Telluride)

Bridal Veil Creek, rising high in Bridal Veil Basin to the south, roars over Bridal Veil Falls, shattering to mist on boulders below. The creek continues northwest toward Telluride, dashing over two-tiered "Middle Bridal Veil Falls" and "Lower Bridal Veil Falls," a horsetail waterfall. On the east side of the valley, Ingram Falls plummets off a high cliff and then frolics over boulders in a frothy cascade, while "Silver Ribbon Falls" freefalls off an overhanging cliff. In moist Mays, as many as ten falls are seen in this cirque of the waterfalls.

See map on page 199.
Start: Bridal Veil Falls Trailhead
Trails: Bridal Veil Falls Trail, Black Bear Road (FR 648)
Difficulty: Moderate up Bridal Veil Trail; easy for descent on Black Bear Road; easy for Black Bear Road to top of falls
Hiking time: About 3 hours for Bridal Veil Trail to Black Bear Road loop hike; add 1 hour for "Extra Credit Hike" to top of Bridal Veil Falls
Distance: 2.8 miles up Bridal Veil Falls Trail and down Black Bear Road (FR 648); 2.0 miles round-trip for "Extra Credit Hike" to top of Bridal Veil Falls from viewpoint at falls base

Elevation trailhead to falls viewpoints: 9,080 to 9,820 feet (+740 feet) for Bridal Veil Falls
Trail surface: Dirt, rocks, gravel road
Restrictions: Hazardous crossing at Ingram Creek; leashed dogs only; pick up pet waste (bags at trailhead); no bikes allowed
Amenities: Services in Telluride
Maps: *DeLorme:* Page 76 A3; Trails Illustrated 603: Telluride [Local Trails]; USGS Telluride
County: San Miguel
Land status/contact: Uncompahgre National Forest, (970) 874-6600; Ouray Ranger District, (970) 240-5300

Finding the trailhead: From downtown Telluride, take CO 145 (East Colorado Avenue) to Columbine Drive on the town's eastern edge. Drive 1.6 miles east on paved CO 145 Spur and then dirt FR 648, passing Idarado Mine, to a parking lot at Bridal Veil Trailhead (GPS: 37 55.4669, -107 46.1664).

The Hike

Telluride, boasting the most spectacular setting of any Colorado town, also offers more waterfalls than any other Colorado town. More than twenty-five waterfalls lie within 6 miles of Telluride, including 365-foot Bridal Veil Falls, the tallest freefalling

Billed as the tallest freefalling waterfall in the state, ▶
Bridal Veil Falls is popular with ice climbers.

Left: Bridal Veil Creek crashes over rock steps into a deep pool at "Lower Bridal Veil Falls."
Center: "Middle Bridal Veil Falls" is a lovely two-tiered waterfall surrounded by cliffs near Telluride.
Right: Ingram Falls puts on a dramatic show on the northern slopes of Ingram Peak near Telluride.

waterfall in Colorado. This excellent hike explores a glaciated cirque southeast of Telluride, climbing the Bridal Veil Trail past two magnificent waterfalls to a viewpoint below Bridal Veil Falls and then returning down Black Bear Road, a famed 4WD track that descends to the trailhead past more waterfalls. The best time to see as many as ten waterfalls is from mid-May to mid-June when snowmelt fills the creeks.

The Bridal Veil Falls area is busy in summer, so consider hiking on weekdays. The parking area fills fast, and the hike's road section has 4WD traffic. It's recommended not to drive to Bridal Veil Falls because of congestion. No uphill vehicles are allowed beyond the waterfall's top. The Bridal Veil Trail, opened in 2020, is a singletrack trail that twists up rocky terrain by Bridal Veil Creek. The rough trail, not recommended for beginner hikers or families, has uneven surfaces and a creek crossing (a bridge is planned).

The trail threads through big boulders and thick woods, passing two stunning waterfalls—"Lower Bridal Veil Falls" and "Middle Bridal Veil Falls." At trail's end is a viewpoint at the thundering base of

Fed by snowmelt on Ajax Peak, "Silver Ribbon Falls" plunges off an overhanging cliff above Black Bear Road.

Bridal Veil Falls. When the falls is gushing, it's impossible to get close, as a powerful spray and soaking mist fill the basin. For extra credit, hike up Black Bear Road from the falls and jog right to a historic power station perched above the falls.

From the base of Bridal Veil Falls, hike down Black Bear Road. Watch for traffic and waterfalls. The track crosses frothy Ingram Creek. Look 1,500 feet up the cascading creek to Ingram Falls, named for J. B. Ingram, who discovered the wealthy Smuggler Mine in 1876. Then pass "Silver Ribbon Falls," a slender thread of water that rumbles down a steep gully before freefalling over 100 feet from a clifftop.

Miles and Directions

0.0 Start at Bridal Veil Falls Trailhead on left side of boulder with mileage sign and map at parking lot. Hike east and bend south next to Black Bear Road. Continue south through boulders and cross Ingram Creek. Do not attempt in high water.

0.5 Reach junction with spur trail on right (GPS: 37 55.4288, -107 46.4462). Go right on spur for 0.03 mile to "Lower Bridal Veil Falls." Arrive at falls (GPS: 37 55.403, -107 46.4545). Return to trail and go right.

0.7 Reach junction with spur on right to "Middle Bridal Veil Falls" (GPS: 37 55.3439, -107 46.4188). Follow trail for 0.03 mile to falls. Arrive at falls (GPS: 37 55.3246, -107 46.409). Return to main trail and go right.

0.8 Reach junction with signed Ingram Spur Trail and views of Ingram Falls (GPS: 37 55.3183, -107 46.3197). Keep right on main trail.

1.2 Arrive at Bridal Veil Falls viewpoint at road's edge (GPS: 37 55.2036, -107 46.2298). Hike northeast down Black Bear Road (FR 648).

1.4 Descend road to hairpin turn and viewpoint of Ingram Falls (GPS: 37 55.3662, -107 46.1225). Continue down gravel road.

1.8 After crossing Ingram Creek, reach viewpoint of "Silver Ribbon Falls" in cliffs above left (GPS: 37 55.4669, -107 46.1664). Continue north and descend five switchbacks to trailhead.

2.8 Arrive back at trailhead (GPS: 37 55.4669, -107 46.1664).

Extra Credit: Hike to Top of Bridal Veil Falls

0.0 Begin at Bridal Veil Falls viewpoint at top of trail (GPS: 37 55.2036, -107 46.2298). Hike up Black Bear Road.

0.4 Reach first switchback. Go straight on short spur to views of upper Ingram Falls (GPS: 37 55.3769, -107 45.987). Side trail continues to Telluride Via Ferrata. Return to road.

0.9 Arrive at gate at fourth switchback. Go right and follow closed road toward Bridal Veil Power Station. Keep off private property.

1.0 Reach viewpoint of upper cascade of Bridal Veil Falls by creek (GPS: 37 55.0933, -107 46.1897). Return to Black Bear Road and descend to viewpoint.

2.0 Arrive back at viewpoint below Bridal Veil Falls. Enjoy the view again, then descend road 1.6 miles to trailhead and parking lot (GPS: 37 55.4669, -107 46.1664).

62 Ames Waterfalls: "Ames (Mystic) Falls," "Lower Ames Falls," and "Upper Ames Falls"

Three gorgeous waterfalls, including "Ames Falls," also known as "Mystic Falls," hide in a cliff-lined canyon above the famed Ames power plant west of Telluride.

Start: Ames Power Plant
Trails: Galloping Goose Trail #499, unnamed trail and road
Difficulty: Easy
Hiking time: About 1 hour
Distance: 1.6 miles out and back
Elevation trailhead to falls viewpoint: 8,705 to 8,829 feet (+124 feet) for Ames Falls; to 9,010 feet (+305 feet) for Upper Ames Falls
Trail surface: Gravel, dirt, rocks

Restrictions: Follow road and trails; stay off signed private property at Upper Ames Falls
Amenities: Services in Telluride; limited services in Ophir
Maps: *DeLorme:* Page 76 B2 and B3; Trails Illustrated 603: Telluride [Local Trails]; USGS Mount Wilson
County: San Miguel
Land status/contact: Uncompahgre National Forest, (970) 874-6600; Norwood Ranger District, (970) 327-4261

Finding the trailhead: From Telluride, drive west on CO 145 to a large roundabout, then turn left (south) on CO 145 South and drive 7.2 miles to an unmarked, sharp right turn on CR 63L. This narrow dirt road descends steeply for 0.9 mile to a sharp left turn on Ames Road. Descend the steep dirt road for 0.3 mile to the Ames Hydroelectric Generating Plant at 699 Ames Rd., on the left. Park off the road at the plant. The hike begins right of the plant at the base of a dirt road (GPS: 37 51.8989, -107 52.9276).

The Hike

This short hike explores three spectacular waterfalls—"Ames Falls" (sometimes called "Mystic Falls"), "Lower Ames Falls," and "Upper Ames Falls"—tucked into sheer canyons carved by the Lake Fork of the San Miguel River above the famed Ames Hydroelectric Generating Plant. "Ames Falls," dubbed "Mystic Falls" on the internet and "Lake Fork Falls," plunges over 100 feet into a cliff-lined gorge, shattering to foam in a plunge pool. "Lower Ames Falls," 190 feet south of "Ames Falls" in a neighboring gorge, also tumbles over 100 feet in a thick ribbon of falling water interrupted midway by a pool on a ledge. Both "Ames Falls" and "Lower Ames Falls" are fed by the Lake Fork, which splits 400 feet upstream from the waterfalls. "Upper Ames Falls" is a 45-foot, horsetail waterfall with two streams in high water. These waterfall names have been used by ice climbers for more than 40 years.

The hike follows 4WD mining roads from Ames Road, but this description encourages visitors to park at an informal trailhead at Ames power station and walk. The two gorges below the falls can be reached by rough social trails that head north

Top left: "Ames Falls," also called "Mystic Falls," plummets over 100 feet into a cul-de-sac canyon. Top right: The Lake Fork feeds "Lower Ames Falls," a two-step waterfall on a broken cliff. Bottom: "Upper Ames Falls," surrounded by mining claims, is a gorgeous waterfall on the Lake Fork of the San Miguel River.

from a log cabin. Do not attempt to hike into the gorge at "Ames Falls" during spring snowmelt or after rain since the Lake Fork runs deep. All waterfall viewpoints are on cliff edges. Use extreme caution above the falls, and control children and pets.

Miles and Directions

0.0 Begin at informal trailhead right of Ames power plant at base of dirt road. Hike south on road past green house, old log cabin, and junction with 4WD road on left.

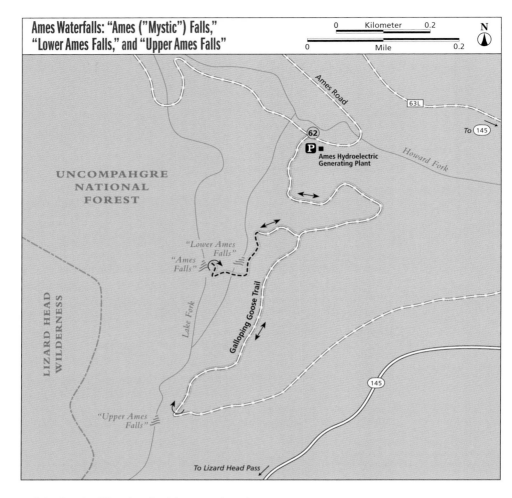

Ames Waterfalls: "Ames ("Mystic") Falls," "Lower Ames Falls," and "Upper Ames Falls"

0.3 Reach a Y-junction. Go right on rough road.

0.4 Reach vehicle turnaround and view of "Lower Ames Falls" in canyon below (GPS: 37 51.7862, -107 53.0042). Hike south on narrow trail along sheer cliff edge past falls. Keep right and cross feeder creek above falls. Walk through trees and keep right to edge of overhanging cliff by "Ames Falls."

0.5 Reach unfenced cliff-edge viewpoint of "Ames Falls" (GPS: 37 51.7543, -107 53.0689). Use extreme caution—dangerous cliff. Control children and dogs.

0.7 Return to Y-junction. Go right on 4WD road (Galloping Goose Trail) and hike uphill past old mining buildings posted "No Trespassing." Continue until road bends left and marked trail continues straight.

1.0 Step right at trail's start to "Upper Ames Falls" viewpoint on cliff edge (GPS: 37 51.5745, -107 53.129). Area around falls is mostly private property, so it's difficult to reach water-fall base.

1.3 Return northeast down road to Y-junction. Keep right on old road.

1.6 Arrive back at trailhead (GPS: 37 51.8989, -107 52.9276).

63 Navajo Trail Waterfalls: "West Dolores River Falls," "Kilpacker Creek Falls," and "Navajo Basin Falls"

Navajo Lake Trail leads to three of Colorado's 14,000-foot peaks, but three trailside waterfalls and a lake make this hike a fine day trip or backpack. The first two falls lie below the trail in a shady hideaway, while the third waterfall starts at the western edge of Navajo Basin and tumbles over 100 feet below El Diente Peak.

Start: Navajo Lake Trailhead
Trail: Navajo Lake Trail #635
Difficulty: Easy/moderate for "West Dolores River Falls" and "Kilpacker Creek Falls"; strenuous for all 3 waterfalls and Navajo Lake
Hiking time: About 2 hours for "West Dolores River Falls" and "Kilpacker Creek Falls"; 7 hours for all 3 waterfalls and Navajo Lake
Distance: 3.4 miles out and back for "West Dolores River Falls"; 3.6 miles out and back for "Kilpacker Creek Falls"; 9.9 miles out and back for all 3 waterfalls and Navajo Lake
Elevation trailhead to falls viewpoints: 9,330 to 9,780 feet (+450 feet) for "West Dolores River Falls" and "Kilpacker Creek Falls"; to 11,000 feet (+1,670 feet) for "Navajo Basin Falls"; to 11,140 feet (+1,810 feet) for Navajo Lake
Trail surface: Dirt, rocks, deadfall
Restrictions: No bicycles or campfires; dogs must be leashed; observe wilderness regulations
Amenities: Backcountry camping; services in Rico and Telluride
Maps: *DeLorme:* page 76 B1; Trails Illustrated 141: Telluride, Silverton, Ouray, Lake City; USGS Dolores Peak
County: Dolores
Land status/contact: San Juan National Forest, (970) 247-4874; Dolores Ranger District, (970) 882-7296

Finding the trailhead: From Telluride, drive west on CO 145 to a large roundabout. Go left and follow CO 145 South for 17.4 miles, over Lizard Head Pass, and turn right on unpaved Dunton Road (CR 38/FR 535). Drive 7.3 miles, passing Kilpacker Trailhead, and turn right toward Navajo Trailhead. Continue 0.1 mile to parking at the trailhead (GPS: 37 48.3062, -108 3.7949).

The Hike

Navajo Basin, a long, glaciated valley drained by the West Dolores River, is surrounded by towering mountains, including 14,159-foot El Diente Peak, 14,017-foot Wilson Peak, and 14,246-foot Mount Wilson. Mountaineers travel the Navajo Lake Trail to access the Fourteeners, so expect to share the trail and backcountry campsites at Navajo Lake during the summer. This is a beautiful trek no matter how far you walk, so if the lake hike is too much, pick a turnaround point and enjoy the alpine beauty and three waterfalls.

Left: Hike the many leaps of "Navajo Basin Falls" to appreciate its impressive size and power. Right: "Navajo Basin Falls" rushes down a stone groove in a whitewater fury.

The trail follows the river into the basin, passing through mixed conifer forest, meadows filled with wildflowers, and views of Dolores Peak and craggy El Diente. The first waterfall, "West Dolores River Falls," is reached by a side trail that leads to the falls base and river. The nearby second waterfall, lovely "Kilpacker Creek Falls," is difficult to reach, requiring a river crossing on a log and a bushwhack up Kilpacker Creek. The seldom-visited third falls, "Navajo Basin Falls," offers impressive leaps filled with thundering water. While you can see it from the trail, a hike from the base to the top requires scrambling around cliffs and thrashing through deadfall and brush. For extra credit and more grand scenery, follow the trail to Navajo Lake, a shimmering pool reflecting sky, clouds, and peaks.

Miles and Directions

0.0 Begin at Navajo Lake Trailhead. Walk past junction with Groundhog Stock Drive Trail (#534) and continue on Navajo Lake Trail with river on left.

0.2 Pass a bridge on left (part of Groundhog Stock Drive Trail) and stay on main trail. Enter Lizard Head Wilderness.

0.8 Go left and cross bridge over West Dolores River.

1.7 Leave main trail and descend a steep social trail to right. Arrive at "West Dolores River Falls" on left (GPS: 37 49.41, -108 3.114). Then go right, cross river on logs, and hike east on faint trail to left of Kilpacker Creek.

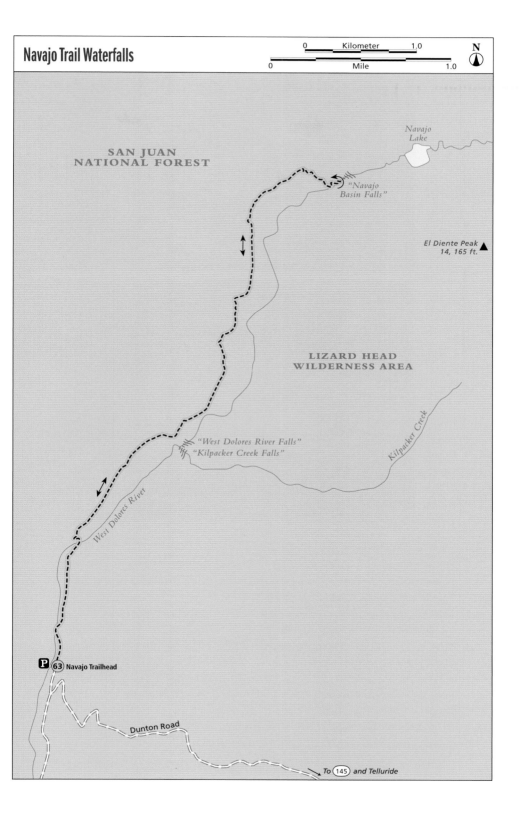

Navajo Trail Waterfalls

0 — Kilometer — 1.0

0 — Mile — 1.0

N

SAN JUAN
NATIONAL FOREST

*Navajo
Lake*

*"Navajo
Basin Falls"*

El Diente Peak
14, 165 ft.

LIZARD HEAD
WILDERNESS AREA

Kilpacker Creek

"West Dolores River Falls"
"Kilpacker Creek Falls"

West Dolores River

P 63 Navajo Trailhead

Dunton Road

To 145 *and Telluride*

"West Dolores River Falls" lies just below the trail in a shady hideaway.

The frothy leaps at "Navajo Basin Falls" are hard to reach but worth the effort.

1.8 Arrive at "Kilpacker Creek Falls" (GPS: 37 49.385, -108 3.072). Return to main trail.

2.4 Pass junction with Kilpacker Trail (#203) on right and stay straight on Navajo Lake Trail.

3.6 Leave main trail and head for waterfall visible in cliffs to right. Use social trails and game trails to work through light brush toward falls.

4.2 Arrive at lower leaps of "Navajo Basin Falls" (GPS: 37 50.6976, -108 2.1289). Hike up trail on left side of river; watch for deadfall.

4.3 Arrive at middle leaps of "Navajo Basin Falls" (GPS: 37 50.705,-108 2.108). Continue to top of falls.

4.4 Arrive at upper leaps of "Navajo Basin Falls" (GPS: 37 50.7188,-108 2.0786). Return on main trail for 8.8-mile out-and-back hike. Alternatively, go north up slopes for 0.1 mile to pick up trail and hike right (east) to lake.

5.0 Arrive at Navajo Lake (GPS: 37 50.8503, -108 1.6976). Return via Navajo Lake Trail.

9.9 Arrive back at trailhead (GPS: 37 48.3062, -108 3.7949).

Oh-be-joyful Creek Waterfalls

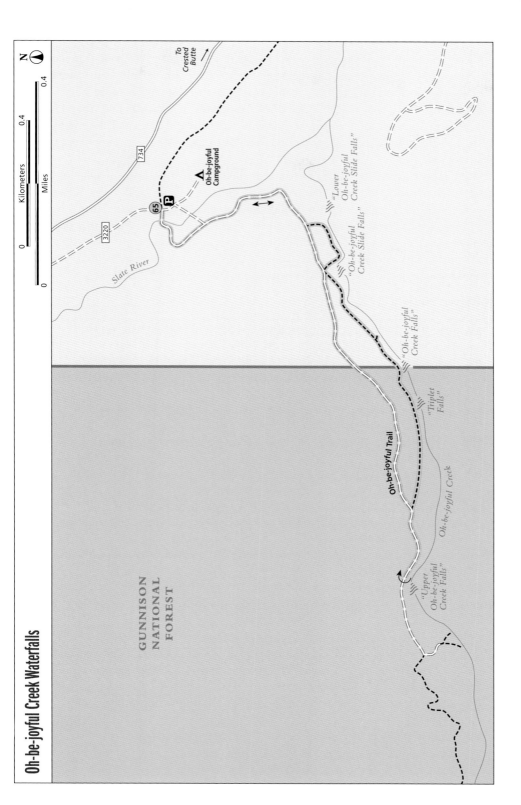

GUNNISON NATIONAL FOREST

Oh-be-joyful Trail

"Upper Oh-be-joyful Creek Falls"

Oh-be-joyful Creek

"Triplet Falls"

"Oh-be-joyful Creek Falls"

"Oh-be-joyful Creek Slide Falls"

"Lower Oh-be-joyful Creek Slide Falls"

Oh-be-joyful Campground

Slate River

To Crested Butte

734

3220

65

P

N

Kilometers
0   0.4

Miles
0   0.4

The described hike follows an unnamed path and the Oh-be-joyful Trail along the north edge of the creek's gorge, stopping at viewpoints of the best waterfalls before turning around at "Upper Oh-be-joyful Creek Falls." To see more waterfalls, continue up the 7-mile trail to Blue Lake, a gorgeous shelf tarn below Afley Peak. Past the turnaround point are more falls alongside the trail and dramatic views of "Redwell Basin Falls," a 700-foot cascade, and "Peeler Basin Falls," a big plunge in a side canyon.

The loop hike climbs the trail to an unnamed path that leads to the edge of the gorge. Below are views of "Lower Oh-be-joyful Creek Slide Falls" and "Oh-be-joyful Creek Slide Falls," an 80-foot slide falls in the narrow canyon. Farther west are more slide falls and "Oh-be-joyful Creek Falls," a gorgeous horsetail that noisily plunges into a deep cauldron. Around the corner is an overlook with "Triplet Falls," three smaller falls dropping over rock ledges. At the turnaround point is the last falls, "Upper Oh-be-joyful Creek Falls," a horsetail in the gorge to the left.

Miles and Directions

0.0 Start at Oh-be-joyful Trailhead right of restrooms. Descend stairs and follow road to left. Cross bridge over Slate River and bend left. Follow trail south and then west.

0.4 Reach junction with trail on left (GPS: 38 54.6421, -107 1.999). Go left and hike to viewpoint above "Lower Oh-be-joyful Creek Slide Falls" (GPS: 38 54.6356, -107 1.9848). Continue west on trail above gorge.

0.5 Reach viewpoint above gorge and "Oh-be-joyful Creek Slide Falls" (GPS: 38 54.6116, -107 2.0843). Go right and climb to main trail.

0.55 Go left from Oh-be-joyful Trail on side trail and descend to edge of gorge. Follow trail west above creek.

0.7 Reach "Upper Oh-be-joyful Creek Slide Falls" on left (GPS: 38 54.5401, -107 2.2343). Continue straight.

0.8 Reach viewpoint above scenic "Oh-be-joyful Creek Falls" (GPS: 38 54.4979, -107 2.3159). To reach base of falls requires downclimbing loose cliff band. Continue straight above creek's north bank.

0.85 Arrive at spectacular viewpoint up creek of "Triplet Falls," three small waterfalls (GPS: 38 54.5027, -107 2.3254).

0.9 Pass unnamed slide falls below cliff on left.

0.95 Pass another unnamed waterfall on left. Continue on trail, gently climbing hillside back to main trail.

1.15 Reach junction with Oh-be-joyful Trail (GPS: 38 54.4879, -107 2.6373). Go left.

1.25 Arrive at viewpoint above "Upper Oh-be-joyful Creek Falls" in gorge on left (GPS: 38 54.4919, -107 2.7515). Turn around here to return to trailhead or continue west on trail to more waterfalls and Blue Lake.

1.4 Return to junction with second waterfall trail to right. Continue straight on Oh-be-joyful Trail.

1.6 Reach junction with start of first waterfall trail to right. Continue straight on main trail.

2.0 Arrive back at trailhead (GPS: 38 54.8827, -107 1.9807).

66 "Lost Lake Falls"

"Lost Lake Falls," reached by the popular Three Lakes Trail, is a magnificent waterfall on Middle Creek that plummets down a steep, cliffed ravine above Lost Lake on the northern edge of the West Elk Mountains.

Start: Three Lakes Trailhead
Trail: Three Lakes Trail
Difficulty: Easy
Hiking time: About 1 hour
Distance: 1.8 miles out and back
Elevation trailhead to falls viewpoint: 9,612 to 9,945 feet (+333 feet)
Trail surface: Dirt, rocks
Restrictions: Open daily; day-use fee; leashed dogs allowed; no mountain bikes

Amenities: All services in Crested Butte; camping at Lost Lake Campground; picnic area by parking area
Maps: *DeLorme:* Page 57 B8; Trails Illustrated 133: Kebler Pass, Paonia Reservoir; USGS Anthracite Range
County: Gunnison
Land status/contact: Gunnison National Forest, Paonia Ranger District, (970) 527-4131

Finding the trailhead: From Crested Butte, drive west on Kebler Pass Road (CR 12) for about 16 miles to FR 706. Turn left (south) and follow narrow FR 706 for 2 miles to Lost Lake Campground at the road's end. From Paonia, drive east on CO 133 for 15 miles and turn right on Kebler Pass Road (CR 12). Follow the dirt road east for 14.5 miles to FR 706, turn right (south), and drive 2 miles to Lost Lake Campground. At the lake, pay the day-use fee and go right on a dirt road to the hiker's parking lot on the right. The signed trailhead is west of campsite #16 (GPS: 38 52.1412, -107. 12.7169).

The Hike

Middle Creek, draining out of an alpine cirque below the northeast flank of 12,342-foot East Beckwith Peak, drops steeply through talus and forest to a cliff-lined ravine where it plunges over 180 feet down "Lost Lake Falls" in at least eight whitewater leaps. The waterfall lies along the Three Lakes Trail, a popular 3.4-mile hike that passes Lost Lake Slough, Lost Lake, and Dollar Lake in the West Elk Mountains. The family-friendly hike to the falls is easy to follow, has gentle grades, and yields spacious views of surrounding mountains.

Miles and Directions

0.0 Start at Three Lakes Trailhead on west side of campsite #16 west of Lost Lake Slough. Hike south through forest on marked Three Lakes Trail (#843).

0.2 Reach a trail junction. Continue straight on marked trail and climb through mixed conifers to aspen groves.

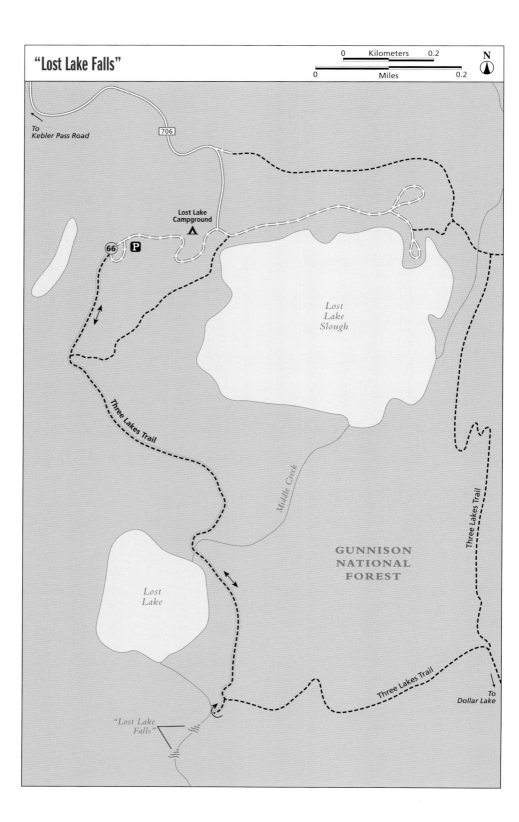

"Lost Lake Falls"

0   Kilometers   0.2

0   Miles   0.2

N

To Kebler Pass Road

706

Lost Lake Campground

66   P

Lost Lake Slough

Three Lakes Trail

Middle Creek

Lost Lake

GUNNISON NATIONAL FOREST

Three Lakes Trail

Three Lakes Trail

"Lost Lake Falls"

To Dollar Lake

With at least eight leaps, "Lost Lake Falls" plunges over 180 feet down a ravine.

0.6 Reach northeast shore of Lost Lake and sign that points left to "The Falls" (GPS: 38 51.7852, -107 12.5834). Balance across logjam plugging Middle Creek, the outlet stream, and hike through spruce and aspen woodland.

0.9 Reach cairn-marked junction at creek. Go right for 125 feet to base of waterfall (GPS: 38 51.6035, -107 12.5666). Return on trail. Alternatively, for a 3.4-mile hike, go right on loop trail to Dollar Lake and back to trailhead.

1.8 Arrive back at trailhead (GPS: 38 52.1412, -107 12.7169).

67 Morrow Point Reservoir Waterfalls: Chipeta Falls and "No Name Falls"

The Morrow Point Boat Tour travels past two remote waterfalls above Morrow Point Reservoir in the canyon heart of Curecanti National Recreation Area.

Start: Pine Creek Trailhead
Trail: Pine Creek Trail
Difficulty: Easy
Hiking time: About 1 hour, plus 1.5-hour boat ride
Distance: 1.8-mile out-and-back hike, plus 14-mile out-and-back boat ride
Elevation trailhead to falls viewpoints: 7,090 to 7,160 feet (+70 feet)
Trail surface: Concrete, wood and stone steps, dirt path

Restrictions: Boat ride is seasonal, fee charged, reservations required; no pets, smoking, firearms, or alcohol
Amenities: Vault toilets at parking; services in Gunnison and Montrose
Maps: *DeLorme:* Page 67 A6 and A7; Trails Illustrated 245: Black Canyon of the Gunnison National Park Map [Curecanti National Recreation Area]; USGS Sapinero
County: Gunnison
Land status/contact: Curecanti National Recreation Area, (970) 641-2337

Finding the trailhead: In Gunnison, follow US 50 West for 25 miles and turn right at mile marker 130, signed "Pine Creek," onto a steep gravel road. This turn is 35 miles east of Montrose via US 50. Drive 1 mile down to a parking lot at the trailhead (GPS: 38 27.0185, -107 20.7147).

The Hike

Two waterfalls—Chipeta Falls and "No Name Falls"—hide above Morrow Point Reservoir in the depths of the upper Black Canyon of the Gunnison River. The once-wild river is tamed by three dams, forming Blue Mesa Reservoir, Morrow Point Reservoir, and Crystal Reservoir. The falls are seen on a ranger-led boat tour twice a day, except Tuesday, from mid-June to mid-September depending on water levels. Reservations are required at Recreation.gov or at the Elk Creek Visitor Center. A fee is charged.

The amusing and informational tour, lasting 1.5 hours, offers views of impressive Chipeta Falls, fed by Corral Creek, on the canyon's north wall and "No Name Falls," fed by seasonal runoff, on the south slope.

On the boat, a park ranger discusses area geology and natural history. The boat swings past Chipeta Falls on the starboard side, and in another mile reaches famed Curecanti Needle, a granite peak jutting almost 800 feet above the lake. In another mile on the port side, "No Name Falls" may or may not make an appearance. This ephemeral waterfall is fed by runoff from Round Corral Creek to the south. The boat turns around after 7 miles at Kokanee Bay and returns to the dock.

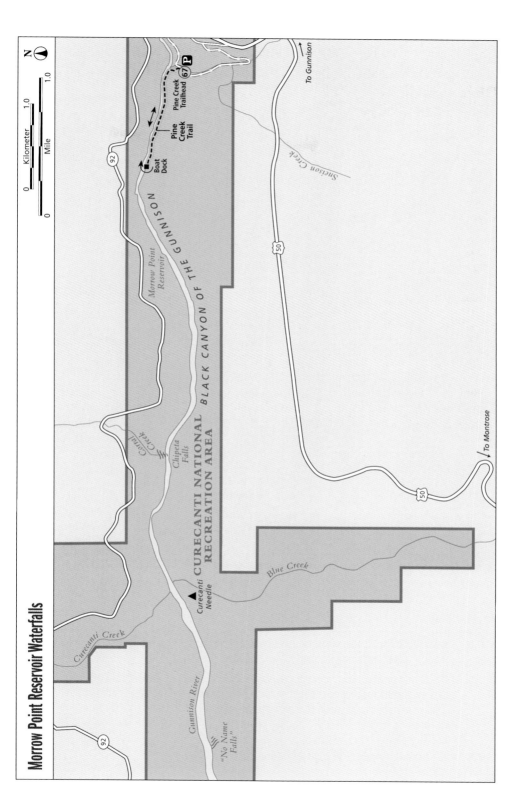

Morrow Point Reservoir Waterfalls

The Morrow Point Boat Tour takes you past Chipeta Falls in the Black Canyon of the Gunnison.

Miles and Directions

0.0 Begin at Pine Creek Trailhead. Hike down path and descend 232 steps and 180 feet.

0.1 At end of steps, hike left along trail to left of river.

0.9 Arrive at Morrow Point Boat Tour dock (GPS: 38 27.239, -107 21.471). Board the boat and enjoy the 14-mile round-trip ride. Chipeta Falls appears to the north (starboard) at 3.1 miles from dock; Curecanti Needle is straight ahead at 4.1 miles; and "No Name Falls" appears to the south (port) at 5.3 miles. Arrive back at boat dock and hike east on trail. Climb steps up to parking lot.

1.8 Arrive back at trailhead (GPS: 38 27.0185, -107 20.7147).

68 Grand Mesa Waterfalls: "Whitewater Falls," "Lands End Falls," and "Coal Creek Falls"

Grand Mesa, lording over western Colorado's desert canyons and valleys, is dotted with more than 300 shining lakes and at least three gorgeous waterfalls that plunge over the airy cliffs lining the mesa's escarpment above Grand Junction.

Start: "Whitewater Falls": unmarked trailhead at FR 102; "Lands End Falls": roadside viewing on Lands End Road (FR 100); "Coal Creek Falls": shoulder parking on FR 100
Trail: FR 102
Difficulty: Very easy/easy
Hiking time: 30 minutes to 1 hour
Distance: 1.8 miles out and back for "Whitewater Falls"; roadside for "Lands End Falls"; 0.1 mile out and back for "Coal Creek Falls"
Elevation trailhead to falls viewpoints: "Whitewater Falls": 9,972 to 9,782 feet (-190 feet) at overlook; "Lands End Falls": 9,752 feet roadside; "Coal Creek Falls": 9,935 to 9,878 feet (-57 feet) at overlook

Trail surface: Dirt, rocks
Restrictions: FR 100 (Lands End Road) is closed during winter, usually Nov to June 1; drive designated roads only; use extreme caution above falls
Amenities: Services in Grand Junction and Cedaredge; campgrounds on Grand Mesa; vault toilet at Lands End Observatory
Maps: *DeLorme* Page 43 E8; Trails Illustrated 136: Grand Mesa; USGS Mesa Lakes
County: Mesa
Land status/contact: Grand Mesa National Forest, Grand Valley Ranger District, (970) 242-8211; Grand Mesa Visitor Center, (970) 856-4153

Finding the trailhead: From I-70 east of Grand Junction, take exit 49 and drive east and south on CO 65, the Grand Mesa Scenic Byway, for 29.8 miles to a right turn on FR 100 (Lands End Road). From Cedaredge to the south, drive north on CO 65 to Grand Mesa Visitor Center. Continue 4.6 miles to a left turn on FR 100.

"Whitewater Falls": Drive 10 miles on FR 100 to a Y-junction with FR 105. Go right on FR 105 and drive 0.1 mile past Lands End Observatory. Continue for 0.4 mile to a junction on the left with FR 102, a 4WD track. Park on the road shoulder opposite the trailhead at FR 102 (GPS: 39 1.7694, -108 13.3126).

"Lands End Falls": Drive 10 miles on FR 100 to a Y-junction with FR 105. Keep left on FR 100, signed Lands End Road, and descend 0.5 mile to the waterfall's base. Park on the road shoulder where it is safe (GPS: 39 1.381, -108 13.0297).

"Coal Creek Falls": Drive 9 miles on FR 100 and park on the road shoulder past a wide bend (GPS: 39 0.4784, -108 11.6353). This parking is 1 mile east of the junction with FR 105.

The Hikes

Grand Mesa, the highest flat-topped mountain in the world, has an average elevation of 10,000 feet and is a summer oasis of cool temperatures, wildflower-filled meadows, thick forests, and more than 300 lakes. It also boasts several seldom-seen waterfalls,

"Whitewater Falls" pours off a basalt cliff on the western edge of Grand Mesa.

including "Whitewater Falls," which plunges over 150 feet off a sheer cliff. The three described waterfalls scatter along the western edge of Grand Mesa, near a point aptly named Lands End. Reach them from Lands End Road (FR 100), a gravel and paved road that runs from Grand Mesa Scenic Byway to Lands End and then descends over 5,000 feet on a twisting dirt road to US 50.

None of the waterfalls—"Whitewater Falls," "Lands End Falls," and "Coal Creek Falls"—have safe overlooks on the rim. The creeks that feed them pour over cliffs as

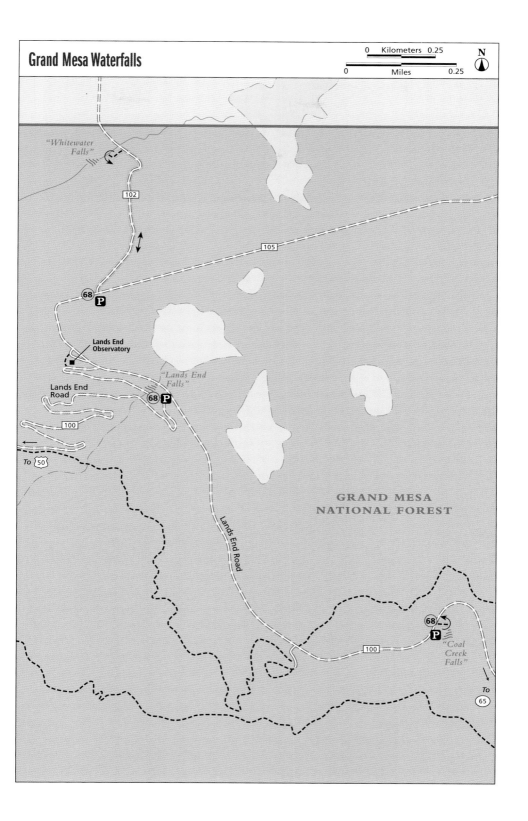

Grand Mesa Waterfalls

"Whitewater Falls"

102

105

68 P

Lands End
Observatory

"Lands End
Falls"

Lands End
Road

68 P

100

To 50

Lands End Road

GRAND MESA
NATIONAL FOREST

68
P
"Coal
Creek
Falls"

100

To
65

Kilometers 0.25
Miles 0.25

N

Left: "Lands End Falls" riffles off a cliff edge above Lands End Road.
Right: Dropping off an overhanging cliff, "Coal Creek Falls" shatters to mist in an amphitheater.

high as 200 feet, so the rimrock viewpoints are airy and scary. Use extreme caution, keep back from cliff edges, and control children and pets.

"Whitewater Falls," fed by Whitewater Creek, which drains from Somerville-McCullah Reservoir, is the most impressive Grand Mesa waterfall. The creek pours over a precipitous basalt cliff onto talus in a deep, cliff-lined amphitheater.

"Lands End Falls," a 50-foot horsetail waterfall, is a roadside attraction on Lands End Road. After the first switchback, continue down the road to talus below the falls. Park where convenient and enjoy the falling water.

"Coal Creek Falls," a mile east of Lands End Observatory, hides in a deep cul-de-sac amphitheater lined with basalt cliffs. Coal Creek, originating in hills north of the waterfall, dashes over the rimrock and falls 40 feet before dropping off an overhanging wall and turning to mist. The waterfall's total height is about 150 feet.

Miles and Directions

"Whitewater Falls"

0.0 Start at informal trailhead at junction of FR 105 and FR 102, a 4WD track, north of Lands End Observatory. Hike north on FR 102, gently losing elevation.

0.8 After descending through a band of spruce, reach junction above Whitewater Creek. Go left on another road to social trail that cuts down to lip of falls and top of high cliff.

0.9 Arrive at top of Whitewater Falls (GPS: 39 2.3199, -108 13.2496). Use extreme caution here. For a better viewpoint, cross creek and hike west on social trails along north rim of amphitheater to a high point and view of plunge waterfall.

1.8 Arrive back at trailhead (GPS: 39 1.7694, -108 13.3126).

"Coal Creek Falls"

0.0 Start at informal trailhead on shoulder of FR 100 east of Lands End Observatory. Hike northeast to canyon's west rim.

0.05 Arrive at viewpoints on canyon rim. Use extreme caution here.

0.1 Return to parking on road (GPS: 39 0.4784, -108 11.6353).

69 Big Dominguez Canyon Waterfalls: "Lower Dominguez Falls," "Middle Dominguez Falls," and Big Dominguez Falls

Big Dominguez Creek sweeps through Big Dominguez Canyon and tumbles down three distinctive falls. The first waterfall, "Lower Dominguez Falls," slides over slickrock in a wide sheet and splashes into a pool, while the second waterfall, "Middle Dominguez Falls," pours down four horsetail leaps and cascades. The final waterfall, Big Dominguez Falls, tucks among cliffs below the trail, dropping abruptly over slabs in a sparkling horsetail spray. A plunge pool and flat rock at the base provide a delightful setting.

Start: Bridgeport Trailhead
Trails: BLM Route 035, Big Dominguez Trail
Difficulty: Easy/moderate
Hiking time: About 2 hours for "Lower Dominguez Falls"; 3 hours for "Middle Dominguez Falls"; 4 hours for Big Dominguez Falls
Distance: 3.6 miles out and back for "Lower Dominguez Falls"; 5.6 miles out and back for "Middle Dominguez Falls"; 6.2 miles out and back for Big Dominguez Falls
Elevation trailhead to falls viewpoints: 4,720 to 4,750 feet (+30 feet) for "Lower Dominguez Falls"; to 4,890 feet (+170 feet) for "Middle Dominguez Falls"; to 4,920 feet (+200 feet) for base of Big Dominguez Falls; to 4,950 feet (+230 feet) for top of Big Dominguez Falls

Trail surface: Gravel, dirt, sand
Restrictions: No bicycles or motor vehicles; river campers must carry personal potties for waste removal and use fire pans for campfires; follow wilderness regulations
Amenities: Backcountry camping; trailhead porta-potty; services in Grand Junction and Delta
Maps: *DeLorme:* Page 55 B6; Trails Illustrated 147: Uncompahgre Plateau North [Uncompahgre National Forest]; USGS Dominguez, Triangle Mesa
County: Mesa
Land status/contact: Dominguez-Escalante National Conservation Area; BLM, Grand Junction Field Office, (970) 244-3000

Finding the trailhead: From the intersection of US 50 and CO 141 in Grand Junction, take US 50 east toward Delta/Montrose. Drive 20 miles and turn right (west) on gravel Bridgeport Road and into the Dominguez-Escalante National Conservation Area. Go 3.3 miles to a parking lot at road's end by railroad tracks. Do not block the gate at the trailhead entrance (GPS: 38 50.947, -108 22.340).

The Hike

Begin at the trailhead on the south side of the parking lot. Hike south on a gravel road on Union Pacific Railroad property. Observe posted warnings about the dangers of the tracks and trains. Follow the road along the Gunnison River and cross the tracks at a designated crossing. After leaving the tracks, cross a footbridge over the river and hike south to Big Dominguez Canyon. Turn right on Big Dominguez Trail

Left: Big Dominguez Falls drops abruptly over slabs in a fantastical horsetail spray.
Right: "Middle Dominguez Falls" pours through a scenic viewing area in a series of leaps and cascades.

to "Lower Dominguez Falls." Formed by a diversion dam, the 20-foot waterfall is best observed from above.

Continue on the trail to the junction of Little Dominguez Canyon and Big Dominguez Canyon. Keep right and follow the trail up Big Dominguez to the second falls, "Middle Dominguez Falls," to the trail's left. Enjoy the playful splatter of the cascades below.

Return to the trail and continue 0.1 mile to a social trail on the left that climbs a rise, drops to the creek bed, and crosses the creek. If conditions allow, follow the path to a viewpoint across from Big Dominguez Falls. If you descend to the waterfall's base, wade up the creek for the best vantage point. Use extreme care, and don't descend to the creek if conditions are icy or the water is high. To view the falls from above, return to the main trail and continue for 0.2 mile to rock slabs on the left, overlooking Big Dominguez Falls. Stay clear of wet and icy slabs above the falls and cliffs.

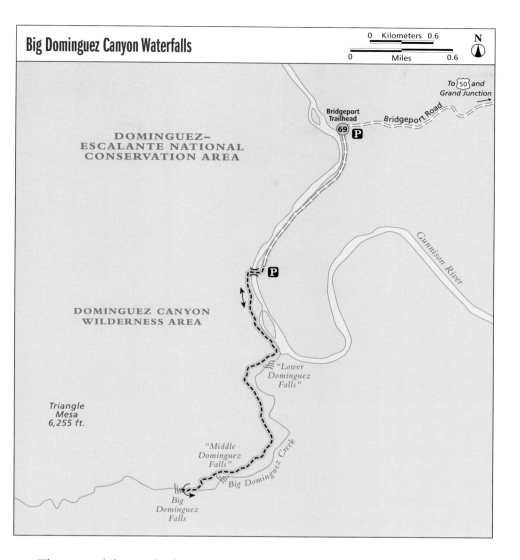

The sunny hike can be hot, with only occasional shade trees by bluffs and boulders. Bring a trekking pole and water shoes if conditions are safe enough to cross the creek to the waterfall's base.

For a longer outing, continue west to ancient Native American petroglyphs on trailside boulders.

Miles and Directions

0.0 Begin at Bridgeport Trailhead and go left on closed gravel road (BLM Route 035) along railroad tracks.

0.3 Cross tracks at designated crossing and continue on road.

"Lower Dominguez Falls" pours off a bedrock bench into a tight canyon.

1.0 Turn right to trail register and info sign. Cross marked footbridge over Gunnison River, then continue hiking south along river's west side.

1.7 Turn right from river and follow Big Dominguez Trail to a kiosk. Enter Big Dominguez Canyon and Dominguez Canyon Wilderness boundary at gate.

1.8 Reach "Lower Dominguez Falls" (GPS: 38 49.725, -108 22.813). Continue on trail.

2.4 Reach junction of Little Dominguez Canyon and Big Dominguez Canyon. Bear right (southwest) and hike trail up Big Dominguez Canyon.

2.8 Reach "Middle Dominguez Falls" (GPS: 38 49.127, -108 23.104). Continue on trail.

2.9 Leave main trail for a social trail to left; hike over ridge and down to creek bed. Cross creek and continue on social trail with creek on your right.

3.1 Arrive at base of Big Dominguez Falls (GPS: 38 49.024, -108 23.369). Alternatively, stay on main trail to top of falls, located left of trail (GPS: 38 49.070, -108 23.332). Do not attempt to reach top of falls from base, or base from top. Use the trails. Return the way you came.

6.2 Arrive back at trailhead (GPS: 38 50.947, -108 22.340).

70 No Thoroughfare Canyon Waterfalls: "Pool Fall," "No Thoroughfare Canyon First Waterfall," and "No Thoroughfare Canyon Second Waterfall"

Three hidden waterfalls lie deep within No Thoroughfare Canyon at Colorado National Monument. The falls, best seen in spring and early summer, plummet over sandstone cliffs. It's an unforgettable experience to hike up a dry canyon to an oasis with a waterfall, tall cottonwoods, and the sweet smell of water.

Start: Devils Kitchen Trailhead
Trail: No Thoroughfare Canyon Trail
Difficulty: Easy for "Pool Fall"; moderate for "First Waterfall" and "Second Waterfall"
Hiking time: About 2 hours for "Pool Fall"; 3 hours for "First Waterfall"; 4 hours for "Second Waterfall"
Distance: 2.2 miles out and back for "Pool Fall"; 3.8 miles out and back for "First Waterfall"; 6.2 miles out and back for "Second Waterfall"
Elevation trailhead to falls viewpoints: 5,020 to 5,070 feet (+50 feet) for "Pool Fall"; to 5,260 feet (+240 feet) for "First Waterfall"; to 5,630 feet (+610 feet) for "Second Waterfall"

Trail surface: Dirt, sand, rocks
Restrictions: Entrance fee; no pets, bicycles, campfires, or alcohol
Amenities: Toilets at Devils Kitchen Picnic Area; Saddlehorn Campground near monument's west entrance; services in Grand Junction
Maps: *DeLorme:* Page 42 E4; Trails Illustrated 208: Colorado National Monument [McInnis Canyons National Conservation Area]; USGS Colorado National Monument
County: Mesa
Land status/contact: Colorado National Monument, (970) 858-3617

Finding the trailhead: From I-70 in Grand Junction, take exit 31 (Horizon Drive) and follow signs to the east entrance of Colorado National Monument. Or, from the intersection of Grand Avenue and North 1st Street in Grand Junction, take Grand Avenue West for 0.9 mile and turn left on Monument Road. Drive 3.5 miles to the east entrance station to the monument. Continue 0.3 mile to parking at Devils Kitchen Trailhead on the road's left side (GPS: 39 01.904, -108 37.840). Additional parking is at Devils Kitchen Picnic Area to the west.

The Hike

No Thoroughfare Canyon, at 8.5 miles long, is Colorado National Monument's longest canyon. Sculpted by No Throughfare Creek, the awesome gash is lined with towering sandstone cliffs, jutting pinnacles, and boulder-strewn shale slopes. The creek also tumbles over dark cliffs, forming three waterfalls.

The first, dubbed "Pool Fall," pours over a cleft into a punchbowl carved in bedrock. Many hikers opt for the easy trek out to this small waterfall, and then return to

No Thoroughfare Canyon Waterfalls

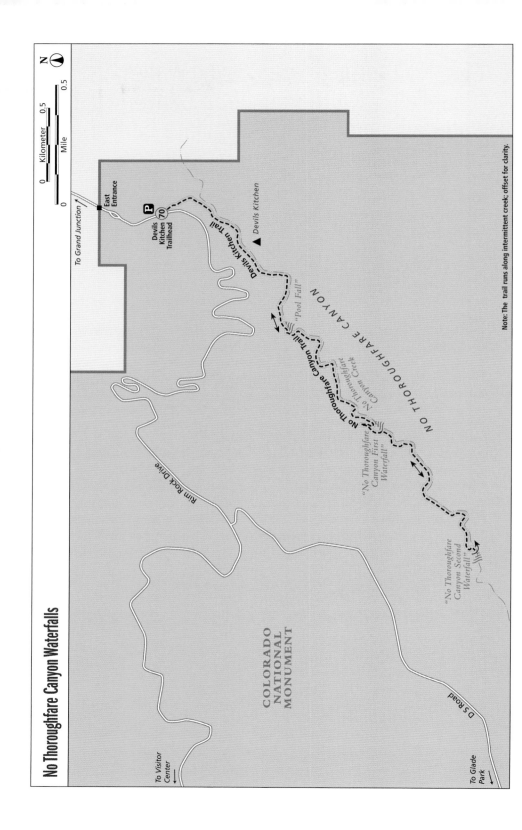

Note: The trail runs along intermittent creek; offset for clarity.

Left: No Thoroughfare Canyon Creek carves a punchbowl into ancient bedrock at "Pool Fall."
Center: Whitewater dances down a cliff at "No Thoroughfare Canyon First Waterfall."
Right: "No Thoroughfare Canyon Second Waterfall" is the hike's turnaround point.

the trailhead. Less than a mile west, the creek drops over 100 feet down a vertical cliff in a plunge, sheet, or ribbon falls—depending on water flow—into a plunge pool below "No Thoroughfare Canyon First Waterfall." More punchbowls adorn the creek's bedrock above these falls. Intrepid hikers continue up the trail to "No Thoroughfare Canyon Second Waterfall," which tumbles over 200 feet in a two-tiered horsetail into a plunge pool, and then return to the trailhead for a three-waterfall hike.

The hike is sunny and hot, with only intermittent shade from cottonwood trees. Bring sun protection, wear a hat, and carry plenty of water. If weather threatens, avoid the hike since flash floods strike quickly.

Miles and Directions

0.0 Begin at Devils Kitchen Trailhead and follow signs for No Thoroughfare Canyon Trail.

0.1 Reach junction with Old Gordon Trail. Keep right on No Thoroughfare Canyon Trail.

0.3 Reach junction with Devils Kitchen Trail on left (GPS: 39 1.7151, -108 37.8393). Go right on No Thoroughfare Canyon Trail.

1.1 Reach "Pool Fall" (GPS: 39 1.411, -108 38.454). Take trail to right with sign for "No Thoroughfare Canyon First Waterfall," climb steps, and follow worn trail west.

1.9 Reach "No Thoroughfare Canyon First Waterfall," the most scenic of the three falls and the end of good trail (GPS: 39 1.054, -108 38.973). Climb steep, unmaintained trail to right; don't dislodge rocks on hikers below. Reach top of second falls.

2.0 View bedrock punchbowls left of trail above falls. Cross slabs, with creek to left, to rejoin trail. Do not go up social trails to right—stay along creek. Follow trail southwest.

3.1 Reach "No Thoroughfare Canyon Second Waterfall" and turnaround point in deep canyon (GPS: 39 00.676, -108 39.604). Return the way you came.

6.2 Arrive back at trailhead (GPS: 39 01.904, -108 37.840).

71 "Little Dolores Falls"

"Little Dolores Falls," a tiered waterfall on the Little Dolores River southwest of Grand Junction, is reached by a short trail down bedrock to several viewpoints and the base of the largest waterfall.

Start: Unmarked trailhead at end of access road
Trail: Unnamed trail
Difficulty: Easy
Hiking time: About 30 minutes
Distance: 0.4 mile out and back
Elevation trailhead to falls base: 6,685 to 6,630 feet (-55 feet)
Trail surface: Dirt, rocks
Restrictions: Park at trailhead or on access road; do not drive closed roads; cliff jumping and swimming not recommended; no glass bottles; unfenced viewpoints; avoid high water
Amenities: Services in Grand Junction and Fruita; camping at Colorado National Monument
Maps: *DeLorme:* Page 54 A2; Trails Illustrated 208: Colorado National Monument [McInnis Canyons National Conservation Area]; USGS Payne Wash, Beiser Creek
County: Mesa
Land status/contact: BLM, Grand Junction Field Office, (970) 244-3000

Finding the trailhead: Approach from Grand Junction by driving CO 340 to a left turn on Monument Road. Drive to the east entrance of Colorado National Monument. A fee is not charged if you are going to Glade Park. Drive up Rim Rock Road for 3.8 miles to a junction past Cold Shivers Point. Turn left on DS Road, marked "Glade Park," and drive 5.7 miles to Glade Park. Continue west on DS Road for 8 miles and turn left (south) on 9⁹⁄₁₀ Road. Drive 2.4 miles on the dirt road to an unmarked right turn. Follow the dirt road, keeping right at the first fork, for 0.2 mile to parking and the trailhead at steel posts and rocks (GPS: 38 57.8506, -108 52.4494).

The Hike

"Little Dolores Falls" offers four leaps that drop into pools in giant potholes sculpted by the Little Dolores River, a 41-mile river that begins on Piñon Mesa and drains into the Dolores River in Utah. The upper falls is a 20-foot cascade through polished potholes to a 3-foot drop into a pool; the middle falls area includes a 15-foot plunge into a huge pothole and a 6-foot falls into a smaller hole; the dramatic lower 25-foot waterfall pours through a chute to the lowest pool. The falls are sculpted in Precambrian basement granite, the remains of a 1.5-billion-year-old mountain range.

Unlike most desert falls, this waterfall oasis, fed by snowmelt and springs, flows year-round. Spring is the best time to visit, when deep water fills the falls. This waterfall, locally called the Potholes, is a popular cliff jumping and swimming hole in summer. A sign above the falls, however, warns of its dangers, including shallow, swift water. Severe injuries and fatalities regularly occur here, so use extreme caution before swimming and remember, there is no cell service for emergency calls.

Above: "Little Dolores Falls" plunges into a deep pool carved into ancient bedrock on the Uncompahgre Plateau.
Right: "Little Dolores Falls," tucked into a narrow canyon, drops over five ledges interrupted by glassy plunge pools.

The easy hike begins at an unmarked trailhead at the end of the access road. Other roads in the area have been closed by the BLM, though closures are ignored by summer visitors. Walk down a closed road to a left turn on an unmarked trail that descends west on bedrock on the waterfall's eastern rim. Check out the falls and potholes below from various viewpoints, but be aware of drop-offs and slick rock to avoid tumbling into the river. A short trail heads north from the bedrock rim and descends through trees to the plunge pool below the lower falls.

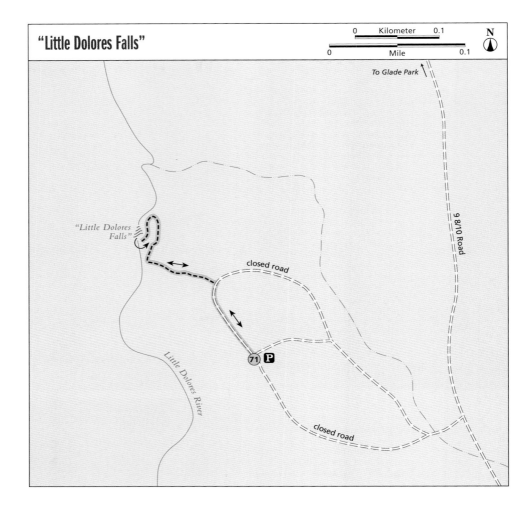

0   Kilometer   0.1

0   Mile   0.1

N

To Glade Park

9 8/10 Road

"Little Dolores Falls"

closed road

71 P

Little Dolores River

closed road

Miles and Directions

0.0   Start at unmarked trailhead by five metal posts and large rocks. Go right down closed road.

0.05 Turn left opposite illegal parking spots and hike west down bedrock to sign that says, "Danger, Steep Cliffs, Shallow and Swift Water." Continue down bedrock.

0.1   Reach overlook above falls on cliff edge (GPS: 38 57.9124, -108 52.5377). Use caution on slippery rock.

0.2   Hike north across bedrock slabs to trail that leads to base of lower falls (GPS: 38 57.9263, -108 52.5415). Return up trail to slabs.

0.3   Reach overlook and go left up trail to closed road.

0.35 Go right on road.

0.4   Arrive back at trailhead (GPS: 38 57.8506, -108 52.4494).

The Northwest
Maybell, Meeker, Steamboat Springs, Rifle, Glenwood Springs, Redstone, and Vail

A whitewater maelstrom rages over Gold Creek Falls in the Mount Zirkel Wilderness.

72 "Vermillion Creek Falls" and "Lower Vermillion Creek Falls"

Fed by Vermillion Creek, "Vermillion Creek Falls" and its smaller neighbor, "Lower Vermillion Creek Falls," offer the sound and scent of falling water in an arid basin northeast of Dinosaur National Monument.

Start: Unofficial trailhead
Trail: Unnamed road
Difficulty: Easy
Hiking time: About 30 minutes
Distance: 0.7 mile out and back
Elevation trailhead to falls base: 5,673 to 5,605 feet (-68 feet)
Trail surface: Dirt
Restrictions: Park off highway; do not drive closed roads; no glass bottles

Amenities: Services in Craig; limited services in Maybell
Maps: *DeLorme:* Page 12 C2 and C3; Trails Illustrated 220: Dinosaur National Monument; USGS Jack Springs
County: Moffat
Land status/contact: BLM, Little Snake Field Office, (970) 826-5000

Finding the trailhead: From Maybell on US 40 between Craig and Dinosaur, turn northwest on CO 318 and drive 40.6 miles to a left turn on an unmarked dirt road after the highway crosses a bridge over Vermillion Creek. Drive 100 feet and park. Do not drive on the closed road because there are sinkholes, some unseen below the surface. Trailhead is at a road closure sign (GPS: 40 43.4134, -108 45.257).

To see "Lower Vermillion Creek Falls," drive 5.6 miles west on CO 318 from the "Vermillion Creek Falls" turnoff to the old Browns Park School. Turn left on dirt CR 34N and drive 0.7 mile to a bridge (GPS: 40 45.4036, -108 49.9418). Park on the shoulder. The falls is below. Scramble down the right side of the creek to the lower falls and pool.

The Hike

"Vermillion Creek Falls" dashes 40 feet off a sandstone shelf into a muddy pool lined with willows, talus, and cliffs in a remote canyon in northwestern Colorado. Vermillion Creek, originating to the north on upland plateaus in southern Wyoming, twists south through cliff-lined canyons before bending northwest to the waterfall and continuing to the Green River in Browns Park. "Vermillion Creek Falls," while far from any towns, is not difficult to see, hiding a short distance from a state highway. It can also be seen from a pullout on the highway's south side 0.3 mile west of the trailhead turnoff.

The hike starts at an informal trailhead at a BLM closure sign, where a rough road to the falls begins. In early 2021 the BLM closed the road to vehicles because "subsurface erosion has resulted in deep sinkholes in the roadbed." The BLM warns that road sections could fall into hidden sinkholes. It is, however, safe to walk on the closed road.

"Vermillion Creek Falls" is a remote desert waterfall near Dinosaur National Monument.

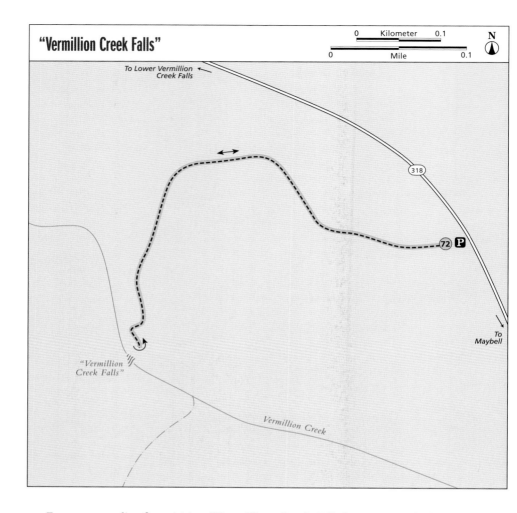

"Vermillion Creek Falls"

For extra credit after visiting "Vermillion Creek Falls," stop at roadside "Lower Vermillion Creek Falls," 5 miles downstream. This cascade over bedrock and concrete chunks, lying below the stone abutments of an old bridge, ends in a 3-foot waterfall off a ledge into a small pool. The cascade is below a road, which heads south to CR 34 and on to the Gates of Lodore in Dinosaur National Monument.

Miles and Directions

0.0 Start at unmarked trailhead at road closure signs in middle of closed dirt road. Hike southwest on dirt road.

0.07 Reach junction. Go right on rutted road and descend edge of bluff. Bend south to pool below falls.

0.35 Reach base of waterfall (GPS: 40 43.3514, -108 45.478). Return on road, gaining 68 feet of elevation.

0.7 Arrive back at trailhead (GPS: 40 43.4134, -108 45.257).

73 Bessies Falls

Cascading down a gully in a glacier-carved valley, Bessies Falls leaps over cliffs and dashes down grassy slopes above Big Fish Lake Trail in the Flat Tops Wilderness.

Start: Big Fish Trailhead
Trail: Big Fish Trail #1819
Difficulty: Moderate
Hiking time: 2–3 hours
Distance: 4.3 miles out and back
Elevation trailhead to falls viewpoints: 8,872 to 9,098 feet (+226 feet) for viewpoint; to 9,620 feet (+748 feet) for top of falls
Trail surface: Dirt
Restrictions: Observe wilderness regulations; no motorized vehicles or equipment; dogs must be under control

Amenities: Vault toilets at Himes Peak Campground
Maps: *DeLorme:* Page 35 A8; Trails Illustrated 150: Flat Tops North; USGS Ripple Creek, Big Marvine Peak
County: Garfield
Land status/contact: Flat Tops Wilderness Area; White River National Forest, (970) 945-2521; Blanco Ranger District, (970) 878-4039

Finding the trailhead: From Meeker, drive northeast on CO 13 for 1 mile and turn right on Rio Blanco CR 8. Drive east up the North Fork of the White River valley for 39 miles. Turn right on Trappers Lake Road (FR 205) and drive 6 miles to the Himes Peak Campground turnoff on the right. Follow the campground access road down to the signed Big Fish Trailhead at the campground entrance and a parking lot (GPS: 40 1.6597, -107 16.305).

The trailhead is also reached on the Flat Tops Trail Scenic Byway from Yampa on CO 131. This 47-mile route follows dirt roads. Allow 2.5 hours to drive from Yampa to the trailhead.

The Hike

Bessies Falls, fed by a spring and snowmelt on the west shoulder of 11,201-foot Himes Peak, cascades down a steep ravine on the eastern wall of a glaciated valley in the Flat Tops Wilderness, Colorado's third-largest wilderness area. The unnamed creek, falling almost 500 feet to the valley floor, is a series of short frothy drops punctuated by several larger leaps, one almost 40 feet high. As the trail heads up the valley, watch for the falls up left. It's best to admire the waterfall from a distance, since the steep mountainside is covered with deadfall. After a waterfall break, continue another mile up the trail to Big Fish Lake, a gorgeous lake tucked in the upper cirque at 9,388 feet, or retrace your footsteps down to the trailhead.

The area was severely burned by the Fish Creek Fire, which began in July 2002 after a lightning strike near Fish Creek Lake ignited deadfall. The fire eventually consumed 17,056 acres in the wilderness area and surrounding mountains, including the Trappers Lake area and the original Trappers Lake Lodge. The Big Fish Trail to the waterfall and Big Fish Lake passes through the burned area with standing dead snags,

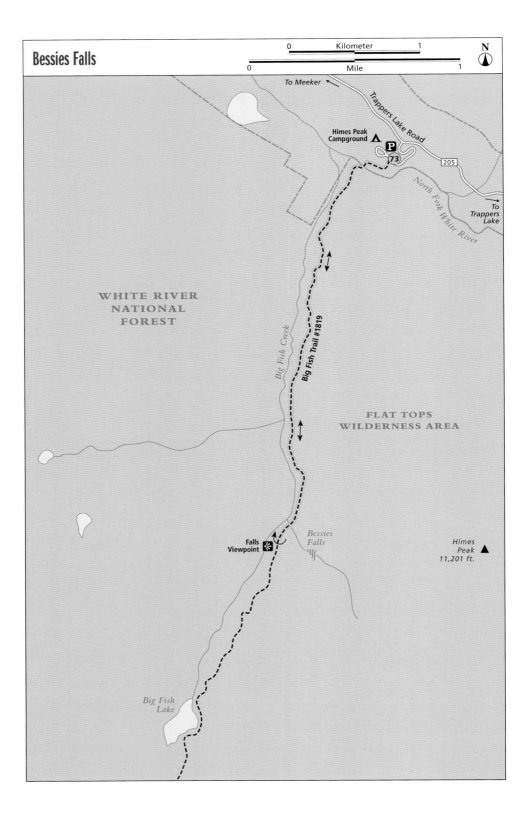

Bessies Falls

0 Kilometer 1

0 Mile 1

N

To Meeker

Trappers Lake Road

Himes Peak Campground

P

73

205

North Fork White River

To Trappers Lake

WHITE RIVER NATIONAL FOREST

Big Fish Creek

Big Fish Trail #1819

FLAT TOPS WILDERNESS AREA

Falls Viewpoint

Bessies Falls

Himes Peak 11,201 ft.

Big Fish Lake

Deadfall from the Fish Creek Fire surrounds cascades and waterfalls at Bessies Falls.

fallen trunks, aspen groves, and open meadows decorated with wildflowers, including masses of columbine, in June and July.

Miles and Directions

0.0 Start at Big Fish Trailhead at Himes Peak Campground. Hike downhill to North Fork White River.

0.15 Cross White River on footbridge and climb hill.

0.2 Reach Flat Tops Wilderness boundary (GPS: 40 1.6304, -107 16.4903). Go through gate and hike south on singletrack trail in meadows left of willow-lined Big Fish Creek. Trail crosses several small side creeks.

2.0 Reach creek crossing below Bessies Falls. Do not attempt in high water.

2.05 Arrive at first viewpoint of falls from meadow next to trail past creek.

2.15 Arrive at second viewpoint of falls by clump of spruce (GPS: 40 0.0794, -107 16.9064). Return the way you came.

4.3 Arrive back at trailhead (GPS: 40 1.6597, -107 16.305).

74 Fish Creek Waterfalls: Fish Creek Falls and "Upper Fish Creek Falls"

A paved overlook and down-and-up hike offer views of the many tiers of Fish Creek Falls. A short, easy hike delights visitors, but the most breathtaking views lie at the upper leaps, more than 1,000 feet higher on Fish Creek Falls National Recreation Trail.

Start: Fish Creek Falls Overlook Trailhead; Fish Creek Falls Trailhead

Trails: Overlook Trail #1102.1A, Fish Creek National Recreation Trail #1102.1

Difficulty: Very easy to overlook and base of Fish Creek Falls; moderate to "Upper Fish Creek Falls" or to combine overlook, falls, and upper falls in a loop

Hiking time: Less than 1 hour for hikes to overlook and base of falls; about 3 hours for hike to upper falls or to combine all 3

Distance: 0.6 mile out and back to falls overlook; 0.6 mile out and back to base of falls; 1.0 mile to combine hikes to overlook and base of falls; 4.4 miles out and back to upper falls; 5.0 miles to combine hikes to overlook, base of falls, and upper falls

Elevation trailhead to falls viewpoints: 7,530 to 7,550 feet (+20 feet) to falls overlook; 7,550 to 7,420 feet (-130 feet) to base of falls; 7,550 to 8,680 feet (+1,130 feet) to upper falls

Trail surface: Paved to overlook; paved and dirt to falls base; dirt and rocks to upper falls

Restrictions: Fee area, self-service pay station; day use only; hours 6 a.m. to 8 p.m.; no bicycles on paved trail; leashed dogs only; observe wilderness regulations

Amenities: Vault toilets; potable water; benches; picnic area; interpretive signs; bicycle rack; wheelchair access to overlook; services in Steamboat Springs

Maps: *DeLorme:* Page 26 A4; Trails Illustrated 117: Clark, Buffalo Pass; USGS Steamboat Springs

County: Routt

Land status/contact: Fish Creek Falls Recreation Area, Routt National Forest, (307) 745-2300; Hahns Peak/Bears Ears Ranger District, (970) 870-2299

Finding the trailhead: In Steamboat Springs, take US 40 (Lincoln Avenue) to 3rd Street. Go north on 3rd Street for 0.1 mile and take the first right onto Fish Creek Falls Road. Follow Fish Creek Falls Road for 2.8 miles to the Fish Creek Falls Recreation Area pay station, and then continue 0.2 mile to the upper parking lot. The trailheads for the Fish Creek Falls Overlook (GPS: 40 28.905, -106 46.608) and the trail to "Upper Fish Creek Falls" (GPS: 40 28.9, -106 46.573) begin here.

The Hike

Hiding in a deep canyon a few minutes from Steamboat Springs, Fish Creek Falls plummets 280 feet in two dramatic leaps into a cliff-lined canyon. The short, paved Overlook Trail, accessible by wheelchairs and strollers, leads to a dramatic overlook. For more adventure, descend Fish Creek Falls National Recreation Trail to a historic

The Overlook Trail offers stunning views of Fish Creek Falls by Steamboat Springs.

bridge with another stunning view, and then continue up Fish Creek Canyon on a strenuous trail to the spectacular upper falls.

The Overlook Trail is an easy, kid-friendly way to enjoy awesome views of an impressive waterfall. There are informative signs to read, and a picnic area off the trail

Fish Creek Waterfalls: Fish Creek Falls and "Upper Fish Creek Falls"

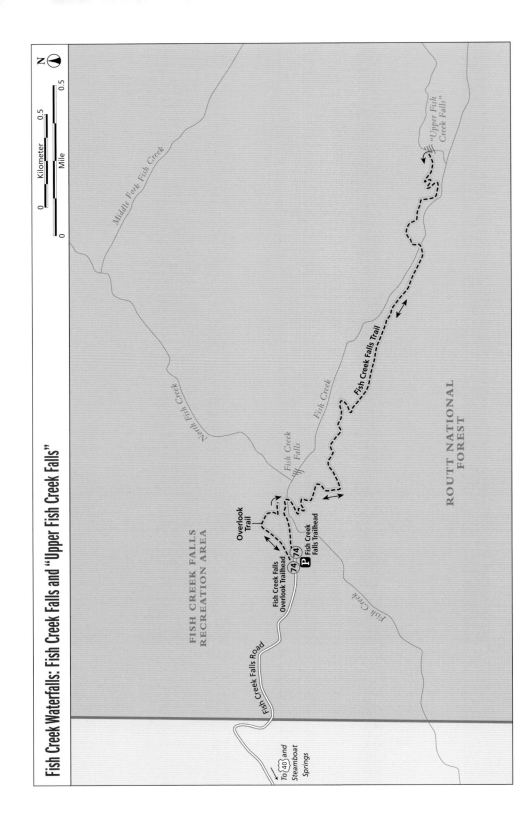

if you packed lunch. For a longer outing, descend 0.2-mile Picnic Trail, passing picnic tables, to the waterfall's base at a footbridge over Fish Creek. Bring a camera, as the shimmering plunge makes a picture-perfect backdrop for family outings.

To reach "Upper Fish Creek Falls," continue from the footbridge or start at Fish Creek Falls Trailhead at the parking lot's eastern edge. From the bridge, Fish Creek Falls National Recreation Trail ascends steeply through the forest along the creek's south side. Pass shady groves of aspen and fir, and then cross a second footbridge to the creek's north bank. The trail grows faint and crosses slabs but listen for the roar of the falls and you'll find them over a rise ahead. The top leap plunges over the hillside and collapses in multiple segments that pool and funnel through rock, then drop into the abyss. This is a waterfall that takes you by surprise with its power and beauty. Sit for a while and enjoy it.

The longer hike to "Upper Fish Creek Falls" is worth the extra effort.

Miles and Directions

Falls Overlook with Option to Base of Falls

0.0   Begin at Overlook Trailhead, located at northeastern edge of parking lot. Walk east on paved Fish Creek Falls Overlook Trail to the overlook, enjoying interpretive signs along the way.

0.3   Arrive at Falls Overlook (GPS: 40 28.9459, -106 46.382). Return the way you came. Alternatively, backtrack to paved Picnic Trail that drops left to restrooms and a picnic area. From there, turn left on dirt Fish Creek Falls Trail and continue 0.12 mile to base of falls, and then return to parking lot.

0.6   Arrive back at trailhead (GPS: 40 28.905, -106 46.608).

Base of Fish Creek Falls and "Upper Fish Creek Falls"

0.0   Begin at Fish Creek Falls Trailhead on east end of parking lot (GPS: 40 28.9001, -106 46.5737). Hike east down Fish Creek Falls Trail. Pass cutoffs to restrooms, picnic area, and overlook.

0.2   Arrive at main bridge over Fish Creek and best viewpoint of Fish Creek Falls (GPS: 40 28.922, -106 46.365). Turn around here and return to trailhead for 0.4-mile round-trip hike, or continue across bridge and follow trail to upper falls.

1.7   Cross second bridge over Fish Creek.

2.2   Reach "Upper Fish Creek Falls" (GPS: 40 28.526, -106 45.059). Return the way you came.

4.4   Arrive back at trailhead (GPS: 40 28.9, -106 46.573).

75 "Gold Creek Falls"

"Gold Creek Falls" is a two-tiered waterfall that pours over rock ledges in a canyon in the heart of the 159,935-acre Mount Zirkel Wilderness north of Steamboat Springs.

Start: Slavonia Trailhead
Trails: Gilpin Trail #1161, Gold Creek Lake Trail #1150.1
Difficulty: Moderate
Hiking time: About 3 hours
Distance: 3.6 miles out and back
Elevation trailhead to falls viewpoints: 8,428 to 8,887 feet (+459 feet)
Trail surface: Dirt, rocks
Restrictions: Observe wilderness regulations; dogs must be under control or on leash; group size limited to 15; stay on trail; no bicycles or motorized vehicles
Amenities: Vault toilets at trailhead; nearby campgrounds and dispersed campsites
Maps: *DeLorme:* Page 17 C5; Trails Illustrated 116: Hahns Peak, Steamboat Lake; USGS Mount Zirkel
County: Routt
Land status/contact: Routt National Forest, (307) 745-2300; Hahns Peak/Bears Ears Ranger District, (970) 870-2299

Finding the trailhead: From Steamboat Springs, drive west on US 40 to Elk River Road (CR 129) on the west edge of Steamboat and turn right. Drive north for 17.6 miles on CR 129, through Clark to Glen Ellen, and turn right on Seedhouse Road (CR 60), which turns into FR 400 in Routt National Forest. Continue northeast on the paved and dirt road for 11.8 miles to Slavonia Trailhead and parking at the road's end (GPS: 40 46.989, -106 43.372).

The Hike

Gold Creek, fed by snowmelt on the western crest of the Park Range south of 12,180-foot Mount Zirkel, runs southwest down a glaciated valley to turbulent "Gold Creek Falls," a double waterfall with a 35-foot drop on the upper falls and 15 feet on the lower. Below the falls, the creek dashes steeply down a narrow canyon in an almost continuous whitewater torrent before joining Gilpin Creek to form the Middle Fork of the Elk River. Come early in June to see the waterfall at peak flow. The popular trail to "Gold Creek Falls" is easy to follow and has gentle grades. It's busy on weekends so arrive early at the trailhead. Another waterfall lies up a tributary creek west of Gold Creek Lake. After reveling in the water's roar, return down the trail or continue up another mile to picturesque 5-acre Gold Creek Lake.

Miles and Directions

0.0 Start at Slavonia Trailhead on northeast side of parking lot. Hike straight on signed Gilpin Trail.

0.15 Reach junction with signed Gold Creek Lake Trail on right. Sign in at register box and go right on Gold Creek Lake Trail. Hike southeast through aspen grove.

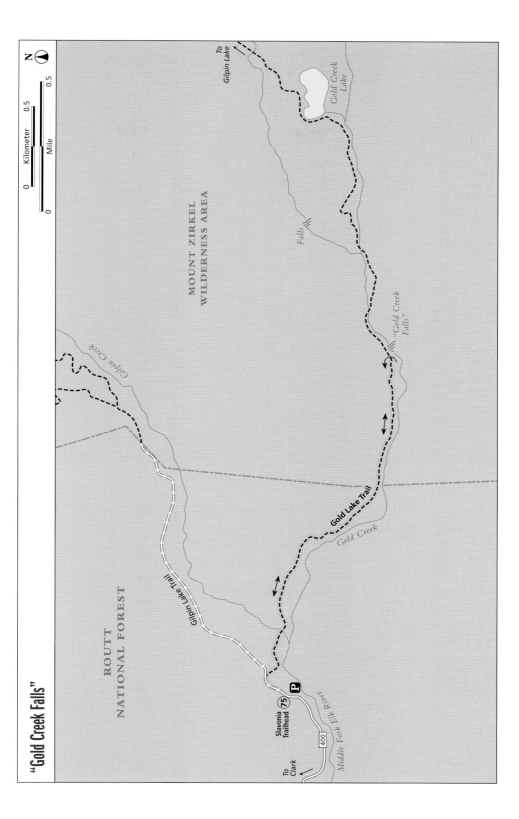

"Gold Creek Falls"

ROUTT NATIONAL FOREST

MOUNT ZIRKEL WILDERNESS AREA

Gilpin Creek

Gilpin Lake Trail

Gold Lake Trail

Gold Creek

"Gold Creek Falls"

Falls

Gold Creek Lake

To Gilpin Lake

Slavonia Trailhead 75

Middle Fork Elk River

To Clark

400

N

0   Kilometer   0.5

0   Mile   0.5

"Gold Creek Falls" is a torrent of whitewater along the Gold Creek Lake Trail.

0.4 Cross rushing Gilpin Creek on footbridge (GPS: 40 47.0078, -106 43.0908). Continue straight.

1.0 Stop at airy overlook atop cliff high above Gold Creek in canyon below.

1.2 Reach Mount Zirkel Wilderness boundary, marked with a wooden sign (GPS: 40 46.7128, -108 42.4928).

1.4 Reach edge of Gold Creek's north bank. Continue east on trail, steadily climbing wooded slopes.

1.8 Arrive at flat rock overlook above "Gold Creek Falls" and plunge pool (GPS: 40 46.6622, -108 41.896). After enjoying falls, return west on trail.

3.6 Arrive back at trailhead (GPS: 40 46.989, -106 43.372).

76 Rifle Falls

Limestone cliffs at Rifle Falls State Park provide a lofty ledge for three dramatic leaps at Rifle Falls. This segmented plunge, fed by East Rifle Creek, is an ostentatious show of waterfall wonder and not to be missed on a hiking tour of Colorado's best falls.

Start: Coyote Trailhead
Trail: Coyote Trail
Difficulty: Very easy
Hiking time: Less than 1 hour
Distance: 0.2 mile out and back to falls base; 0.7-mile loop for Coyote Trail
Elevation trailhead to falls viewpoints:
Minimal to base of falls; 6,510 to 6,610 feet (+100 feet) to top of falls on Coyote Trail
Trail surface: Dirt, rocks, paved walk, catwalk
Restrictions: Fee area, self-serve kiosk if no attendant at gate; pets allowed on 6-foot leash maximum except in wildlife area

Amenities: Wheelchair access to base of falls; park campground, restrooms, picnic areas; trailside benches and interpretive signs; Rifle Gap State Park Visitor Center 4 miles south of Rifle Falls; services in Rifle
Maps: *DeLorme:* Page 34 D4; Trails Illustrated 151: Flat Tops South; USGS Rifle Falls
County: Garfield
Land status/contact: Rifle Falls State Park, (970) 625-1607

Finding the trailhead: From Rifle, take Railroad Avenue north and bear right on CO 13 North. Go 2 miles and turn right on CO 325 North. Drive 9.6 miles to Rifle Falls State Park, on the right. The parking lot and trailhead are at the end of the paved road (GPS: 39 40.580, -107 41.955).

Left: The Coyote Trail offers unique views of the flowing waters of Rifle Falls.
Center: East Rifle Creek plunges over a 70-foot cliff at Rifle Falls State Park.
Right: Limestone cliffs provide a lofty ledge for three dramatic leaps at Rifle Falls.

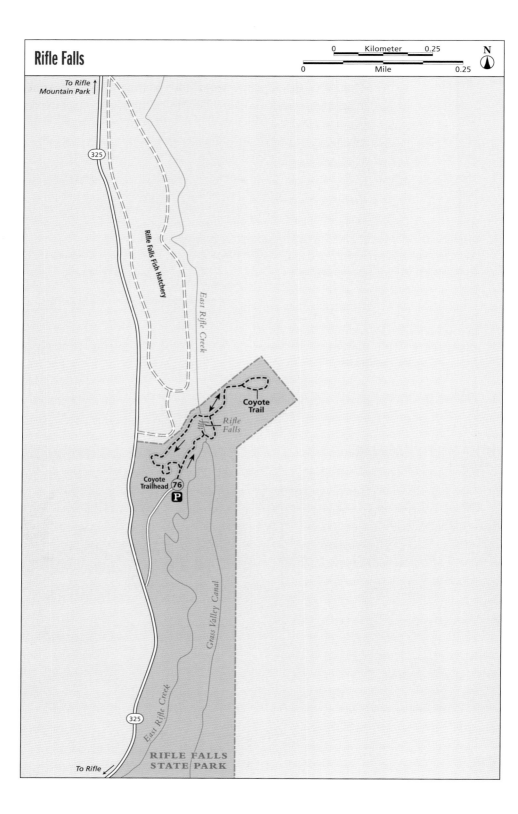

Rifle Falls

The Hike

East Rifle Creek rushes down a limestone canyon before pouring over a travertine curtain in three 70-foot waterfalls at Rifle Falls State Park. The water thunders off broken rocks below, filling the air with fine mist. Park rangers call the idyllic park "Colorado's Hawaii," with ferns filling moist crevices, thick mats of spray-drenched grass and moss on boulders beneath the falls, garter snakes and frogs in wet grass, and the air perfumed with the smell of water. The falls are unnatural, created in the 1920s when a small power plant diverted the creek's flow over the cliff.

The first section of the Coyote Trail is paved and ADA wheelchair accessible to the waterfall's base. Follow a paved walkway along the creek for a closer look below the falls. The rest of the hike wraps around the right side of a cliff, passing shallow caves, and climbs to a fenced catwalk with view platforms overlooking the waterfall. Make sure on the descent to take a side trail to an amazing lookout behind the west falls. Expect to get wet!

Miles and Directions

0.0 Begin at Coyote Trailhead at parking lot. Walk north up paved trail to Rifle Falls. Go left on paved trail along creek for a closer waterfall look (GPS: 39 40 642, -107 41.906), then climb steps to backside of left falls. Return to main trail, following signs for "Coyote Trail."

0.1 Turn left on Coyote Trail and hike along cliff base past caves in the cliff. Trail bends left and climbs to clifftop. Hike southwest.

0.5 Reach top of the three falls and fenced overlooks. Continue left on trail and descend slopes to trailhead. Alternatively, take detour to a spectacular viewpoint beneath falls. This adds 0.2 mile to the hike.

0.7 Arrive back at trailhead (GPS: 39 40.580, -107 41.955).

Three waterfalls form Rifle Falls, one of Colorado's best waterfalls.

77 Hanging Lake Trail Waterfalls: Bridal Veil Falls and "Spouting Rock"

The East Fork of Dead Horse Creek topples south into Glenwood Canyon, leaping off moss-covered rock in two bridal veil plunges at Hanging Lake. The hike is steep, but the reward is mesmerizing, with an emerald pool and waterfall at this hidden gem.

Start: Hanging Lake Trailhead
Trail: Hanging Lake Trail #1650
Difficulty: Moderate
Hiking time: About 3 hours
Distance: 2.9 miles out and back
Elevation trailhead to falls viewpoint: 6,120 to 7,157 feet (+1,037 feet) for Bridal Veil Falls; to 7,330 feet (+1,210 feet) for "Spouting Rock"
Trail surface: Paved, dirt, rocks
Restrictions: Open year-round, weather dependent; permit required year-round; hikers must carry permit; reserve permits at www.visit glenwood.com/hanginglake; hourly reservation times 6:30 a.m. to 5:30 p.m.; free shuttles from 110 Wulfsohn Rd., Glenwood Springs, May 1 to Oct 31; personal vehicles not allowed at trailhead during those months; no toilets at lake or on trail; no cell service; do not stand on log, swim, or fish; no dogs, pets, or bicycles; pack out trash; forecasted rain may lead to closure and trail evacuation due to terrain damage from 2020 wildfire.
Amenities: Restrooms and water at trailhead; services in Glenwood Springs
Maps: *DeLorme:* Page 35 E8; Trails Illustrated 151: Flat Tops South; USGS Shoshone
County: Garfield
Land status/contact: White River National Forest, (970) 945-2521; Eagle–Holy Cross Ranger District, (970) 827-5715; Hanging Lake Call Center, (970) 384-6309

Finding the trailhead: During peak season (May 1 to Oct 31), personal vehicles are not allowed to drive to the trailhead except by prior reservation. Because of limited parking, arrive within 15 minutes before or after your reservation time; otherwise you won't be allowed to park. Alternatively, park in Glenwood Springs at Hanging Lake Welcome Center in peak season and ride the shuttle (6:45 a.m. to 5 p.m.) to the trailhead. Return shuttles operate until 8 p.m. During off-peak season (Nov 1 to Apr 30), vehicles are allowed at the trailhead, but hiking permits are required. Be advised that dates, times, and requirements are subject to change.

To reach the trailhead from Glenwood Springs, drive 9 miles east on I-70 East and take exit 125 for Hanging Lake. There is no direct exit to Hanging Lake from westbound I-70. Rather, take exit 121 for Grizzly Creek, go 0.2 mile and turn left to merge onto I-70 East, then drive 3.8 miles to exit 125 for Hanging Lake. There is no reentry to I-70 East from Hanging Lake; rather, take I-70 West to exit 121 (Grizzly Creek) to get onto I-70 East. Parking is 0.4 mile from the Hanging Lake exit (GPS: 39 35.361, -107 11.406).

Top left: Thin streams of water pour over Bridal Veil Falls into Hanging Lake, a shelf lake perched above Glenwood Canyon.
Top Right: "Spouting Rock" gushes through a hole in a limestone cliff above Hanging Lake.
Bottom: Bridal Veil Falls and Hanging Lake form one of Colorado's natural wonders.

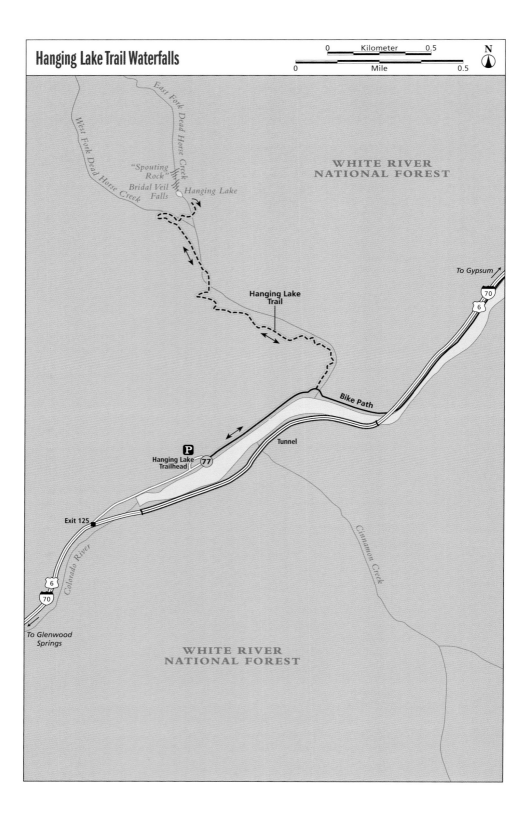

Hanging Lake Trail Waterfalls

0   Kilometer   0.5

0   Mile   0.5

N

East Fork Dead Horse Creek

West Fork Dead Horse Creek

WHITE RIVER NATIONAL FOREST

"Spouting Rock"

Bridal Veil Falls

Hanging Lake

Hanging Lake Trail

To Gypsum

70

6

Bike Path

P

Tunnel

Hanging Lake Trailhead

77

Exit 125

6

70

Colorado River

Cinnamon Creek

To Glenwood Springs

WHITE RIVER NATIONAL FOREST

The Hike

Bridal Veil Falls pours into Hanging Lake, forming one of Colorado's iconic beauty spots. The shallow lake, a designated National Natural Landmark, is a rare formation— a small, clear lake formed by a travertine or calcium carbonate dam that perches atop a cliff in a narrow side canyon above Glenwood Canyon. Fed by Dead Horse Creek, "Spouting Rock," a unique 70-foot waterfall that gushes through a hole in a limestone cliff above the lake, and 20-foot Bridal Veil Falls are not only gorgeous but also popular.

Hanging Lake became so popular, with visitation jumping from 99,000 in 2014 to almost 200,000 in 2018, that the US Forest Service instituted restrictions to keep the lake and falls from being loved to death. The number of daily hikers is limited, and a permit is required for hiking and parking. Be advised that the trail, damaged in 2021 floods, may be rebuilt and rerouted at a future time.

Begin on a paved walkway along the north side of the Colorado River in Glenwood Canyon, and head northeast to Hanging Lake Trail. Leave the walkway and turn left up the winding trail that climbs through Dead Horse Creek Canyon. Hikers gain nearly 1,400 feet of elevation on this relatively short trail, so expect steep portions. Trekking poles are useful, especially on the descent.

The final trail section climbs steps with a safety railing up an exposed cliff. Finish at a boardwalk with benches that let you rest your legs and soak in the stunning scenery. After viewing Bridal Veil Falls, follow the boardwalk to the top of the trail and turn right to hike 400 feet up a spur trail to "Spouting Rock," a spectacular bonus waterfall.

Miles and Directions

0.0   Begin at trailhead at east end of parking lot. Hike northeast on paved trail along river.

0.4   Leave sidewalk and hike up signed Hanging Lake Trail on left (GPS: 39 35.562, -107 11.053).

0.7   Junction with Dead Horse Trail on right (GPS: 39 35.716, -107 11.049). Go straight on Hanging Lake Trail up canyon.

1.4   Reach boardwalk at Hanging Lake and benches to view Bridal Veil Falls (GPS: 39 36.0755, -107 11.4963).

1.45 Reach end of the boardwalk and closest view of waterfall (GPS: 39 36.08, -107 11.46). Return the way you came. Alternatively, continue up main trail to "Spouting Rock."

2.9   Arrive back at trailhead (GPS: 39 35.361, -107 11.406).

78 Hayes Creek Falls

A short trail leads from CO 133 south of Redstone to Hayes Creek Falls, a photogenic waterfall tumbling over boulders and benches in a cliff-lined amphitheater.

Start: Hayes Creek Falls Trailhead
Trail: Hayes Creek Falls Trail
Difficulty: Very easy
Hiking time: About 5 minutes
Distance: 0.04 mile out and back
Elevation trailhead: 7,348 feet
Trail surface: Dirt, rocks
Restrictions: No bicycles, horses, or motor vehicles

Amenities: Services in Redstone and Carbondale
Maps: *DeLorme:* Page 45 D8; Trails Illustrated 128: Maroon Bells, Redstone, Marble Map; USGS Placita
County: Pitkin
Land status/contact: White River National Forest, (970) 945-2521

Finding the trailhead: From the junction of CO 82 and CO 133 on the north side of Carbondale, drive south on CO 133 toward McClure Pass for 19.2 miles to a pullout signed "Hays Creek Falls" (misspelled waterfall name) on the right (west) side of the highway (GPS: 39 9.496, -107 15.0951). The pullout is 1.8 miles south of Redstone.

The Hike

Hayes Creek Falls, a 60-foot slide and horsetail waterfall, is a terrific roadside attraction. Beginning at 10,400 feet on the east flank of Huntsman Ridge, Hayes Creek steeply drops 4,050 feet in 3.5 miles down a narrow, twisting canyon, forming an almost continuous cataract of cascades and occasional small waterfalls that culminates in rushing Hayes Creek Falls near the Crystal River. The falls plunges over a cliff band of red sandstone that towers above the highway and parking strip before emptying under the highway into the river.

The three-tiered waterfall, reached by walking 125 feet from car to falls, is fed by snowmelt, so the best time to visit is May to July. By autumn the waterfall slows to a trickle. During high water, use caution crossing the creek below the falls. After enjoying the waterfall, visit historic Redstone, the nineteenth-century Redstone Coke Oven Historic District, and natural Penny Hot Springs to the north.

Hayes Creek Falls plunges into a sandstone ▷
amphitheater along the Crystal River.

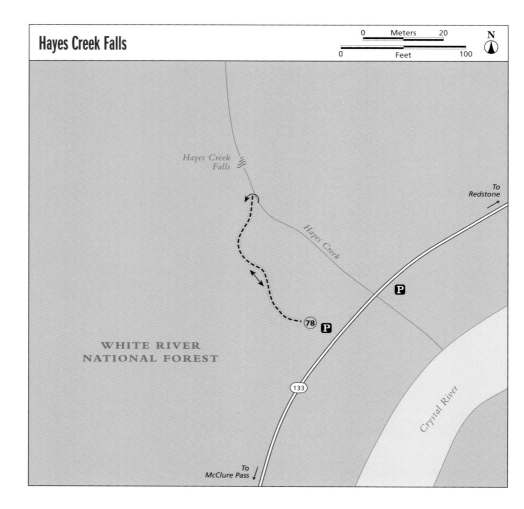

Miles and Directions

0.0 Start at trailhead on left side of parking area and left of Hayes Creek. Hike west along rocky left bank of creek.

0.02 After 125 feet, reach base of waterfall (GPS: 39 9.5116, -107 15.1062).

0.04 Arrive back at trailhead (GPS: 39 9.496, -107 15.0951).

79 Booth Creek Falls

On the southern edge of the Gore Range, Booth Creek slips down mountainsides, pools in scenic lakes, and then careens down a cliff, forming popular Booth Creek Falls, a frothy horsetail in a trailside chasm.

Start: Booth Lake Trailhead
Trail: Booth Creek Trail #2011
Difficulty: Moderate
Hiking time: About 3 hours
Distance: 4.0 miles out and back
Elevation trailhead to falls viewpoint: 8,460 to 9,750 feet (+1,290 feet)
Trail surface: Dirt, rocks
Restrictions: No bicycles or motorized vehicles; dogs must be leashed; parking limited at trailhead; no parking on streets by trailhead; no overnight parking; follow wilderness rules; limit group sizes to 15
Amenities: Services in Vail
Maps: *DeLorme:* Page 37 D8; Trails Illustrated 602: Vail [Local Trails]; USGS Vail East
County: Eagle
Land status/contact: White River National Forest, (970) 945-2521; Eagle–Holy Cross Ranger District, (970) 827-5715

Finding the trailhead: From I-70 West in Vail, take exit 180 and turn right on Big Horn Road, then left on Frontage Road. Drive 0.8 mile and turn right on Booth Falls Road. From the eastbound lane of I-70, take exit 176, keep left, and at a traffic circle take the 3rd exit onto Frontage Road. Go 3 miles and turn right on Booth Falls Road. Drive 0.2 mile on Booth Falls Road to parking at road's end. The trailhead is at a closed gate (GPS: 39 39.053,-106 19.265).

To alleviate trailhead parking problems, it's recommended (and required in summer) to park free at Vail Village or Lionshead and take the free East Vail blue line shuttle from Vail Transportation Center. Ride to the Booth Falls bus stop and walk up Booth Falls Road 0.25 mile to the trailhead.

The Hike

The Booth Creek Trail ascends a steep canyon to Booth Creek Falls, a 60-foot plunge over a sharp cliff, before continuing to Booth Lake, a pristine pond tucked against 12,163-foot Booth Mountain. The trail is busy in summer, especially on weekends. To lessen traffic congestion and parking problems, the trailhead is closed to vehicles in summer. Hikers must park in Vail and take a free shuttle bus to the trailhead. Consider hiking to the falls on a weekday to avoid crowds. After reaching the waterfall, extend the hike by continuing for another 2.4 miles to Booth Lake and views of the rugged Gore Range.

The trail offers a view of Booth Creek dashing over Booth Creek Falls. PHOTO BY MICHAEL MOORE

Booth Creek Falls cuts through a trailside chasm in a frosty horsetail waterfall.

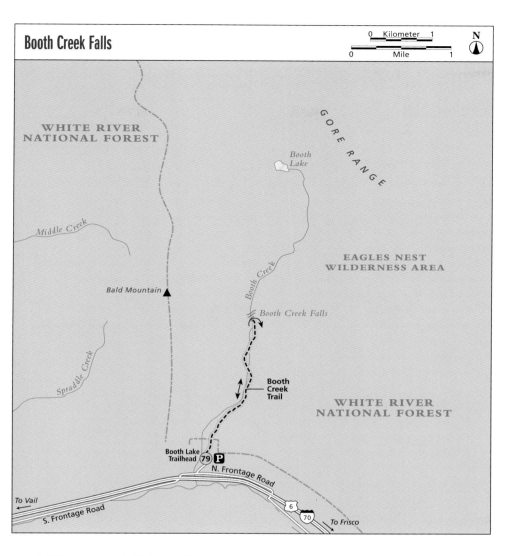

Booth Creek Falls

WHITE RIVER
NATIONAL FOREST

GORE RANGE

Booth
Lake

Middle Creek

EAGLES NEST
WILDERNESS AREA

Bald Mountain

Booth Creek

Booth Creek Falls

Booth
Creek
Trail

WHITE RIVER
NATIONAL FOREST

Spraddle Creek

Booth Lake
Trailhead 79 P

N. Frontage Road

To Vail

S. Frontage Road

6

70

To Frisco

Miles and Directions

0.0 Begin at Booth Lake Trailhead. Follow trail uphill by creek.

0.2 Enter Eagles Nest Wilderness and continue north on trail through aspens.

1.8 Pass trail sign on left and switchback to right and up steep trail.

2.0 Cut off trail to rocky overlook above Booth Creek Falls (GPS: 39 40.348, -106 18.680). Return the way you came.

4.0 Arrive back at trailhead (GPS: 39 39.053, -106 19.265).

80 Pitkin Creek Trail Waterfalls: "Upper Pitkin Creek Falls" and "Lower Pitkin Creek Falls"

Originating from Pitkin Lake below the crest of the Gore Range, Pitkin Creek splashes over two waterfalls before draining south to the Vail Valley.

Start: Pitkin Creek Trailhead
Trail: Pitkin Creek Trail #2012
Difficulty: Strenuous
Hiking time: About 4 hours
Distance: 7.0 miles out and back
Elevation trailhead to falls viewpoints: 8,455 to 9,120 feet (+665 feet) for "Lower Pitkin Creek Falls"; to 10,415 feet (+1,960 feet) for "Upper Pitkin Creek Falls"
Trail surface: Dirt, rocks
Restrictions: Wilderness rules apply; dogs must be leashed; group size limited to 15; parking limited at trailhead; no parking on street by trailhead; no sleeping in cars at trailhead; porta-potty at trailhead
Amenities: Services in Vail
Maps: *DeLorme:* Page 37 D8; Trails Illustrated 602: Vail [Local Trails]; USGS East Vail
County: Eagle
Land status/contact: White River National Forest, (970) 945-2521; Eagle–Holy Cross Ranger District, (970) 827- 5715

Finding the trailhead: From I-70 in Vail, take exit 180. On the north side of I-70, turn right on Fall Line Drive and go 0.3 mile to the trailhead on the left at road's end (GPS: 39 38.5817, -106 18.1841). Limited parking is on both sides of the road.

Alternatively, to alleviate trailhead parking problems, park free at Vail Village or Lionshead and take the free East Vail blue line shuttle from Vail Transportation Center. Ride to the Falls at Vail bus stop and walk east on the road for 0.25 mile to the trailhead.

The Hike

The popular Pitkin Creek Trail, climbing north up a narrow valley east of Vail, passes two waterfalls before switchbacking up to Pitkin Lake in an alpine cirque at 10,385 feet. Like the Booth Creek Trail in the next valley to the west, the trail is busy in summer and on weekends. Limited parking is a problem, so to ease congestion, park in Vail and take a free shuttle bus to the trailhead. Also, hike on weekdays to avoid crowds.

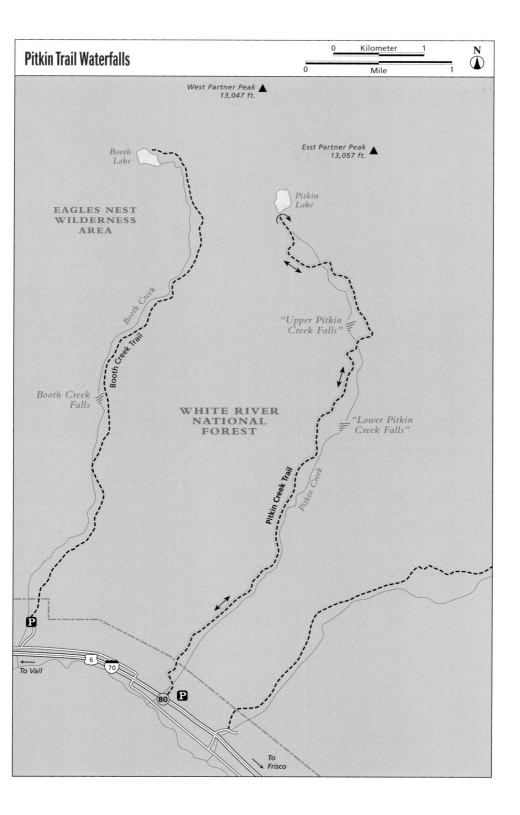

Pitkin Trail Waterfalls

0   Kilometer   1
0   Mile   1

N

West Partner Peak ▲
13,047 ft.

Esst Partner Peak ▲
13,057 ft.

Booth Lake

Pitkin Lake

EAGLES NEST
WILDERNESS
AREA

Booth Creek

Booth Creek Trail

"Upper Pitkin Creek Falls"

Booth Creek Falls

WHITE RIVER
NATIONAL
FOREST

"Lower Pitkin Creek Falls"

Pitkin Creek Trail

Pitkin Creek

P

6   70

To Vail

80   **P**

To Frisco

Left: Pitkin Creek, draining from an alpine cirque, drops noisily over boulders at "Upper Pitkin Creek Falls."
Right: Seen from Pitkin Creek Trail, "Lower Pitkin Creek Falls" splashes down a groove in a broken cliff.

Miles and Directions

0.0   Start at Pitkin Creek Trailhead on north side of parking lot. Hike north on trail.

0.25 Cross a footbridge and enter Eagles Nest Wilderness. Trail passes through avalanche debris and then follows creek up steep valley.

2.5   Reach viewpoint of "Lower Pitkin Creek Falls" gushing down a cliff (GPS: 39 40.1932, -106 17.0179). Enjoy waterfall from large boulder on trail or descend social trail for a closer look. Continue up trail.

3.4   View of "Upper Pitkin Creek Falls" spilling down broken cliffs ahead. Continue on trail and cross side creek on rocks.

3.5   Reach best view of falls (GPS: 39 40.788, -106 16.7116). Turn around here or continue up steep trail for 1.3 miles to glistening Pitkin Lake, then return for a 9.6-mile hike.

7.0   Arrive back at trailhead (GPS: 39 38.5817, -106 18.1841).

Northern Colorado

Walden and Fort Collins

Open woods surrounded Big Creek Falls before wildfire ravaged the area.

81 Big Creek Falls

The Big Creek Lakes attracts boaters, hunters, hikers, and anglers from Colorado and nearby Wyoming, and the wetlands here attract a variety of wildlife. Big Creek pours through the nearby wilderness and tosses its waters over calico slabs at Big Creek Falls.

Start: Seven Lakes Trailhead
Trail: Seven Lakes Trail #1125.1
Difficulty: Easy/moderate
Hiking time: About 3 hours
Distance: 4.8 miles out and back
Elevation trailhead to falls viewpoint: 9,020 to 9,180 feet (+160 feet)
Trail surface: Dirt, rocks, boardwalk
Restrictions: Fee area; dogs must be on voice command or on leash; observe wilderness regulations

Amenities: Campsites; vault toilets; potable water; leashed dogs on first trail section; services in Walden
Maps: *DeLorme:* Page 17 B5; Trails Illustrated 116: Hahns Peak, Steamboat Lake: USGS Pearl, Davis Peak
County: Jackson
Land status/contact: Routt National Forest, (307) 745-2300; Parks Ranger District, (970) 723-2700

Finding the trailhead: From Walden, take CO 125 north for 9 miles to Cowdrey and turn left (west) on CR 6W at the sign for Big Creek Lakes. Drive 18.7 miles on CR 6W (road is unpaved at 5.2 miles and winter maintenance ends at 11.6 miles) and turn left on Big Creek Lakes Road (CR 6A/FR 600). Drive 4.9 miles on Big Creek Lakes Road, then bear left at the sign for Big Creek Lakes. Go 0.7 mile to an intersection and continue straight, past the lakes on your left and through the campground, on CR 6C for another 0.7 mile, then bear left to parking at the trailhead (GPS: 40 55.88, -106 37.193).

The Hike

Big Creek Falls, one of the best waterfalls in the Mount Zirkel Wilderness, topples 45 feet off a rock outcrop into a pool hidden in a valley on the east flank of the Park Range. The waterfall lies in secluded Jackson County, Colorado's only county with no stoplights and a mere 1,700 residents. The falls is southwest of a remote campground 10 miles south of the Wyoming border, so it's best to camp overnight at Big Creek Lake and combine the waterfall hike with other activities. The twin lakes and surrounding wetlands are one of Colorado's best spots to see moose browsing in marshes or walking by the campground.

The Big Creek Lakes area, including the falls, was extensively burned by the 37,627-acre Beaver Creek Fire in 2016, so watch for deadfall. Much of the area was covered with trees killed by pine beetles, which burned fast and hot, leaving a decimated forest that is slowly regenerating.

Seven Lakes Trailhead, at the southwest end of Big Creek Lakes Campground, is the starting point for the hike. The first 1.3 miles of the trail is also called Red

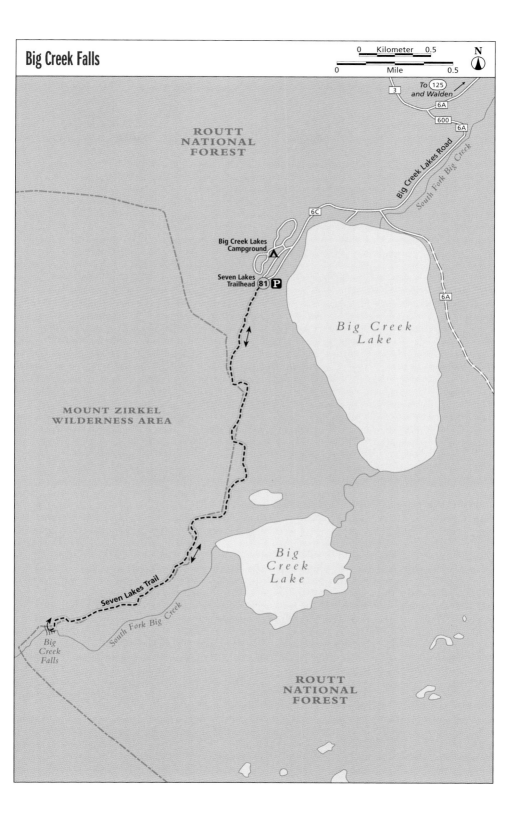

Big Creek Falls

0 Kilometer 0.5
0 Mile 0.5

N

To 125
and Walden

3
6A
600
6A

Big Creek Lakes Road

South Fork Big Creek

ROUTT
NATIONAL
FOREST

6C

Big Creek Lakes
Campground

Seven Lakes
Trailhead 81 P

6A

Big Creek
Lake

MOUNT ZIRKEL
WILDERNESS AREA

Big
Creek
Lake

Seven Lakes Trail

Big
Creek
Falls

South Fork Big Creek

ROUTT
NATIONAL
FOREST

Big Creek Falls crashes over a cliff into a deep pool.

Elephant Nature Trail, featuring twenty-five numbered stops keyed to a brochure. The trail follows the west side of Big Creek Lakes, edging past wetlands and beaver ponds. The wettest trail sections have boardwalks to keep your feet high and dry.

Miles and Directions

0.0 Begin at Seven Lakes Trailhead at southwest end of campground. Hike southwest on Seven Lakes Trail through marshes and standing burned trees on lake's west side.

1.2 Reach signed trail junction (GPS: 40 54.9904, -106 37.3722). Keep right on Seven Lakes Trail toward Big Creek Falls. Left trail is Big Creek Lakes Loop (#1125.1A); good option for return hike.

2.3 Enter Mount Zirkel Wilderness and go left from main trail on social trail down to waterfall base and plunge pool.

2.4 Arrive at Big Creek Falls (GPS: 40 54.535, -106 38.234). Return on trail.

4.8 Arrive back at trailhead (GPS: 40 55.88, -106 37.193).

82 Poudre Falls

The Cache la Poudre River, originating at Poudre Lake in Rocky Mountain National Park, carves a deep runnel through upper Poudre Canyon where a highway pullout gives scenic views of the rushing leaps and gushing cascades at Poudre Falls.

Start: Poudre Falls Overlook on CO 14
Trail: None
Difficulty: Very easy
Hiking time: Less than 1 hour
Distance: Roadside
Elevation trailhead to falls viewpoint: Minimal
Trail surface: Dirt, rocks
Restrictions: None posted

Amenities: Limited services on CO 14; services in Walden and Fort Collins
Maps: *DeLorme:* Page 18 D4; Trails Illustrated 112: Poudre River, Cameron Pass; USGS Boston Peak
County: Larimer
Land status/contact: Roosevelt National Forest, (970) 295-6600; Canyon Lakes Ranger District, (970) 295-6700

Finding the trailhead: From Walden, take CO 14 East (Poudre Canyon Highway) for 40.9 miles and park at the pullout on the right side of the highway. From Fort Collins, follow CO 14 West (Poudre Canyon Highway) for 55.3 miles and park at the pullout on the left side of the highway (GPS: 40 38.806, -105 48.583). Carefully cross the highway to the overlook.

The Hike

The pullout and overlook for Poudre Falls is marked by a small sign at the side of the highway east of Cameron Pass. Below the asphalt, the Cache la Poudre River crashes through a narrow cliff-lined gorge, tumbling around boulders and sliding over the rocky riverbed in three long leaps. Social trails allow for a closer look at the falls and the steep-sided west wall of the canyon. Use caution when crossing the highway here, and keep pets and children close at hand.

Miles and Directions

0.0 Begin at Poudre Falls Overlook. Enjoy falls from above or descend social trails for a closer look.

0.1 Arrive back at trailhead (GPS: 40 38.806, -105 48.583).

Granite cliffs force the Cache la Poudre River down a narrow channel at Poudre Falls. PHOTO BY IAN GREEN

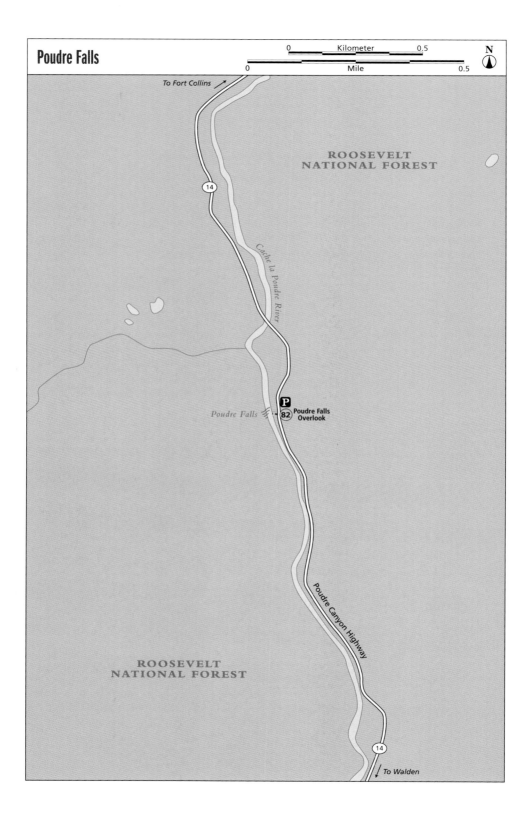

Poudre Falls

0   Kilometer   0.5

0   Mile   0.5

N

To Fort Collins

ROOSEVELT
NATIONAL FOREST

14

Cache la Poudre River

Poudre Falls

82

Poudre Falls
Overlook

Poudre Canyon Highway

ROOSEVELT
NATIONAL FOREST

14

To Walden

83 Horsetooth Falls

Spring Creek, rising from the north flank of Horsetooth Mountain west of Fort Collins, drops northwest down a wooded canyon before plunging 25 feet into a cliff-lined alcove.

Start: Horsetooth Mountain Trailhead
Trails: Horsetooth Rock Trail, Horsetooth Falls Trail
Difficulty: Easy
Hiking time: About 1 hour
Distance: 2.4 miles out and back
Elevation trailhead to falls viewpoint: 5,787 to 5,824 feet (+37 feet)
Trail surface: Dirt, rocks
Restrictions: Trailhead open 24 hours a day; entrance fee charged; park only in designated spots; leashed dogs allowed; stay on trail; mountain bikers and equestrians share trail; no fires, fireworks, or glass containers
Amenities: Services in Fort Collins
Maps: *DeLorme:* Page 20 E2; Trails Illustrated: none; USGS Horsetooth Reservoir
County: Larimer
Land status/contact: Larimer County Department of Natural Resources, (970) 619-4570

Finding the trailhead: From Denver, drive north on I-25 and take exit 265 (Harmony Road/Timnath). Turn left and drive west on Harmony Road for 7 miles to its intersection with Taft Hill Road. Continue west on the road, which becomes CR 38E, for about 4 miles to a junction on the southwest side of Horsetooth Reservoir. Keep left on CR 38E and follow it for 4.6 miles around the south end of the lake, passing Blue Sky Trailhead, to a right turn into the marked Horsetooth Mountain Trailhead. The trailhead is on the north side of the parking lot (GPS: 40 31.4415, -105 10.8677).

The Hike

Horsetooth Falls, the closest waterfall to Fort Collins, is reached by a popular trail in Horsetooth Mountain Open Space, a 2,711-acre preserve with 29 miles of trails. The falls is a lovely plunge waterfall that freefalls from a deep notch in cliffs to a shiny pool below. Springtime or after a rain is the best time to see the falls. The trailhead has limited parking, so plan on hiking during the week or arriving in the morning or evening on weekends and holidays.

While Spring Creek is a small, joyful stream, the creek flooded in late July 1997 after a thunderstorm dropped 14.5 inches of rain, a year's worth of precipitation, on Horsetooth Mountain. The resulting wall of water killed five people and caused over $200 million of damage in Fort Collins. The waterfall must have been quite a sight that night.

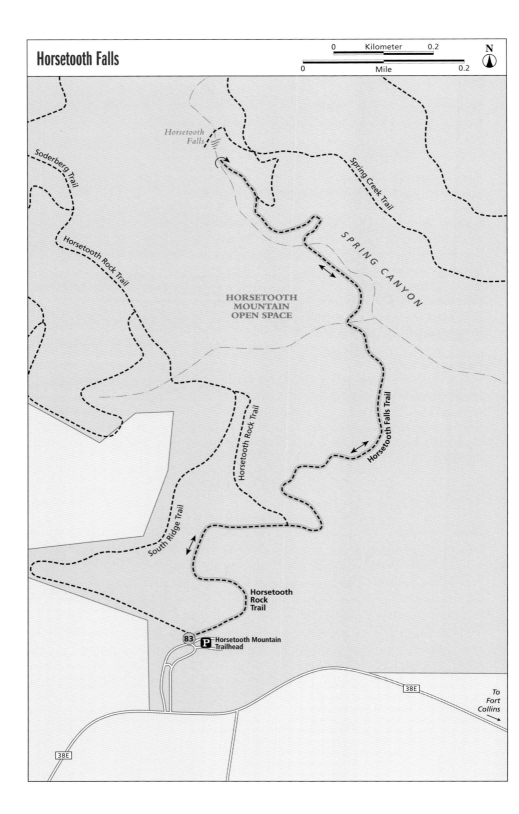

Horsetooth Falls

0   Kilometer   0.2

0   Mile   0.2

N

Horsetooth Falls

Soderberg Trail

Horsetooth Rock Trail

Spring Creek Trail

SPRING CANYON

HORSETOOTH
MOUNTAIN
OPEN SPACE

Horsetooth Rock Trail

Horsetooth Falls Trail

South Ridge Trail

Horsetooth
Rock
Trail

83   P   Horsetooth Mountain
Trailhead

38E

38E

To
Fort
Collins

Spring Creek freefalls off a cliff at Horsetooth Falls near Fort Collins. PHOTO BY IAN GREEN

Miles and Directions

0.0   Start at Horsetooth Mountain Trailhead. Hike north on Horsetooth Rock Trail up a hillside.

0.3   Reach a junction (GPS: 40 31.56, -105 10.7453). Go right on Horsetooth Falls Trail and descend grassy slopes into Spring Canyon. Dip across Spring Creek on a bridge and follow trail above rocky gorge toward cliffs.

1.2   Arrive at base of Horsetooth Falls below cliffs (GPS: 40 31.9503, -105 10.8259). Return the way you came.

2.4   Arrive back at trailhead (GPS: 40 31.4415, -105 10.8677).

Rocky Mountain National Park

Grand Lake, Allenspark, Lyons, and Estes Park

Ribbon Falls slides down a granite slab in Glacier Gorge.

84 East Inlet Trail Waterfalls: Adams Falls, "Footbridge Falls," and "East Inlet Falls"

The scenic East Inlet Trail, heading east from Grand Lake into Rocky Mountain National Park, passes three waterfalls—Adams Falls, "Footbridge Falls," and "East Inlet Falls."

Start: East Inlet Trailhead
Trails: East Inlet Trail, Adams Falls Trail
Difficulty: Very easy for Adams Falls; easy/moderate for "Footbridge Falls"; moderate for "East Inlet Falls"
Hiking time: About 1 hour for Adams Falls; 3 hours for "Footbridge Falls"; 4 hours for "East Inlet Falls"
Distance: 0.6 mile out and back (or 1.0-mile loop) for Adams Falls; 4.4 miles out and back for "Footbridge Falls"; 6.2 miles out and back for "East Inlet Falls"
Elevation trailhead to falls viewpoints: 8,400 to 8,450 feet (+50 feet) for Adams Falls; to

8,620 feet (+220 feet) for "Footbridge Falls"; to 9,020 feet (+620 feet) for "East Inlet Falls"
Trail surface: Dirt, stone steps
Restrictions: Fee area; no dogs; wilderness regulations apply
Amenities: Vault toilets; backcountry camping; Kawuneeche Visitor Center; services in Grand Lake
Maps: *DeLorme:* Page 28 C4; Trails Illustrated 200: Rocky Mountain National Park; USGS Shadow Mountain
County: Grand
Land status/contact: Rocky Mountain National Park, (970) 586-1206

Finding the trailhead: From US 34 in Grand Lake, drive to a Y-junction at the Grand Lake Visitor Center, bear right on West Portal Road (CO 278) and drive northeast for 0.3 mile to an intersection with Grand Avenue. Bear left and continue straight on West Portal Road. Drive 2 miles on the paved and unpaved road to a parking lot and East Inlet Trailhead on the road's left side (GPS: 40 14.3658, -105 47.9935).

The Hike

The trail follows East Inlet, a creek that runs from the north slopes of 13,118-foot Isolation Peak to Grand Lake, Colorado's largest natural lake. It winds through a conifer forest, crosses footbridges, climbs to vantage points with lake views, and passes several waterfalls. Like many waterfall trails, East Inlet Trail can flood, so pack appropriate footwear. In winter a trekking pole and microspikes may be required to cross icy bridges and frozen trail sections.

The first waterfall, Adams Falls, is an easy hike for families, with a developed overlook. Segmented at the top, Adams Falls cascades down and runs through a narrow chute. "Footbridge Falls," the second falls, is so close to the trail you'll want to stick your fingers in the rushing water. The segmented waterfall flows in dual cascades around a trailside boulder. "East Inlet Falls," the farthest east waterfall, is a trailside

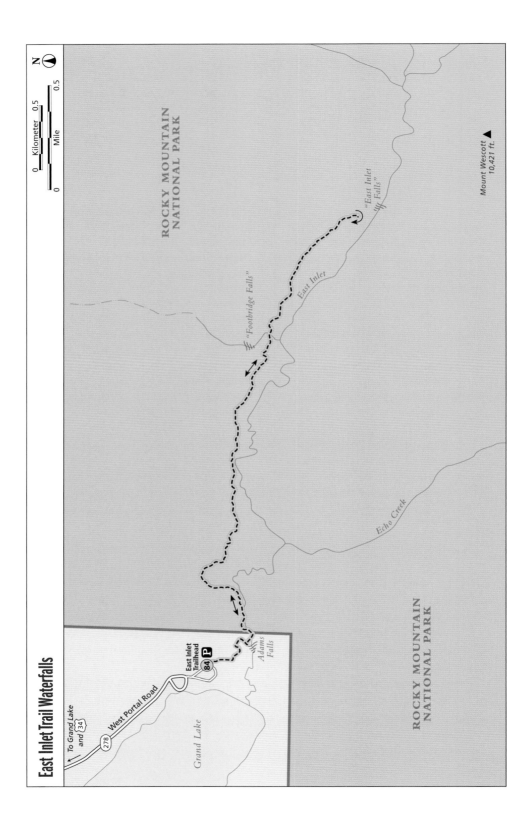

East Inlet Trail Waterfalls

To Grand Lake
and 34

278 West Portal Road

Grand Lake

East Inlet
Trailhead
84 P

Adams
Falls

ROCKY MOUNTAIN
NATIONAL PARK

"Footbridge Falls"

East Inlet

"East Inlet
Falls"

Echo Creek

ROCKY MOUNTAIN
NATIONAL PARK

Mount Wescott
10,421 ft.

N

Kilometer 0 0.5

Mile 0 0.5

wonder that pours over a cliff into a gorge. Hidden off the trail, it takes a bit of route finding to see the falls. The top is below the trail, and it's a long way down to the creek. Use care in this area, as a slip would be fatal. After returning to the trail, continue to stone steps that wrap around a rocky buttress. On the trail's left side, look for a cairn and flat outcrop that provides an ideal lunch spot with views of Grand Lake and the surrounding mountains.

East Inlet Trail continues east for miles, heading to Lone Pine Lake and Lake Verna, while the creek rises to Spirit Lake, Fourth Lake, and Fifth Lake below the Continental Divide.

Miles and Directions

0.0 Begin at East Inlet Trailhead and hike southeast on trail.

0.3 Leave main trail at junction. Go right and descend stone steps on Adams Falls Trail, an 815-foot path, to reach viewing area for Adams Falls (GPS: 40 14.197, -105 47.886). Climb steps left of falls to return to East Inlet Trail.

0.5 Arrive back at East Inlet Trail and go right to continue to next waterfall. For a 1.0-mile loop back to trailhead, turn left here.

2.2 Arrive at second footbridge and "Footbridge Falls" to trail's left (GPS: 40 14.146, -105 46.311).

3.0 Hike down through trees and around left side of rock outcropping. Use extreme care and avoid loose, wet, or icy rocks.

3.1 Reach top of "East Inlet Falls" (GPS: 40 13.768, -105 45.58). Return on trail.

6.2 Arrive back at trailhead (GPS: 40 14.3658, -105 47.9935).

Top: Adams Falls cascades in segments, turns abruptly, and flows into a long, narrow chute. Bottom: The East Inlet Trail is crossed with many unnamed cascades.

85 North Inlet Trail Waterfalls: Cascade Falls, "Snake Dance Falls," "Big Pool Falls," Sun Dance Falls," "Rain Dance Falls," War Dance Falls, and North Inlet Falls

Six waterfalls line the North Inlet Trail at Grand Lake, with a seventh waterfall tucked into a hillside above the trail. From 13,153-foot Taylor Peak and Lake Nokoni, North Inlet flows west to the lake, spilling down a series of cascades, chutes, horsetails, and plunges that provide a wonderous waterfall hike.

Start: North Inlet Trailhead
Trail: North Inlet Trail #813
Difficulty: Moderate for Cascade Falls; moderate/strenuous for "Snake Dance Falls," "Big Pool Falls," "Sun Dance Falls," and "Rain Dance Falls"; strenuous for North Inlet Falls; very strenuous for War Dance Falls
Hiking time: About 4 hours for Cascade Falls; 5 hours for "Snake Dance Falls"; 6 hours for "Big Pool Falls" and "Sun Dance Falls"; 7 hours for "Rain Dance Falls"; 10 hours for North Inlet Falls or War Dance Falls; 11 hours for all 7 falls
Distance: 7.0 miles out and back for Cascade Falls; 9.0 miles out and back for "Snake Dance Falls"; 9.8 miles out and back for "Big Pool Falls"; 10.0 miles out and back for "Sun Dance Falls"; 11.4 miles out and back for "Rain Dance Falls"; 14.0 miles out and back for War Dance Falls; 15.4 miles out and back for North Inlet Falls (not including War Dance Falls); 15.9 miles out and back for all 7 falls

Elevation trailhead to falls viewpoints: 8,510 to 8,760 feet (+250 feet) for Cascade Falls; to 8,940 feet (+430 feet) for "Snake Dance Falls"; to 9,040 feet (+530 feet) for "Big Pool Falls"; to 9,070 feet (+560 feet) for "Sun Dance Falls"; to 9,200 feet (+690 feet) for "Rain Dance Falls"; to 9,490 feet (+980 feet) for North Inlet Falls; to 9,630 feet (+1,120 feet) for War Dance Falls
Trail surface: Dirt, rocks, stone steps
Restrictions: Fee area; no dogs; wilderness regulations apply
Amenities: Vault toilets; Kawuneeche Visitor Center; services in Grand Lake
Maps: *DeLorme:* Pages 28 C4 and 29 C5; Trails Illustrated 200: Rocky Mountain National Park; USGS Grand Lake, McHenrys Peak
County: Grand
Land status/contact: Rocky Mountain National Park, (970) 586-1206

Finding the trailhead: From US 34 in Grand Lake, drive to a Y-junction at the Grand Lake Visitor Center, bear right on West Portal Road (CO 278) and drive northeast for 0.3 mile to an intersection with Grand Avenue. Bear left and continue straight on West Portal Road. Drive 0.8 mile around the north edge of Grand Lake and turn left on unpaved CR 663, signed "Tonahutu and North Inlet Trailheads." Continue 0.2 mile past Tonahutu Trailhead at the top of a hill and then right to a small parking lot at North Inlet Trailhead (GPS: 40 15.392, -105 48.877). An additional parking lot is past the trailhead at road's end.

North Inlet Falls pours over boulders into a narrow slot canyon at the hike's end.

The Hike

This waterfall–rich hike follows North Inlet Trail along a long, curving valley carved by ancient glaciers and North Inlet Creek in the southwest part of Rocky Mountain National Park. Hiking to all of these waterfalls is a major undertaking, and most hikers turn around at Cascade Falls, the first one, rather than continuing deep into the backcountry. If you plan on day hiking to see all seven waterfalls, bring snacks, water, and rain gear, and start early. Parking at the North Inlet Trailhead is limited, so if the lots are full, park at the bottom of the hill and hike to the trailhead. Parts of North

North Inlet Trail Waterfalls

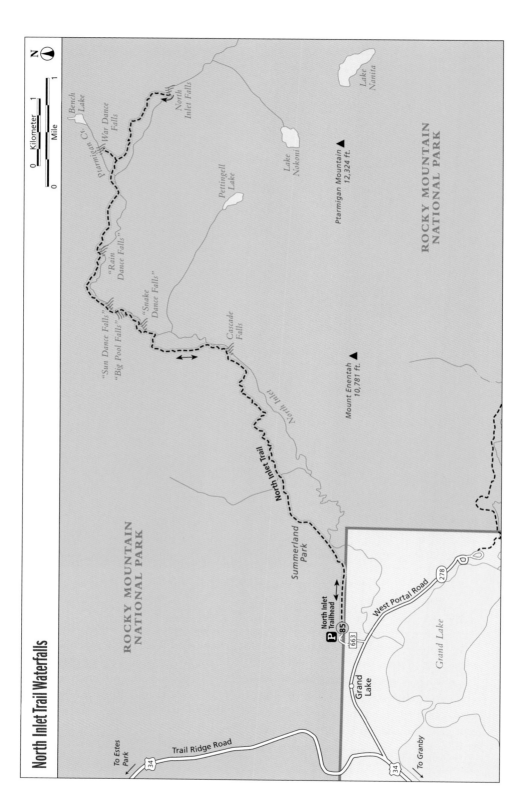

Inlet Trail were burned by the East Troublesome Fire in 2020. Check with the park before hiking for possible trail and area closures.

The first waterwall is signed "Cascade Falls" and reached by a side trail on the right. Loop upstream to see the falls tumbling over dark boulders stacked in the creek bed. Past it is 9,723-foot "Cascade Falls Point" on the left and the upper rapids of the falls on the right. "Snake Dance Falls" gushes down a steep chute into a shallow plunge pool below. Farther up the trail is "Big Pool Falls," which drops into a large pool of frigid, shallow water. The waterfall's top is right of the trail. Note that the creek has carved scalloped edges into the bedrock below. Next is "Sun Dance Falls." Climb onto a broad rock above the waterfall for a closer look. After a footbridge, the trail reaches the long cascades of "Rain Dance Falls" and then an unnamed lake. War Dance Falls, a long cascade through deadfall, lies past North Inlet Group Campsite. The trail to it is faint and gains 340 feet of elevation—with no switchbacks. Best to skip War Dance and admire it from a distance. The hike's last waterfall, North Inlet Falls, is the best. The falls plunges in a gleaming, liquid curtain through a rocky gorge, with views on either side of the falls and from a bridge. Take a good rest here before returning to the trailhead—you've earned it.

Miles and Directions

0.0   Begin at North Inlet Trailhead. Hike east down gravel road past private property and horse pastures.

3.5   Depart main trail and go right to Cascade Falls on short path (GPS: 40 16.283, -105 45.941). Return to main trail.

4.5   At a hard left switchback, step right off trail to see "Snake Dance Falls" dropping into a shallow plunge pool (GPS: 40 16.918, -105 45.746). Continue on main trail.

4.9   Arrive at "Big Pool Falls" to right of trail (GPS: 40 17.11, -105 45.525). Continue on main trail.

5.0   Pass Big Pool Campsite and reach "Sun Dance Falls" to right of trail (GPS: 40 17.214, -105 45.503). Continue on trail.

5.7   Cross a footbridge and arrive at "Rain Dance Falls" to right of trail (GPS: 40 17.271, -105 44.941). Continue on main trail.

6.7   Cross another footbridge and pass North Inlet Group Campsite to junction on left with rough trail that climbs to War Dance Falls. Assess your energy and time before attempting this difficult route. (If you skip this waterfall, continue on main trail.)

7.0   After steep ascent, arrive at War Dance Falls (GPS: 40 17.246, -105 43.859). Return to main trail and continue southeast up valley.

8.0   Reach trail junction. Left fork leads to Flattop Mountain and Bear Lake; keep right toward Lakes Nokoni and Nanita.

8.2   Arrive at North Inlet Falls (GPS: 40 16.734, -105 43.281). Return on North Inlet Trail.

15.9   Arrive back at trailhead (GPS: 40 15.392, -105 48.877).

86 Granite Falls

Snowmelt pools below the Continental Divide and flows west in Tonahutu Creek. At Granite Falls, the water slides down granite slabs then continues to Big Meadows and Grand Lake.

Start: Green Mountain Trailhead
Trails: Green Mountain Trail, Tonahutu Creek Trail
Difficulty: Moderate/strenuous
Hiking time: About 5 hours
Distance: 10.2 miles out and back
Elevation trailhead to falls viewpoint: 8,800 to 9,740 feet (+940 feet)
Trail surface: Dirt, rocks
Restrictions: Fee area; no dogs, bicycles, or motorized vehicles; wilderness rules apply

Amenities: Vault toilets; overnight parking and backcountry camping by permit only; Kawuneeche Visitor Center; services in Grand Lake
Maps: *DeLorme:* Page 28 C4; Trails Illustrated 200: Rocky Mountain National Park; USGS Grand Lake
County: Grand
Land status/contact: Rocky Mountain National Park, (970) 586-1206

Finding the trailhead: From Grand Lake, drive north on US 34 East (Trail Ridge Road) for 1.8 miles to Rocky Mountain National Park's west entrance. Continue 2.5 miles to a paved parking lot on the right and the Green Mountain Trailhead (GPS: 40 18.445, -105 50.471).

The Hike

Granite Falls slips down polished granite bedrock in several tiers and then cascades downstream between mossy banks in the remote Tonahutu Creek Valley (Tonahutu means "Big Meadow" in Arapaho) on the western side of Rocky Mountain National Park. A plunge pool at the bottom completes this pretty waterfall. This recommended hike passes through burned forests and Big Meadows, the park's largest montane ecosystem and home to mule deer and elk, before reaching the 50-foot-high slide waterfall.

It's a long hike to the falls, so consider backpacking to nearby wilderness campsites, including Granite Falls, Lower Granite Falls, Sunrise, and Sunset. Although the hike gains nearly 1,000 feet of elevation, the rise is spread out, making a gradual ascent that never gets too steep. The area from the trailhead to the Continental Divide east of Granite Falls was burned by the East Troublesome Fire in October 2020. Check with the park before hiking for restrictions and closures.

Miles and Directions

0.0 Begin at Green Mountain Trailhead and hike east through woods on Green Mountain Trail.

1.8 Reach junction with Tonahutu Creek Trail on west side of Big Meadows (GPS: 40 18.6551, -105 48.7184). Go left on it and hike north, keeping meadows to right. Watch for moose in meadows and on trail.

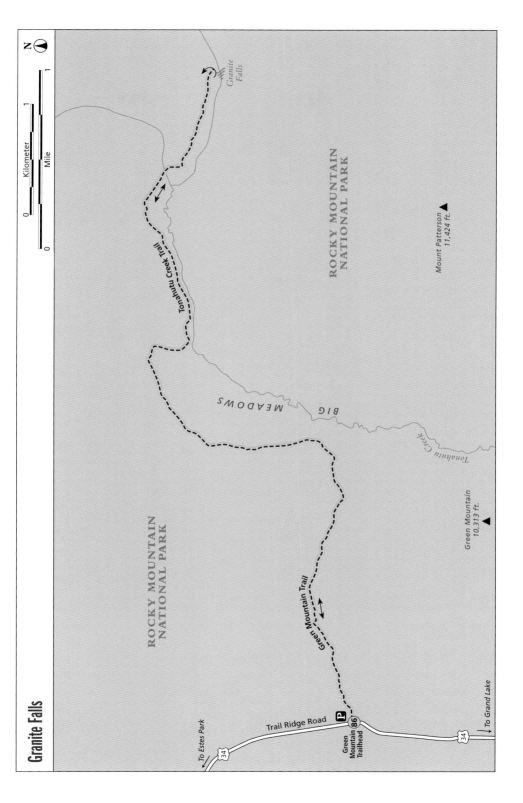

Granite Falls

Trail Ridge Road

To Estes Park

Green Mountain Trailhead

34

86

34

To Grand Lake

Green Mountain Trail

Green Mountain
10,313 ft.

ROCKY MOUNTAIN
NATIONAL PARK

BIG   MEADOWS

Tonahutu Creek

Tonahutu Creek Trail

Granite
Falls

ROCKY MOUNTAIN
NATIONAL PARK

Mount Patterson
11,424 ft.

N

0   Kilometer   1

0   Mile   1

Granite Falls slides down granite slabs before entering Big Meadows.

2.3 Reach junction with Onahu Creek Trail at north end of meadows. Keep right on Tonahutu Creek Trail toward Flattop Mountain and hike east.

3.0 Cross creek on footbridge.

4.4 Reach second creek crossing on footbridge.

5.1 Arrive at signed Granite Falls (GPS: 40 19.119, -105 46.371). Return the way you came.

10.2 Arrive back at trailhead (GPS: 40 18.445, -105 50.471).

87 Wild Basin Trail Waterfalls: Lower Copeland Falls, Upper Copeland Falls, "Lovers Leaps," Calypso Cascades, and Ouzel Falls

Five waterfalls make this Wild Basin hike a waterfall lover's favorite. Enjoy Lower and Upper Copeland Falls, two sheet falls; two horsetail cascades on Cony Creek called "Lovers Leaps"; and lovely Calypso Cascades. Finally, be dazzled by Ouzel Falls, a plunge and veil waterfall at the turnaround point.

Start: Wild Basin Trailhead
Trail: Thunder Lake Trail
Difficulty: Easy for Copeland Falls and "Lovers Leaps"; moderate for Calypso Cascades and Ouzel Falls
Hiking time: About 1 hour for Copeland Falls; 2 hours for "Lovers Leaps"; 3 hours for Calypso Cascades; 4 hours for Ouzel Falls
Distance: 0.8 mile out and back for Lower Copeland Falls; 1.0 mile out and back for Upper Copeland Falls; 2.8 miles out and back for "Lovers Leaps"; 3.6 miles out and back for Calypso Cascades; 5.4 miles out and back for Ouzel Falls; 5.5 miles out and back for all 5 waterfalls
Elevation trailhead to falls viewpoints: 8,500 to 8,532 feet (+32 feet) for Lower Copeland Falls; to 8,575 feet (+75 feet) for Upper

Copeland Falls; to 8,870 feet (+370 feet) for "Lovers Leaps"; to 9,280 feet (+780 feet) for Calypso Cascades; to 9,460 feet (+960 feet) for Ouzel Falls
Trail surface: Dirt, rocks
Restrictions: Fee area; day use only; no campfires, bicycles, or dogs; wilderness rules apply
Amenities: Trailhead vault toilets; Wild Basin Ranger Station (seasonal); limited services in Allenspark; full services in Lyons and Estes Park
Maps: *DeLorme:* Page 29 D6; Trails Illustrated 200: Rocky Mountain National Park; USGS Allens Park
County: Boulder
Land status/contact: Rocky Mountain National Park, (970) 586-1206

Finding the trailhead: From US 36 in Lyons, take Main Street west for 0.2 mile and turn left on 5th Avenue (CO 7). Drive west on South St. Vrain Highway (CO 7) for 20.8 miles past Allenspark and turn left on Wild Basin Road (CR 84). From the intersection of CO 34 and CO 36 in Estes Park, drive 13.1 miles south on CO 7 to the turnoff. Drive 0.4 mile west on CR 84 and take a right on Road 115. Stop at the Wild Basin Entrance Station and continue 2.2 miles to the Wild Basin Ranger Station and parking. Wild Basin Trailhead is on the left side of the parking area (GPS: 40 12.462, -105 33.992).

The Hike

Wild Basin in southern Rocky Mountain National Park offers one of Colorado's best waterfall hikes. Beginning at the ranger station, the Thunder Lake Trail passes Lower and Upper Copeland Falls, "Lovers Leaps," and Calypso Cascades, and ends at Ouzel

Wild Basin Trail Waterfalls, Thunder Lake Trail Waterfalls, Lion Lake Trail Waterfalls

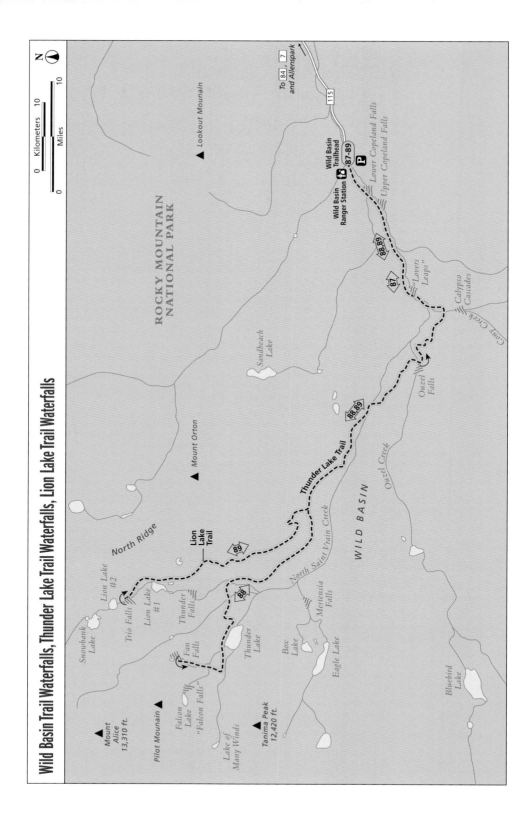

Left: Ouzel Falls, the turnaround point on the hike, is a majestic 50-foot waterfall.
Right: Three footbridges over Cony Creek provide views of tumultuous Calypso Cascades.

Falls, one of the national park's prettiest waterfalls. Both Lower and Upper Copeland Falls, cascades and short waterfalls on North St. Vrain Creek, are easily reached by spur trails. "Lovers Leaps," an unofficially named waterfall, is by a footbridge on the trail. Calypso Cascades, a wide waterfall seen from a boardwalk, is named for the purple calypso orchids, or "fairy slippers," that line Cony Creek in the springtime. Last is Ouzel Falls, a gorgeous waterfall that drops 50 feet over steep granite ledges into a plunge pool. The falls is named for the American dipper, or "water ouzel," a gray bird that bobs up and down in the creek in search of aquatic insects. The trail is easy to follow and well maintained with bridges, steps, and grading to ease your progress.

Miles and Directions

0.0 Begin at Wild Basin Trailhead, located across parking lot from ranger station. Hike west on Thunder Lake Trail along North St. Vrain Creek.

0.3 Go left off main trail on a signed spur toward Lower Copeland Falls.

0.4 Arrive at Lower Copeland Falls (GPS: 40 12.3, -105 34.253). Return to trail and go left toward Upper Copeland Falls (signed).

0.5 Arrive at Upper Copeland Falls (GPS: 40 12.233, -105 34.355). Continue on side trail to rejoin signed main trail.

0.6 Rejoin Thunder Lake Trail and go left (signed) up wide trail right of creek.

Top: North St. Vrain Creek splishes and splatters over rocks at Upper Copeland Falls.
Bottom: North St. Vrain Creek treats hikers to the first of five waterfalls, Lower Copeland Falls,
on this Wild Basin hike.

1.5 Trail bends left and crosses creek on footbridge to "Lovers Leaps" (GPS: 40 11.972, -105 35.305). Continue uphill on trail alongside Cony Creek.

1.8 Reach junction with signed Allenspark–Wild Basin Trail on left. Go right on three bridges over Calypso Cascades (GPS: 40 11.731, -105 35.461). Continue west across wooded slopes on Thunder Lake Trail.

2.8 Arrive at footbridge with Ouzel Falls to left. Scramble up left on a short side trail on the left side of Ouzel Creek to the base of Ouzel Falls (GPS: 40 11.921, -105 36.028). After viewing, return east on Thunder Lake Trail to parking lot.

5.5 Arrive back at trailhead (GPS: 40 12.462, -105 33.992).

88 Thunder Lake Trail Waterfalls: Mertensia Falls, Fan Falls, and "Falcon Falls"

This hike climbs to Thunder Lake in a high basin below the Continental Divide. The trail passes Mertensia Falls, a long cascade below Eagle and Box Lakes; "Falcon Falls," a horsetail splash fed by Falcon Lake; and boisterous Fan Falls, which splatters and spills down a playful cascade to Thunder Lake.

See map on page 292.
Start: Wild Basin Trailhead
Trail: Thunder Lake Trail
Difficulty: Strenuous for Mertensia Falls; strenuous/very strenuous for "Falcon Falls" and Fan Falls
Hiking time: About 7 hours for Mertensia Falls; 10 hours for "Falcon Falls" and Fan Falls
Distance: 11.2 miles out and back for Mertensia Falls; 15.4 miles out and back for "Falcon Falls" and Fan Falls, or all 3 waterfalls
Elevation trailhead to falls viewpoints: 8,500 to 10,370 feet (+1,870 feet) for Mertensia Falls; to 11,030 feet (+2,530 feet) for "Falcon Falls" and Fan Falls
Trail surface: Dirt, rocks

Restrictions: Fee area; wilderness rules apply; backcountry camping by permit; no bicycles or dogs
Amenities: Trailhead vault toilets; Wild Basin Ranger Station (seasonal); limited services in Allenspark; full services in Lyons and Estes Park
Maps: *DeLorme:* Page 29 D6, D5, C6, and C5; Trails Illustrated 200: Rocky Mountain National Park; 301: Longs Peak: Rocky Mountain National Park [Bear Lake, Wild Basin]; USGS Allens Park, Isolation Peak
County: Boulder
Land status/contact: Rocky Mountain National Park, (970) 586-1206

Finding the trailhead: From US 36 in Lyons, take Main Street west for 0.2 mile and turn left on 5th Avenue (CO 7). Drive west on South St. Vrain Highway (CO 7) for 20.8 miles past Allenspark and turn left on Wild Basin Road (CR 84). From the intersection of CO 34 and CO 36 in Estes Park, drive 13.1 miles south on CO 7 to the turnoff. Drive 0.4 mile west on CR 84 and take a right on Road 115. Stop at the Wild Basin Entrance Station and continue 2.2 miles to the Wild Basin Ranger Station and parking. Wild Basin Trailhead is on the left side of the parking area (GPS: 40 12.462, -105 33.992).

The Hike

This long, hard hike climbs to an alpine cirque nestled against the Continental Divide below 12,420-foot Tanima Peak in upper Wild Basin. Following the Thunder Lake Trail, the hike passes Copeland Falls, Calypso Cascades, and Ouzel Falls before busting northwest up North St. Vrain Creek to Thunder Lake and three gorgeous waterfalls. Mertensia Falls is a whitewater cascade down a steep chute to North St. Vrain Creek. Above Thunder Lake, the hike reaches "Falcon Falls," a horsetail waterfall squeezed between granite cliffs, while nearby Fan Falls rumbles over bedrock below Pilot Mountain.

Left: Fan Falls splatters and spills in a playful cascade above Thunder Lake.
Right: Mertensia Falls dances down a tumbling cascade from Eagle Lake and Box Lake.

Miles and Directions

0.0 Begin at Wild Basin Trailhead. Hike west on Thunder Lake Trail on creek's north side, passing Copeland Falls and "Lovers Leaps." Go uphill by Cony Creek.

1.8 Reach signed junction with Allenspark–Wild Basin Trail on left (GPS: 40 11.731, -105 35.461). Go right and cross three footbridges at Calypso Cascades. Follow trail west.

2.7 Cross footbridge over Ouzel Creek below Ouzel Falls (GPS: 40 11.9257, -105 35.9752).

3.1 Reach junction with Bluebird Lake Trail on left (GPS: 40 12.0958, -105 36.2057). Stay straight on main trail.

4.7 Reach junction with Lion Lake Trail to right (GPS: 40 12.7739, -105 37.4975). Continue straight toward Thunder Lake.

5.6 View Mertensia Falls through trees left of trail to west. Viewpoint is 0.4 mile from waterfall (GPS: 40 12.999,-105 38.102).

6.5 Reach sign for Thunder Lake. Bear left and descend stone steps. Pass stock pen on right and descend to a patrol cabin and Thunder Lake. Hike along lake's north side through conifer forest.

7.2 Reach flat clearing on right and listen for the sound of Fan Falls. Cut off main trail on path and hike north toward falls. Cross two creeks and continue uphill toward falls through deadfall with creek on left. Route is steep, loose, and intermittent. Alternatively, continue on main trail and view falls from about 0.2 mile up trail.

7.7 Arrive at Fan Falls and viewpoint of "Falcon Falls" in cliffs to south-southwest (GPS: 40 13.76,-105 39.077). Return the way you came.

15.4 Arrive back at trailhead (GPS: 40 12.462, -105 33.992).

89 Lion Lake Trail Waterfalls: Thunder Falls and Trio Falls

The Lion Lake Trail reaches two secluded waterfalls in the northern part of Wild Basin below towering Chiefs Head Peak and Mount Alice. This hike to Thunder Falls and Trio Falls, the hardest waterfall hike in Rocky Mountain National Park, is perfect for a backpacking trip to falls and pristine lakes in a striking alpine basin.

See map on page 292.
Start: Wild Basin Trailhead
Trails: Thunder Lake Trail, Lion Lake Trail
Difficulty: Strenuous/very strenuous
Hiking time: About 10 hours
Distance: 14.8 miles out and back for both waterfalls
Elevation trailhead to falls viewpoints: 8,500 to 11,000 feet (+2,500 feet) for Thunder Falls; to 11,260 feet (+2,760 feet) for Trio Falls
Trail surface: Dirt, rocks
Restrictions: Fee area; wilderness rules apply; backcountry camping by permit only; no bicycles or dogs

Amenities: Trailhead vault toilets; Wild Basin Ranger Station (seasonal); limited services in Allenspark; full services in Lyons and Estes Park
Maps: *DeLorme:* Page 29 D6, C6, and C5; Trails Illustrated 200: Rocky Mountain National Park; 301: Longs Peak: Rocky Mountain National Park [Bear Lake, Wild Basin]; USGS Allens Park, Isolation Peak
County: Boulder
Land status/contact: Rocky Mountain National Park, (970) 586-1206

Finding the trailhead: From US 36 in Lyons, take Main Street west for 0.2 mile and turn left on 5th Avenue (CO 7). Drive west on South St. Vrain Highway (CO 7) for 20.8 miles past Allenspark and turn left on Wild Basin Road (CR 84). From the intersection of CO 34 and CO 36 in Estes Park, drive 13.1 miles south on CO 7 to the turnoff. Drive 0.4 mile west on CR 84 and take a right on Road 115. Stop at the Wild Basin Entrance Station and continue 2.2 miles to the Wild Basin Ranger Station and parking. Wild Basin Trailhead is on the left side of the parking area (GPS: 40 12.462, -105 33.992).

The Hike

This excellent hike follows the Thunder Lake and Lion Lake Trails to four lakes and two waterfalls in a lofty cirque below the south face of 13,579-foot Chiefs Head in the heart of Rocky Mountain National Park. Rugged and remote Wild Basin is one of the park's most beautiful spots with flower-filled meadows, glacier-scraped cliffs, shining tarns, and falling water at Thunder Falls and Trio Falls. Thunder Falls roars down a hidden trailside chasm, while Trio Falls, fed by Lion Lake #2, is a segmented bridal veil waterfall with triple leaps.

Left: Waters plunge over steep rock in a hidden trailside chasm at Thunder Falls.
Right: Trio Falls pours over a sculpted granite bench high in Wild Basin.

The hike's first section follows Thunder Lake Trail, passing Copeland Falls, "Lover's Leap," Calypso Cascade, and Ouzel Falls, and continues up North St. Vrain Creek to the junction with Lion Lake Trail where it veers right. Lion Lake Trail is steep, rocky, and hard to follow at times on granite slabs and wooded slopes. Expect solitude with few other hikers and stunning scenery at the waterfalls and lakes. Consider getting a backcountry permit and backpacking to the lower lake.

Miles and Directions

0.0   Begin at Wild Basin Trailhead. Hike west on Thunder Lake Trail on creek's north side, passing Copeland Falls and "Lovers Leaps." Go uphill by Cony Creek.

1.8   Reach signed junction with Allenspark–Wild Basin Trail on left (GPS: 40 11.731, -105 35.461). Go right and cross three footbridges at Calypso Cascades. Follow trail west.

2.7   Cross footbridge over Ouzel Creek below Ouzel Falls (GPS: 40 11.9257, -105 35.9752).

3.1   Reach junction with Bluebird Lake Trail on left (GPS: 40 12.0958, -105 36.2057). Stay straight on main trail.

4.7   Reach junction with Lion Lake Trail to right (GPS: 40 12.7739, -105 37.4975). Go right and hike steep trail toward Lion Lake #1.

5.2   Cross slabs and follow cairns as trail fades and bends to right.

6.5   Cut off trail to left for 0.1 mile to view upper leaps of Thunder Falls rushing down a smooth slab. More dramatic falls are downstream but difficult to reach (GPS: 30 13.669, -105 38.357). Return to main trail and continue north to Lion Lake #1.

7.0   Reach southeast edge of Lion Lake #1 (GPS: 40 13.8988, -105 38.2655). Follow trail along right side of lake and head up steep slopes right of creek, scrambling over slabs toward Trio Falls. An unnamed plunge falls is in cliffs to northeast.

7.5   Arrive at base of lower Trio Falls (GPS: 40 14.12, -105 38.4166). To see upper leaps, continue up right of falls. For extra credit, hike slabs for 0.2 mile from waterfall base to Lion Lake #2. Return on main trail.

14.8   Arrive back at trailhead (GPS: 40 12.462, -105 33.992).

90 East Longs Peak Trail Waterfalls: Columbine Falls and "Chasm Lake Falls"

Two beautiful waterfalls, alpine lakes, and Rocky Mountain National Park's highest peak make this hike one of the best! Below Longs Peak, Chasm Lake tips its waters east, cascading down a jumble of rocks at "Chasm Lake Falls." Shortly after, the water spills again into a long plunge down Columbine Falls.

Start: East Longs Peak Trailhead
Trails: East Longs Peak Trail, Chasm Lake Trail
Difficulty: Strenuous
Hiking time: About 5 hours
Distance: 7.8 miles out and back for Columbine Falls; 8.0 miles out and back for "Chasm Lake Falls" or both waterfalls
Elevation trailhead to falls viewpoints: 9,400 to 11,570 feet (+2,170 feet) for Columbine Falls; to 11,600 feet (+2,200 feet) for "Chasm Lake Falls"
Trail surface: Dirt, rocks

Restrictions: Fee area; limited parking; additional parking on road; wilderness rules apply; no dogs
Amenities: Trailhead toilets; Longs Peak Ranger Station; campground; no overnight parking; full services in Lyons and Estes Park
Maps: *DeLorme:* Page 29 C6; Trails Illustrated 301: Longs Peak: Rocky Mountain National Park [Bear Lake, Wild Basin]; USGS Longs Peak
Counties: Larimer, Boulder
Land status/contact: Rocky Mountain National Park, (970) 586-1206

Finding the trailhead: From US 36 in Lyons, take Main Street west for 0.2 mile and turn left on 5th Avenue (CO 7 West). Go straight on CO 7 for 24.3 miles, passing Allenspark, and turn left on signed Longs Peak Road. From the intersection of CO 34 and CO 36 in Estes Park, drive 9 miles south on CO 7 and turn right toward the trailhead. Drive 1 mile to the parking lot at Longs Peak Ranger Station. The Longs Peak Trailhead is in front of the ranger station (GPS: 40 16.329, -105 33.409).

The Hike

This hike follows trails to an atmospheric cirque below the East Face of 14,259-foot Longs Peak. The glacier-carved cirque is a world of soaring cliffs, two lakes, and two alpine waterfalls—Columbine Falls and "Chasm Lake Falls." Falling below Chasm Lake Trail, Columbine Falls is a scenic horsetail waterfall that drops down a broken cliff to a bowl before rollicking down a cliff. "Chasm Lake Falls," draining from its namesake lake, riffles and rolls down a polished trough above the trail.

The hike's first section follows East Longs Peak Trail, the standard climbing route up the mountain. Since it's popular with hikers, mountaineers, and rock climbers, expect a crowded parking lot and to share the trail. A privy, short on privacy but big on views, is at the junction of the trail and Chasm Lake Trail. Besides the waterfalls, check out the blue-green "eye" of Peacock Pool below Columbine Falls, and make

East Longs Peak Trail Waterfalls

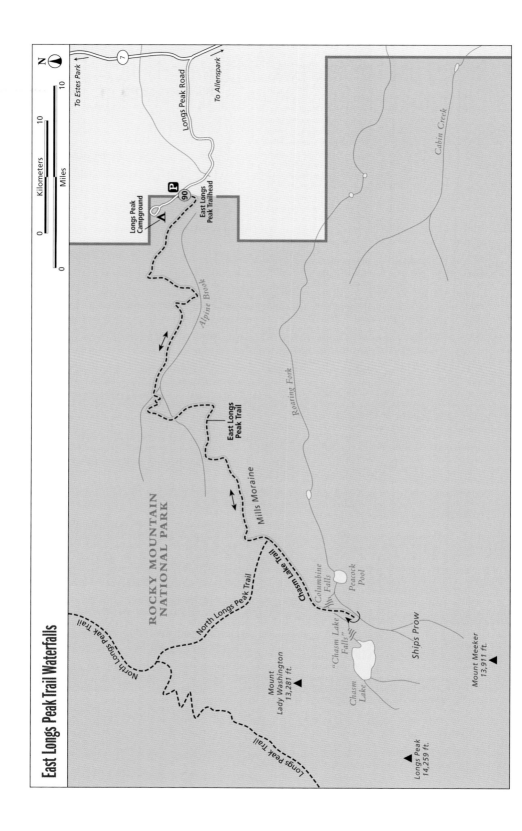

N

To Estes Park
7
Longs Peak Road
To Allenspark

0   Kilometers   10
0   Miles   10

Longs Peak Campground
P
90
East Longs Peak Trailhead

Alpine Brook

Roaring Fork

Cabin Creek

East Longs Peak Trail

ROCKY MOUNTAIN NATIONAL PARK

North Longs Peak Trail

Chasm Lake Trail

Mills Moraine

North Longs Peak Trail

Longs Peak Trail

Columbine Falls

Peacock Pool

"Chasm Lake" Falls

Ships Prow

Mount Lady Washington 13,281 ft.

Chasm Lake

Mount Meeker 13,911 ft.

Longs Peak 14,259 ft.

Left: The aqueous display of Columbine Falls drops east through the Roaring Fork drainage. Right: Chasm Lake tips its waters over a jumble of rocks at "Chasm Lake Falls."

sure to hike past the upper falls to Chasm Lake, a sprawling tarn below Longs Peak's famous East Face.

Miles and Directions

0.0 Begin at East Longs Peak Trailhead. Hike up East Longs Peak Trail through lodgepole pines, following signs for Chasm Lake.

0.5 Reach junction with Eugenia Mine Trail on right. Keep left toward Chasm Lake and hike up hill to bridge over Larkspur Creek. Continue to bridge over Alpine Brook.

2.6 Reach trail junction. Keep left toward Chasm Lake.

3.3 Reach junction with Chasm Lake Trail at 11,550 feet. East Longs Peak Trail to summit goes right and a privy is to the left. Go left on signed Chasm Lake Trail.

3.9 Arrive at Columbine Falls (GPS: 40 15.652, -105 35.976). Continue on trail toward "Chasm Lake Falls" visible ahead.

4.0   View "Chasm Lake Falls" (GPS: 40 15.552, -105 36.03). Stay on trail and off tundra. Return the way you came. Alternatively, continue to Chasm Lake.

8.0 Arrive back at trailhead (GPS: 40 16.329, -105 33.409).

91 Alberta Falls

At Alberta Falls, Glacier Creek pours down a steep chute in a powerful horsetail, fills a punchbowl, and cascades past the trail and overlook.

Start: Glacier Gorge Trailhead
Trail: Glacier Gorge Trail
Difficulty: Easy
Hiking time: About 1 hour
Distance: 1.6 miles out and back
Elevation trailhead to falls viewpoint: 9,180 to 9,400 feet (+220 feet)
Trail surface: Dirt, rocks
Restrictions: Fee area; day use only; no bicycles or dogs; wilderness rules apply; backcountry camping by permit only

Amenities: Trailhead vault toilets; nearby Beaver Meadows Visitor Center, picnic areas, and seasonal concessions; no overnight parking; full services in Estes Park
Maps: *DeLorme:* Page 29 C6; Trails Illustrated 200: Rocky Mountain National Park; 301: Longs Peak: Rocky Mountain National Park [Bear Lake, Wild Basin]; USGS McHenrys Peak
County: Larimer
Land status/contact: Rocky Mountain National Park, (970) 586-1206

Finding the trailhead: From Estes Park, take US 36 West for 3.8 miles to the Beaver Meadows Entrance Station. Drive 0.2 mile and turn left (south) on Bear Lake Road, then go 8.1 miles to a paved parking area on the road's left side at Glacier Gorge Trailhead. The lot quickly fills in summer and on weekends. Avoid parking problems by boarding the Bear Lake shuttle at the Park and Ride opposite Glacier Basin Campground and ride to Glacier Basin Bus Stop and Trailhead (GPS: 40 18.621, -105 38.421).

The Hike

Alberta Falls, a 30-foot-high horsetail waterfall fed by Glacier Creek, is one of Rocky Mountain National Park's most popular waterfalls, with an easy hike and grand scenery. The family-friendly hike has only 160 feet of elevation gain, making it perfect for hikers of all abilities. The waterfall is named for Alberta Sprague, who, with husband Abner, was one of the first settlers in the Estes Park area after homesteading in Moraine Park in 1874.

Reach the falls from Glacier Gorge Trailhead on Bear Lake Road. Hike southwest on Glacier Gorge Trail to Glacier Gorge Junction and go left. Alternatively, start at Bear Lake Trailhead and follow a connector trail for 0.4 mile down to Glacier Gorge Junction. This route is 0.2 mile longer and has more elevation gain. The Glacier Gorge Trail continues past Alberta Falls to more waterfalls in Glacier Gorge and on the Loch Vale Trail.

Miles and Directions

0.0   Begin at Glacier Gorge Trailhead. Hike south on Glacier Gorge Trail.

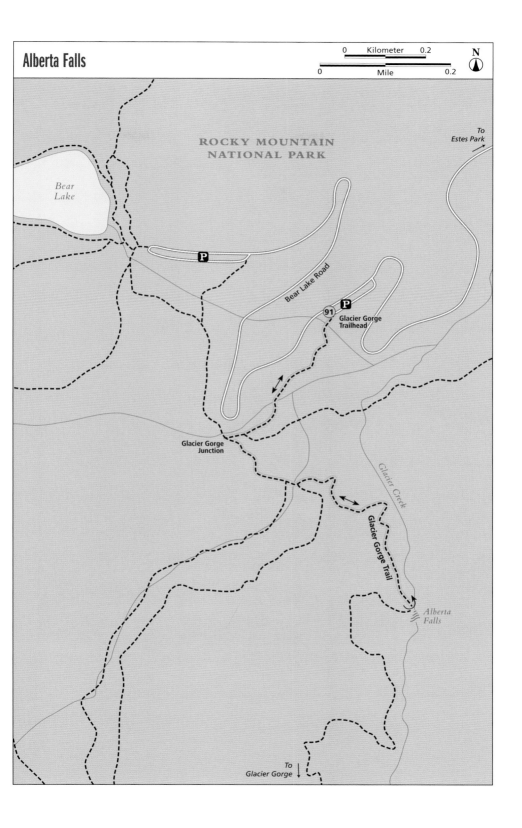

Alberta Falls

0   Kilometer   0.2

0   Mile   0.2

N

To Estes Park

ROCKY MOUNTAIN
NATIONAL PARK

Bear Lake

P

Bear Lake Road

P

91

Glacier Gorge Trailhead

Glacier Gorge Junction

Glacier Creek

Glacier Gorge Trail

Alberta Falls

To Glacier Gorge

Glacier Creek spills off a granite chute at Alberta Falls, one of the park's most popular waterfalls.

0.3 Reach Glacier Gorge Junction. Turn left at signed junction toward Alberta Falls.

0.8 Arrive at Alberta Falls viewpoint (GPS: 40 18.233, -105 38.291). Hike back on same trail.

1.6 Arrive back at trailhead (GPS: N40 18.621, W105 38.421).

92 Glacier Gorge Trail Waterfalls: Glacier Falls, "Shelf Falls," "Solitude Falls," "Blue Lake Falls," "Slide Falls," Ribbon Falls, and "Black Lake Falls"

Glacier Gorge, a gorgeous valley in the heart of Rocky Mountain National Park, offers seven waterfalls from five water sources. Glacier Falls tumbles through boulders below Mills Lake. "Shelf Falls" and "Solitude Falls" hang in cliffs below Thatchtop and Arrowhead, while "Blue Lake Falls" is a segmented horsetail below its namesake lake. Lovely "Slide Falls" slips for 100 feet down a granite slab in a sweeping flourish; Ribbon Falls is a slick slide of frothy delight below Black Lake; and "Black Lake Falls" spills from Frozen Lake in horsetail tiers above the lake.

Start: Glacier Gorge Trailhead
Trail: Glacier Gorge Trail
Difficulty: Moderate for Glacier Falls; strenuous for other falls
Hiking time: About 3 hours for Glacier Falls; 5 hours for "Shelf Falls" and "Solitude Falls"; 6 hours for "Blue Lake Falls," "Slide Falls," and Ribbon Falls; 7 hours for "Black Lake Falls"
Distance: 4.4 miles out and back for Glacier Falls; 8.0 miles out and back for "Shelf Falls"; 8.2 miles out and back for "Solitude Falls"; 8.4 miles out and back for "Blue Lake Falls"; 9.2 miles out and back for "Slide Falls"; 9.4 miles out and back for Ribbon Falls; 9.8 miles out and back for "Black Lake Falls"; 9.8 miles out and back for all waterfalls
Elevation trailhead to falls viewpoints: 9,180 to 9,880 feet (+700 feet) for Glacier Falls; to 10,310 feet (+1,130 feet) for "Shelf Falls" and "Solitude Falls"; to 10,350 feet (+1,170 feet) for "Blue Lake Falls"; to 10,500 feet (+1,320 feet) for "Slide Falls"; to 10,580 feet (+1,400 feet) for Ribbon Falls; to 10,660 feet (+1,480 feet) for "Black Lake Falls"
Trail surface: Dirt, rocks
Restrictions: Fee area; day use only; no dogs; wilderness rules apply
Amenities: Trailhead vault toilets; shuttle service; Beaver Meadows Visitor Center; full services in Estes Park
Maps: DeLorme: Page 29 C5 and C6; Trails Illustrated 200: Rocky Mountain National Park; USGS McHenrys Peak
County: Larimer
Land status/contact: Rocky Mountain National Park, (970) 586-1206

Finding the trailhead: From Estes Park, take US 36 West for 3.8 miles to the Beaver Meadows Entrance Station. Drive 0.2 mile and turn left (south) on Bear Lake Road, then go 8.1 miles to a paved parking area on the road's left side at Glacier Gorge Trailhead. The lot quickly fills in summer and on weekends. Avoid parking problems by boarding the Bear Lake shuttle at the Park and Ride opposite Glacier Basin Campground and ride to Glacier Basin Bus Stop and Trailhead (GPS: 40 18.621, -105 38.421).

Left: A slick slide of frothy white delight flows over black and orange granite at Ribbon Falls. Right: "Black Lake Falls" spills from Frozen Lake in horsetail tiers over high granite walls.

The Hike

Besides glorious waterfalls, the Glacier Gorge Trail offers skyscraping mountains, spruce and pine forests, glistening lakes, and rushing streams. Beginning at Glacier Gorge Trailhead, the trail is popular with hikers. Plan on a full-day adventure to see all the waterfalls and reach the trail's end at Black Lake. Bring extra clothes, rain gear, water, snacks, and trekking poles.

The hike climbs on a well-traveled trail to a junction with North Longs Peak Trail below East Glacier Knob. The trail then heads west and reaches a junction with Loch Vale Trail. Go left here on Glacier Gorge Trail and climb to Glacier Falls in a deep gorge, then continue to Mills Lake, named for Enos Mills, father of Rocky Mountain. The trail hugs the lake's east side, passing Jewel Lake and stepping through wetlands on split logs. Look for ephemeral waterfalls fed by snowmelt cascading off jagged peaks. From Jewel Lake to Black Lake, watch for the big waterfalls, including "Shelf Falls, "Solitude Falls," and "Blue Lake Falls." These inaccessible waterfalls cascade down steep slopes surrounded by cliffs and forest. Trailside falls are "Slide Falls" and pretty Ribbon Falls. At Black Lake, a high lake tucked against McHenrys Peak, look southwest at "Black Lake Falls" on streaked cliffs.

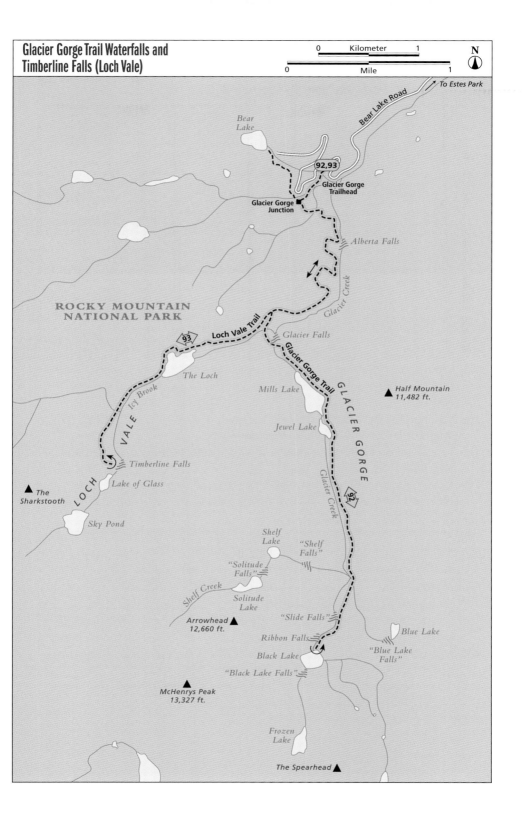

Glacier Gorge Trail Waterfalls and Timberline Falls (Loch Vale)

0   Kilometer   1

0   Mile   1

N

To Estes Park

Bear Lake Road

Bear Lake

92,93

Glacier Gorge Trailhead

Glacier Gorge Junction

Alberta Falls

Glacier Creek

ROCKY MOUNTAIN NATIONAL PARK

93   **Loch Vale Trail**

Glacier Falls

The Loch

Icy Brook

Glacier Gorge Trail

Mills Lake

▲ *Half Mountain* 11,482 ft.

Jewel Lake

GLACIER GORGE

Timberline Falls

Lake of Glass

V A L E

L O C H

▲ *The Sharkstooth*

Sky Pond

Glacier Creek

92

Shelf Lake

"Shelf Falls"

"Solitude Falls"

Shelf Creek

Solitude Lake

Arrowhead ▲ 12,660 ft.

"Slide Falls"

Ribbon Falls

Blue Lake

"Blue Lake Falls"

Black Lake

"Black Lake Falls"

▲ *McHenrys Peak* 13,327 ft.

Frozen Lake

The Spearhead ▲

"Slide Falls" slip-slides over low-angle granite in a sweeping flourish.

Miles and Directions

0.0 Begin at Glacier Gorge Trailhead. Hike south on Glacier Gorge Trail.

0.3 Reach Glacier Gorge Junction. Go straight and turn left at signed junction toward Alberta Falls.

0.8 Pass Alberta Falls (GPS: 40 18.233, -105 38.291). Continue on trail.

1.6 Reach junction with North Longs Peak Trail on left (GPS: 40 17.984, -105 38.389). Go straight on Glacier Gorge Trail toward Mills Lake.

2.1 Reach junction with Loch Vale Trail (GPS: 40 17.845, -105 38.76). Go left toward Mills Lake. Cross bridge.

2.2 Hike up slab left of trail for views of Glacier Falls. Arrive at viewpoint above Glacier Falls (GPS: 40 17.688, -105 38.775). Return to trail and continue south, crossing footbridge over Glacier Creek.

2.5 Reach Mills Lake and follow trail around left (east) side. Hike on trail through deadfall.

4.0 View of "Shelf Falls" right of trail in cliffs (GPS: 40 16.509, -105 38.211).

4.1 View of "Solitude Falls" right of trail in cliffs (GPS: 40 16.449, -105 38.215).

4.2 Arrive at "Blue Lake Falls" above trail to right (GPS: 40 16.388, -105 38.198).

4.5 Leave main trail and go right to "Slide Falls."

4.6 Arrive at "Slide Falls" (GPS: 40 16.141, -105 38.335). Return to main trail and continue south.

4.8 Arrive at Ribbon Falls (GPS: 40 16.045, -105 38.399). Climb trail on steps. "Black Lake Falls" is visible ahead. Follow trail if dry or rock-hop up creek edge.

5.0 Arrive at Black Lake and view of "Black Lake Falls" in cliffs below McHenrys Peak (GPS: 40 15.984, -105 38.431). Return north, following trail back.

9.8 Arrive back at trailhead (GPS: 40 18.621, -105 38.421).

93 Timberline Falls (Loch Vale)

Melting snow from Taylor Glacier trickles into Sky Pond, spills into Lake of Glass, and plunges over cliffs at Timberline Falls in upper Loch Vale. The falls is a picture-perfect waterfall in a storybook setting, and one of the best in Rocky Mountain National Park.

See map on page 307.
Start: Glacier Gorge Trailhead
Trails: Glacier Gorge Trail, Loch Vale Trail
Difficulty: Strenuous
Hiking time: About 5 hours
Distance: 8.2 miles out and back
Elevation trailhead to falls viewpoint: 9,180 to 10,660 feet (+1,480 feet)
Trail surface: Dirt, rocks, stone steps, talus
Restrictions: Fee area; day use only; no dogs; follow wilderness regulations

Amenities: Trailhead vault toilets; Beaver Meadows Visitor Center; shuttle service; full services in Estes Park
Maps: *DeLorme:* Page 29 C5; Trails Illustrated 200: Rocky Mountain National Park; USGS McHenrys Peak
County: Larimer
Land status/contact: Rocky Mountain National Park, (970) 586-1206

Finding the trailhead: From Estes Park, take US 36 West for 3.8 miles to the Beaver Meadows Entrance Station. Drive 0.2 mile and turn left (south) on Bear Lake Road, then go 8.1 miles to a paved parking area on the road's left side at Glacier Gorge Trailhead. The lot quickly fills in summer and on weekends. Avoid parking problems by boarding the Bear Lake shuttle at the Park and Ride opposite Glacier Basin Campground and ride to Glacier Basin Bus Stop and Trailhead (GPS: 40 18.621, -105 38.421).

The Hike

Timberline Falls, one of Rocky Mountain National Park's highest-elevation waterfalls, splatters off a cliff in Loch Vale, a spectacular glaciated valley surrounded by soaring granite mountains. Reached by the Glacier Gorge and Loch Vale Trails, the popular hike to the falls is tough with plenty of elevation gain.

It's a full-day expedition to hike to the 75-foot, tiered, horsetail falls and then to scramble to the upper basin, one of Colorado's most beautiful spots. The basin is floored by Lake of Glass and Sky Pond, with a tableau of saw-toothed peaks including Sharkstooth and the Petit Grepon punctuating the northern horizon. Plan on an early start to avoid the daily afternoon thunderstorms in summer. Bring extra clothes, rain gear, water, food, and trekking poles.

Starting at Glacier Gorge Trailhead, the hike follows Glacier Gorge Trail past Alberta Falls and East Glacier Knob before bending west and joining Loch Vale Trail. This trail heads uphill along Icy Brook, a clear stream filled with cascades and small waterfalls, to The Loch, a gorgeous lake rimmed by outcrops. The hike continues past the lake and up wooded slopes below the towering Cathedral Spires to a steep final

Beginning from Taylor Glacier, Icy Brook fills Sky Pond and Lake of Glass before plunging over Timberline Falls in upper Loch Vale.

ascent to the misty falls. Look for a flat rock below the falls and enjoy 360-degree views of peaks, meadows, and dark forests.

Miles and Directions

0.0   Begin at Glacier Gorge Trailhead. Hike south on Glacier Gorge Trail.

0.3   Reach junction with trail from Bear Lake. Go straight and turn left at next junction toward Alberta Falls.

0.8   Arrive at Alberta Falls (GPS: 40 18.233,-105 38.291). Continue south on trail.

1.6   Reach junction with North Longs Peak Trail on left (GPS: 40 17.984, -105 38.389). Go straight on Glacier Gorge Trail.

2.1   Reach junction with Loch Vale Trail (GPS: 40 17.845, -105 38.76). Go right up Loch Vale.

2.8   Arrive at The Loch. Hike around right (north) side of lake and follow Icy Brook.

3.5   Climb stone and timber steps and cross two creeks on footbridges.

3.7   Reach junction with Andrews Glacier Trail. Stay straight toward Sky Pond.

3.9   Falls come into view in cliffs. Climb steps up steep slopes to falls.

4.1   Arrive at Timberline Falls (GPS: 40 16.993,-105 39.887). Return the way you came.

8.2   Arrive back at trailhead (GPS: 40 18.621, -105 38.421).

94 Fern Lake Trail Waterfalls: "Windy Gulch Cascades," "Spruce Creek Falls," Fern Falls, Marguerite Falls, and Grace Falls

Five waterfalls pour through Odessa Gorge in Rocky Mountain National Park. The first, "Windy Gulch Cascades," hides off the trail. "Spruce Creek Falls" tumbles in leaps below the trail. Fern Falls roars over a trailside cliff. Marguerite Falls, not accessed by trail, offers leaps below Fern Lake. The hike's sparkling gem hangs above Odessa Lake where snowmelt spills over cliffs at Grace Falls.

Start: Fern Lake Trailhead

Trail: Fern Lake Trail

Difficulty: Easy for "Windy Gulch Cascades"; moderate for "Spruce Creek Falls" and Fern Falls; strenuous for Marguerite Falls; very strenuous for Grace Falls

Hiking time: About 1 hour for "Windy Gulch Cascades;" 3 hours for "Spruce Creek Falls;" 4 hours for Fern Falls; 5 hours for Marguerite Falls; 8 hours for Grace Falls; 9 hours for all waterfalls

Distance: 1.0 mile out and back for "Windy Gulch Cascades"; 4.4 miles out and back for "Spruce Creek Falls"; 5.4 miles out and back for Fern Falls; 7.8 miles out and back for Marguerite Falls; 12.0 miles out and back for Grace Falls and all others

Elevations trailhead to falls viewpoints: 8,155 to 8,580 feet (+425 feet) for "Windy Gulch Cascades"; to 8,500 feet (+345 feet) for "Spruce Creek Falls"; to 8,800 feet (+645 feet) for Fern Falls; to 9,440 feet (+1,285 feet) for Marguerite Falls; to 10,510 feet (+2,355 feet) for Grace Falls

Trail surface: Dirt, rocks, talus

Restrictions: Fee area; day use only; no dogs; follow wilderness rules

Amenities: Trailhead vault toilets; Beaver Meadows Visitor Center; no overnight parking; full services in Estes Park

Maps: *DeLorme:* Page 29 B5 and B6; Trails Illustrated 200: Rocky Mountain National Park; USGS McHenrys Peak

County: Larimer

Land status/contact: Rocky Mountain National Park, (970) 586-1206

Finding the trailhead: From Estes Park, take US 36 West for 3.8 miles to the Beaver Meadows Entrance Station. Drive 0.2 mile and turn left (south) on Bear Lake Road. Drive 1.2 miles and turn right toward Moraine Park Campground. Drive 0.5 mile and turn left on Fern Lake Road. Drive 1.5 miles to Cub Lake Trailhead. Continue 0.7 mile to Fern Lake Trailhead (GPS: 40 21.292, -105 37.863). Avoid parking problems by boarding the Moraine Park shuttle at the Park and Ride opposite Glacier Basin Campground and ride to Fern Lake Bus Stop. Hike 0.8 mile to the trailhead (adds 1.6 miles to hike mileage).

Turn page: Fern Falls roars over a trailside cliff, protected ▷
by dense, green shrubs and Engelmann spruce.

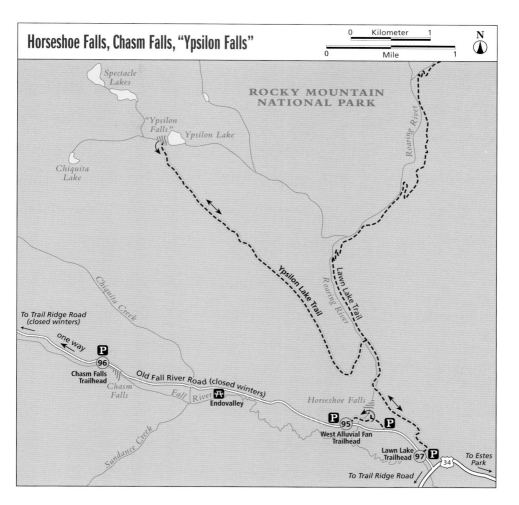

0   Kilometer   1

0   Mile   1

N

Spectacle
Lakes

ROCKY MOUNTAIN
NATIONAL PARK

Rearing River

"Ypsilon
Falls"   Ypsilon Lake

Chiquita
Lake

Ypsilon Lake Trail

Lawn Lake Trail

Roaring River

Chiquita Creek

To Trail Ridge Road
(closed winters)

one way

P
96

Chasm Falls
Trailhead

Old Fall River Road (closed winters)

Chasm
Falls

Fall River

Endovalley

Horseshoe Falls

P
95

P

West Alluvial Fan
Trailhead

Sundance Creek

Lawn Lake
Trailhead   97   P

34

To Estes
Park

To Trail Ridge Road

Miles and Directions

0.0 Begin at West Alluvial Fan Trailhead at west parking lot. Follow trail northeast, cross a bridge, and hike to waterfall viewpoint on paved trail (GPS: 40 24.6649, -105 38.0647).

0.2 For more adventure, scramble north to base of falls (GPS: 40 24.696, -105 38.071). Return the way you came.

0.4 Arrive back at trailhead (GPS: 40 24.641, -105 38.215).

*A massive flash flood in 1982 formed Horseshoe
Falls and the alluvial fan below it.*

96 Chasm Falls

Old Fall River Road climbs west to Fall River Pass before joining Trail Ridge Road, the highest continuous paved roadway in the United States. At the road's eastern end, tucked into a roadside gorge, the Fall River pours down a dramatic chute waterfall at Chasm Falls.

See map on page 317.
Start: Chasm Falls Trailhead
Trail: Chasm Falls Trail
Difficulty: Very easy
Hiking time: Less than 1 hour
Distance: 0.12 mile out and back
Elevation trailhead to falls viewpoint: 9,065 to 9,000 feet (-65 feet)
Trail surface: Paved, dirt, rocks
Restrictions: Fee area; no dogs; park in lot, not on road

Amenities: Picnic tables and vault toilets at Endovalley Picnic Area; Fall River Visitor Center and Alpine Visitor Center
Maps: *DeLorme:* Page 29 B5; Trails Illustrated 200: Rocky Mountain National Park; USGS Trail Ridge
County: Larimer
Land status/contact: Rocky Mountain National Park, (970) 586-1206

Finding the trailhead: From Estes Park, take US 34 West (Fall River Road) for 4.7 miles to the Fall River Entrance to Rocky Mountain National Park. Continue 2.1 miles on US 34 and turn right on Old Fall River Road. Drive 3.2 miles, passing the East and West Alluvial Fan parking on the right and the Endovalley Picnic Area on the left. After the road becomes unpaved, pass a secondary trailhead for Chasm Falls on the road's left side at a switchback. Continue to roadside parking at the trailhead (GPS: 40 25.020, -105 40.366).

The Hike

Chasm Falls, a 30-foot waterfall, drops over a granite ledge into a narrow slot canyon below Old Fall River Road. From the roadside parking area, descend short, steep switchbacks to a viewing platform near the base of the waterfall. The overlook is small, and usually crowded in the summer when Old Fall River Road is open. In the off-season, Old Fall River Road may be closed at the West Alluvial Fan parking area, so plan on a longer hike—about 2.4 miles in each direction.

The historic dirt road leading to the trailhead is one-way uphill, narrow, and has no guardrails. If you do not want to enjoy the scenic drive to Trail Ridge Road, park at Endovalley Picnic Area and hike up the road to the falls.

If you opt for the drive, look for bonus waterfalls. At 3.5 miles beyond Chasm Falls, there's a seasonal cascade in the cliffs across the valley to the left. The road here is a shelf, so find a safe parking spot to enjoy the view. Continue another 0.2 mile to a roadside cascade and more waterfalls. Farther up the road are scenic pullouts, the Alpine Visitor Center, and Trail Ridge Road. Go left toward Estes Park or right to Grand Lake.

The Fall River pours its bounty in a dramatic chute falls of subtle resplendence at Chasm Falls.

Miles and Directions

0.0   Begin at Chasm Falls Trailhead. Descend paved and dirt trail.

0.06 Arrive at viewing platform near base of falls (GPS: 40 25.006, -105 40.327). Return the way you came.

0.12 Arrive back at trailhead (GPS: 40 25.020, -105 40.366).

97 "Ypsilon Falls"

The Spectacle Lakes hide below 13,514-foot Ypsilon Mountain in the Mummy Range. Their outlet stream drops south through a ravine in multitiered horsetails amid mossy rocks and greenery, spilling into a shimmering pool at "Ypsilon Falls."

See map on page 317.
Start: Lawn Lake Trailhead
Trails: Lawn Lake Trail, Ypsilon Lake Trail
Difficulty: Strenuous
Hiking time: About 6 hours
Distance: 9.0 miles out and back
Elevation trailhead to falls viewpoint: 8,540 to 10,590 feet (+2,050 feet)
Trail surface: Dirt, rocks

Restrictions: Fee area; no dogs
Amenities: Vault toilets; Fall River Visitor Center
Maps: *DeLorme:* Page 29 A5 and B6; Trails Illustrated 200: Rocky Mountain National Park; USGS Trail Ridge
County: Larimer
Land status/contact: Rocky Mountain National Park, (970) 586-1206

Finding the trailhead: From Estes Park, take US 34 West (Fall River Road) for 4.7 miles to the Fall River Entrance to Rocky Mountain National Park. Continue 2.1 miles on US 34 and turn right on Old Fall River Road. Drive 0.1 mile to the Lawn Lake Trailhead parking area on the right (GPS: 40 24.4327, -105 37.5704).

The Hike

Ypsilon Mountain, the national park's fifth-highest peak at 13,514 feet, lifts a glaciated brow above the Spectacle Lakes and Ypsilon Lake. "Ypsilon Falls," a segmented, two-tiered waterfall, tucks into a cliff-lined canyon just west of its namesake lake. The water fills a shiny plunge pool, then squeezes through a granite gap. After hiking to the lake, find the falls by hiking from the lake's southwest shore to a bridge. Listen for the sound of falling water and hike left to the falls. The mountain is named for the gullies on its east face that form a Y, or the letter Ypsilon in Greek.

Miles and Directions

0.0 Begin at Lawn Lake Trailhead. Hike north on Lawn Lake Trail, and after 0.1 mile bear left at a trail junction. Follow trail up gorge carved by the Lawn Lake flood.

1.5 Reach junction with Ypsilon Lake Trail. Go left on it, crossing footbridge over Roaring River and then ascending timber steps. Trail climbs steadily northwest through forest with limited views.

4.0 Reach pretty Chipmunk Lake on right. Continue on trail past backcountry campsites.

4.4 Arrive at Ypsilon Lake's southern shore. Cross footbridge and turn left to falls.

4.5 Arrive at "Ypsilon Falls" (GPS: 40 26.615, -105 39.964). Return the way you came.

9.0 Arrive back at trailhead (GPS: 40 24.4327, -105 37.5704).

Water flows in multitiered horsetails and spills into a shimmering pool at "Ypsilon Falls."

98 MacGregor Falls

Black Canyon Creek, flowing southeast from Mummy Mountain, empties into the Big Thompson River in Estes Park. At MacGregor Falls the creek cascades through a narrow passage, twists through boulders, and slip-slides over a granite slab in a frothy sheet.

Start: Lumpy Ridge Trailhead
Trails: Lumpy Ridge Trail, Black Canyon Trail, McGregor Falls Trail
Difficulty: Moderate
Hiking time: About 4 hours
Distance: 6.2 miles out and back
Elevation trailhead to falls viewpoint: 7,870 to 8,330 feet (+460 feet)
Trail surface: Dirt

Restrictions: Fee area; no dogs or bicycles
Amenities: Vault toilets; services in Estes Park
Maps: *DeLorme:* Page 29 B6; Trails Illustrated 200: Rocky Mountain National Park; USGS Estes Park
County: Larimer
Land status/contact: Rocky Mountain National Park, (970) 586-1206

Finding the trailhead: From Estes Park, drive north on Wonderview Avenue past the Stanley Hotel and turn right on MacGregor Avenue, which becomes Devils Gulch Road at 0.5 mile. Drive 1.3 miles and turn left on signed Lumpy Ridge Road. Continue 0.3 mile to a parking lot and the Lumpy Ridge Trailhead (GPS: 40 23.793, -105 30.793).

The Hike

Black Canyon Creek dashes southeast down deep Black Canyon before rumbling over 20-foot McGregor Falls below craggy cliffs at Lumpy Ridge. The hike, following Black Canyon Trail and then the unmarked McGregor Falls Trail, is not hard to follow, but bring a map and pay attention as you hike to find the crucial, unsigned cutoff left at the junction with The Pear climber's path.

Miles and Directions

0.0   Begin at Lumpy Ridge Trailhead and hike west on Lumpy Ridge Trail over a ridge to Black Canyon Trail.

0.6   Reach junction with Black Canyon Trail (GPS: 40 24.1061, -105 31.2162). Go left on Black Canyon Trail and hike through grassland toward The Pear, passing obvious Lumpy Ridge rock formations like the Twin Owls.

0.7   Cross a closed road and rejoin trail on other side, then arrive at trail junction. Stay left on Black Canyon Trail.

1.5   Reach trail junction with climbing routes to right; continue straight.

1.8   Reach a pole where a social trail meanders straight ahead; bear right.

Black Canyon Creek twists through boulders and slip-slides over a granite slab in a frothy, frozen sheet at MacGregor Falls.

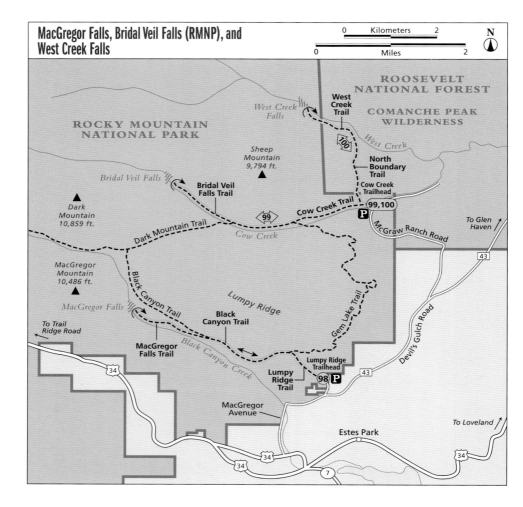

MacGregor Falls, Bridal Veil Falls (RMNP), and West Creek Falls

1.9 Reach junction on right with climber's trail to The Pear (GPS: 40 24.2371, -105 32.4005). The Pear is right and Black Canyon Trail continues straight. Look left for a cairn and follow faint trail southwest across meadow for 320 feet; join closed dirt road on other side (GPS: 40 24.2291. -105 32.4683). Walk west up ranch road.

2.3 Road ends at Black Canyon Creek (GPS: 40 24.3166, -105 32.8775). Continue west on trail to right (signed for MacGregor Falls). Follow trail along creek to left.

3.1 Arrive at base of MacGregor Falls in shady, rock-walled alcove (GPS: 40 24.619, -105 33.667). After viewing falls, return east on approach trails.

6.2 Arrive back at trailhead (GPS: 40 23.793, -105 30.793).

99 Bridal Veil Falls (Rocky Mountain National Park)

Waterfall lovers delight at this falls that tumbles down as a cascade, slips across low-angle rock as a slide, and finally spreads falling waters in a frothy veil. The hike follows Cow Creek in northern Rocky Mountain National Park.

See map on page 324.
Start: Cow Creek Trailhead
Trails: Cow Creek Trail, Bridal Veil Falls Trail
Difficulty: Moderate
Hiking time: About 4 hours
Distance: 6.2 miles out and back
Elevation trailhead to falls viewpoint: 7,820 to 8,800 feet (+980 feet)
Trail surface: Dirt, rocks

Restrictions: No fees; parking limited; don't park on road; no dogs or bicycles
Amenities: Vault toilet; services in Estes Park
Maps: *DeLorme:* Page 29 A7 and A6; Trails Illustrated 200: Rocky Mountain National Park; USGS Estes Park
County: Larimer
Land status/contact: Rocky Mountain National Park, (970) 586-1206

Finding the trailhead: From Estes Park, drive north on Wonderview Avenue and turn right on MacGregor Avenue, which becomes Devils Gulch Road at 0.5 mile. Continue for 3 miles and keep left on gravel McGraw Ranch Road. Drive 2.2 miles and park in a designated area along the road. The trailhead is past the parking area (GPS: 40 25.876, -105 30.061).

The Hike

This Bridal Veil Falls, one of seven Bridal Veil Falls in Colorado, is a lovely 20-foot waterfall that pours over a granite bench below cliffs into a tight gorge. Bordering the trail below the falls is a continuous cascade that includes a slide falls and two pretty falls—"Bridal Bath" and "Bridal Shower." Above the main falls are small cascades gushing into pothole pools, which are accessed by scrambling up slopes left of Bridal Veil.

The hike begins at Cow Creek Trailhead at McGraw Ranch, a former cattle and dude ranch, passing ranch buildings and heading west up a wide valley. While this part of the park is quiet and secluded, the trailhead parking is limited. Don't park on the road or your car may be towed. Instead, wait for a spot or hike elsewhere. An alternate route to the falls is from Lumpy Ridge Trailhead. This increases the hike to 12.8 miles out and back.

Miles and Directions

0.0 Begin at Cow Creek Trailhead. Hike past buildings at old McGraw Ranch and toilet.
0.1 Reach junction with North Boundary Trail at ranch. Go straight on Cow Creek Trail. Right turn goes to West Creek Falls. Continue west on old road that becomes singletrack trail.

Top left: Cow Creek tumbles, slides, and spreads its waters in a frothy veil at Bridal Veil Falls.
Top right: The creek riffles over smooth boulders at "Bridal Shower."
Bottom: "Bridal Bath," a small trailside waterfall, pours into a clear, cold pool.

1.2 Junction with Gem Lake Trail. Continue straight. Left heads to Gem Lake and Lumpy Ridge Trailhead.

1.9 Reach trail junction in bottom of valley. Go right on Bridal Veil Falls Trail. Left turn is Cow Creek Connector Trail, which leads to Black Canyon Trail.

2.9 Pass horse hitch and start up steep, rocky trail. Pay attention to stay on trail.

3.1 Reach base of Bridal Veil Falls (GPS: 40 26.116, -105 33.03). Return the way you came.

6.2 Arrive back at trailhead (GPS: 40 25.876, -105 30.061).

100 West Creek Falls

West Creek flows southeast from Mummy Mountain to Glen Haven where it joins the North Big Thompson River. Deep within the creek's drainage, surrounded by stone walls, a horsetail falls pours over granite, filling a punchbowl at West Creek Falls.

See map on page 324.
Start: Cow Creek Trailhead
Trails: Cow Creek Trail, North Boundary Trail, West Creek Trail
Difficulty: Moderate
Hiking time: About 3 hours
Distance: 4.6 miles out and back
Elevation trailhead to falls viewpoint: 7,820 to 8,100 feet (+280 feet)
Trail surface: Dirt, rocks

Restrictions: Observe wilderness regulations; no dogs; limited parking at trailhead
Amenities: Toilet at ranch; services in Estes Park
Maps: *DeLorme:* Page 29 A7 and A6; Trails Illustrated 200: Rocky Mountain National Park; USGS Estes Park
County: Larimer
Land status/contact: Rocky Mountain National Park, (970) 586-1206; Roosevelt National Forest, (970) 295-6600

Finding the trailhead: From Estes Park, drive north on Wonderview Avenue and turn right on MacGregor Avenue, which becomes Devils Gulch Road at 0.5 mile. Continue for 3 miles and keep left on gravel McGraw Ranch Road. Drive 2.2 miles and park in a designated area along the road. The trailhead is past the parking area (GPS: 40 25.876, -105 30.061).

The Hike

West Creek Falls is a hidden horsetail near the eastern edge of Rocky Mountain National Park. The creek, twisting down a deep canyon, reaches a granite cliff where it slides over water-polished rock before dropping 25 feet into a deep pool. On the trail to the falls, look left in the canyon for "Twin Falls," a short, sheet fall tumbling down granite into a small punchbowl. The hike, mostly in the Comanche Peak Wilderness, gains over 600 feet from the trailhead to a ridge between Cow Creek and West Creek. The route is reversed on the return hike for a heart-pounding day.

The trailhead is at McGraw Ranch, a former dude ranch with historic ranch buildings. While this part of the park is quiet and secluded, the trailhead parking is limited. Don't park on the road or your car may be towed. Instead, wait for a spot or pick another hike.

Miles and Directions

0.0 Begin at Cow Creek Trailhead. Hike west through McGraw Ranch on Cow Creek Trail.

0.1 On west side of buildings, reach junction and turn right (north) on signed North Boundary Trail.

West Creek fills a punchbowl at West Creek Falls.

0.3   Enter Comanche Peak Wilderness, hike over ridge, descend into West Creek drainage, and cross footbridge over creek.

1.4   Reach junction and turn left on signed North Boundary Trail.

1.6   Reach junction and turn left toward West Creek Falls on signed side trail.

2.0   Enter Rocky Mountain National Park.

2.3   Pass "Twin Falls" and arrive at West Creek Falls (GPS: 40 27.084, -105 31.0097). Return the way you came.

4.6   Arrive back at trailhead (GPS: 40 25.876,-105 30.061).

Appendix: Land Status Contact Information

Bureau of Land Management Field Offices

Grand Junction Field Office
2815 H Rd.
Grand Junction, CO 81506
(970) 244-3000
www.blm.gov/office/grand-junction-field-office

Gunnison Field Office
210 W. Spencer Ave.
Gunnison, CO 81230
(970) 642-4940
www.blm.gov/office/gunnison-field-office

Royal Gorge Field Office
3028 E. Main St.
Cañon City, CO 81212
(719) 269-8500

San Luis Valley Field Office
1313 E. Hwy. 160
Monte Vista, CO 81144
(719) 852-7074
www.blm.gov/office/san-luis-valley-field-office

Campgrounds

Recreation.gov
(877) 444-6777 (Reservations)
www.recreation.gov

City, County, State, and National Monuments, Open Spaces, Parklands, Parks, and Recreation Areas

Boulder County Parks & Open Space
5201 St. Vrain Rd.
Longmont, CO 80503
(303) 678-6200
www.bouldercounty.org/departments/parks-and-open-space/

Castlewood Canyon State Park
2989 Hwy. 83
Franktown, CO 80116
(303) 688-5242
https://cpw.state.co.us/placestogo/parks/CastlewoodCanyon

City of Boulder Open Space & Mountain Parks
PO Box 791
Boulder, CO 80306
(303) 441-3440
www.bouldercolorado.gov

City of Idaho Springs
1711 Miner St.
Idaho Springs, CO 80452
(303) 567-4421
https://cityofidahosprings.colorado.gov

City of Ouray Parks and Recreation
320 6th Ave.
Ouray, CO 81427
(970) 325-7211
www.cityofouray.com

Colorado National Monument
1750 Rim Rock Dr.
Fruita, CO 81521-0001
(970) 858-3617
www.nps.gov/colm

Colorado Springs Department of Parks, Recreation & Cultural Services
1401 Recreation Way
Colorado Springs, CO 80905
(719) 385-5940
www.springsgov.com

Curecanti National Recreation Area
102 Elk Creek
Gunnison, CO 81230
(970) 641-2337 x205
www.nps.gov/cure/index.htm

Dominguez-Escalante National Conservation Area
5524 650 Rd.
Delta, CO 81416
(970) 244-3000
www.blm.gov/programs/national-conservation-lands/colorado/dominguez
-escalante-nca

Eldorado Canyon State Park
9 Kneale Rd., PO Box B
Eldorado Springs, CO 80025
(303) 494-3943
https://cpw.state.co.us/placestogo/parks/EldoradoCanyon

El Paso County Parks
2002 Creek Crossing St.
Colorado Springs, CO 80905
(719) 520-7529
https://communityservices.elpasoco.com/parks-and-recreation/

Green Mountain Falls
10615 Green Mountain Falls Rd.
Green Mountain Falls, CO 80819
(719) 684-9414
https://greenmountainfalls.colorado.gov

Rocky Mountain National Park
1000 Hwy. 36
Estes Park, CO 80517-8397
(970) 586-1206
www.nps.gov/romo

Telluride Parks and Recreation
113 W. Columbia Ave., PO Box 397
Telluride, CO 81435
(970) 728-2173
www.telluride-co.gov

Arapaho & Roosevelt National Forests
2150 Centre Ave., Bldg. E
Fort Collins, CO 80526
(970) 295-6600
www.fs.usda.gov/arp

Grand Mesa, Uncompahgre & Gunnison National Forests
2250 S. Main St.
Delta, CO 81416
(970) 874-6600
www.fs.usda.gov/gmug

Pike & San Isabel National Forests
2840 Kachina Dr.
Pueblo, CO 81008
(719) 553-1400
www.fs.usda.gov/psicc

Rifle Falls State Park
5775 Hwy. 325
Rifle, CO 81650
(970) 625-1607
https://cpw.state.co.us/placestogo/parks/RifleFalls

Rio Grande National Forest
1803 W. Hwy. 160
Monte Vista, CO 81144
(719) 852-5941
www.fs.usda.gov/riogrande

Roosevelt National Forest
2150 Centre Ave., Bldg. E
Fort Collins, CO 80526
(970) 295-6600
www.fs.usda.gov/arp

Routt National Forest
2468 Jackson St.
Laramie, WY 82070
(307) 745-2300
www.fs.usda.gov/mbr

San Isabel National Forest
2840 Kachina Dr.
Pueblo, CO 81008
(719) 553-1400
www.fs.usda.gov/psicc

San Juan National Forest
15 Burnett Ct.
Durango, CO 81301
(970) 247-4874
ww.fs.usda.gov/sanjuan

Uncompahgre National Forest
2250 Hwy. 50
Delta, CO 81416
(970) 874-6600
www.fs.usda.gov/gmug

White River National Forest
900 Grand Ave.
Glenwood Springs, CO 81601
(970) 945-2521
www.fs.usda.gov/whiteriver

Passes

CORSAR Card
https://dola.colorado.gov/sar/cardPurchase.jsf

National Parks Pass
www.nps.gov/planyourvisit/passes.htm
https://shop.usparkpass.com

State Parks & Wildlife Areas Pass
https://cpw.state.co.us/buyapply/Pages/ParksPassInfo.aspx

Private Lands

Seven Falls
The Broadmoor
(855) 923-7272
www.broadmoor.com/broadmoor-adventures/seven-falls/

Aspen–Sopris Ranger District
620 Main St.
Carbondale, CO 81623
(970) 963-2266

Blanco Ranger District
220 E. Market St.
Meeker, CO 81641
(970) 878-4039

Boulder Ranger District
2140 Yarmouth Ave.
Boulder, CO 80301
(303) 541-2500

Canyon Lakes Ranger District
2150 Centre Ave., Bldg. E
Fort Collins, CO 80526
(970) 295-6700

Clear Creek Ranger District
2060 Miner St.
Idaho Springs, CO 80452
(303) 567-3000

Columbine Ranger District
367 Pearl St.
Bayfield, CO 81122
(970) 884-2512

Conejos Peak Ranger District
15571 County Rd. T.5
La Jara, CO 81140
(719) 274-8971

Dillon Ranger District
680 Blue River Pkwy.
Silverthorne, CO 80498
(970) 468-5400

Divide Ranger District

13308 W. Hwy. 160
Del Norte, CO 81132
(719) 657-3321

Divide Ranger District—Creede Office

304 S. Main St.
Creede, CO 81130
(719) 658-2556

Dolores Public Lands Office

29211 CO 184
Dolores, CO 81323
(970) 882-7296

Eagle–Holy Cross Ranger District

24747 US Hwy. 24
Minturn, CO 81645
(970) 827-5715

Grand Valley District Office

1010 Kimball Ave.
Grand Junction, CO 81501
(970) 242-8211

Gunnison Ranger District

216 N. Colorado
Gunnison, CO 81230
(970) 641-0471

Hahns Peak / Bears Ears Ranger District

925 Weiss Dr.
Steamboat Springs, CO 80487-9315
(970) 870-2299

Leadville Ranger District

810 Front St.
Leadville, CO 80461
(719) 486-0749

Ouray Ranger District

2505 S. Townsend
Montrose, CO 81401
(970) 240-5300

Pagosa Ranger District

180 Pagosa St.
Pagosa Springs, CO 81147
(970) 264-2268

Paonia Ranger District

N. Rio Grande Ave.
Paonia, CO 81428
(970) 527-4131

Parks Ranger District

100 Main St.
Walden, CO 80480
(970) 723-2700

Pikes Peak Ranger District

601 S. Weber St.
Colorado Springs, CO 80903
(719) 636-1602

Saguache Ranger District

46525 CO Hwy. 114
Saguache, CO 81149
(719) 655-2547

Salida Ranger District

5575 Cleora Rd.
Salida, CO 81201
(719) 539-3591

San Carlos Ranger District

3028 E. Main St.
Cañon City, CO 81212
(719) 269-8500

Silverton Public Lands Center
1246 Blair St.
Silverton, CO 81433
(970) 387-5530

South Park Ranger District
320 Hwy 285
Fairplay, CO 80440
(719) 836-2031

Colorado Parks and Wildlife Headquarters
6060 Broadway
Denver, CO 80216
(303) 291-7227
https://cpw.state.co.us

About the Authors

Susan Joy Paul has traveled around the United States and beyond to 47 hot springs, more than 150 waterfalls, and to the summits of more than 700 peaks. Her memorable adventures include hikes and climbs on the Keyhole Route on Longs Peak, the Knife-edge on Capitol Peak, the Mountaineer's Route on Mount Whitney, the East Arête on Mount Russell, Otto's Route on Independence Monument, the Emmons Glacier on Mount Rainier, the Gooseneck Glacier on Gannett Peak, the Jamapa Glacier on Pico de Orizaba, the Ayoloco Glacier on Iztaccihuatl, and the Whymper Route on Chimborazo. Her books include *Touring Colorado Hot Springs*, the first edition of *Hiking Waterfalls Colorado*, *Climbing Colorado's Mountains*, and *Woman in the Wild: The Everywoman's Guide to Hiking, Camping, and Backcountry Travel*. Susan lives independently in Colorado Springs, Colorado.

Stewart M. Green has hiked, climbed, photographed, and traveled across the American West as well as the world in search of memorable images and experiences to document. Based in Colorado Springs, Stewart, a freelance writer and photographer for Globe Pequot and FalconGuides, has written and photographed over forty-five travel and outdoor adventure books, including *Best Easy Day Hikes Colorado Springs*, *Scenic Driving Colorado*, *Best Hikes Colorado Springs*, *Best Climbs Moab*, *Best Hikes Albuquerque*, *Rock Climbing Colorado*, *Scenic Driving New England*, and *Rock Art: The Meanings and Myths Behind Ancient Ruins in the Southwest and Beyond*. His photographs and writing are also published in many magazines, books, catalogs, and ads. Stewart is also a professional rock climbing and hiking guide for Front Range Climbing Company. Visit green1109.wix.com/stewartmgreenphoto for images and information.

THE TEN ESSENTIALS OF HIKING

American Hiking Society

American Hiking Society recommends you pack the "Ten Essentials" every time you head out for a hike. Whether you plan to be gone for a couple of hours or several months, make sure to pack these items. Become familiar with these items and know how to use them. Learn more at **AmericanHiking.org/hiking-resources**.

1. Appropriate Footwear

6. Safety Items (light, fire, and a whistle)

2. Navigation

7. First Aid Kit

3. Water (and a way to purify it)

8. Knife or Multi-Tool

4. Food

9. Sun Protection

5. Rain Gear & Dry-Fast Layers

10. Shelter

PROTECT THE PLACES YOU LOVE TO HIKE

Become a member today and take $5 off an annual membership using the code **Falcon5**.

AmericanHiking.org/join

American Hiking Society is the only national nonprofit organization dedicated to empowering all to enjoy, share, and preserve the hiking experience.